WORLD TRAVEL DICTIONARY

The Dictionary for the Travel Industry

ISBN: 1–902221–21–4

Columbus Publishing Limited, Columbus House,
28 Charles Square, London, N1 6HT, United Kingdom
Tel: +44 (0)171 417 0700
Fax: +44 (0)171 417 0710
E-mail: booksales@columbus-group.co.uk

Editor
Richard English

Assistant Editor
Stewart Wild

Contributors
David Burles, Jim Maynard, Ned Middleton, Patrick Thorne, Penny Locke

Design and Production
Space Design and Production Services Ltd, London N1

Publisher
Pete Korniczky

Printed by
Croxsons Sheetfed, Watford

The publishers would like to thank all the organisations and individuals who have assisted in the preparation of this edition, with particular thanks to Brookson's Travel, Maureen Hill, Alan Beaver, the staff at Lunn Poly in Reigate and World Wide Words <htpp//www.quinion.com/words/>

Contents

An Introduction
To The Dictionary

Welcome to the second edition of the World Travel Dictionary.

Although the first edition proved very popular, we listened to what you said and for this new edition have included many of your suggestions for improvement. The alphabetical listing is now larger and contains over 3000 terms. We have also made several amendments to the contents including giving the country of origin of many of the terms, especially American ones. Furthermore, there is now a substantial appendix that gives the translation of nearly 400 words from UK English to US English and vice versa.

Certain historical terms have been included such as "Perpendicular" since reference to these is often made in guide books and brochures and is rarely explained in them. Furthermore, because of the increasing popularity of sporting holidays, a select number of sporting terms has also been included in this edition,

especially those relating to skiing and diving.

Names or terms of foreign origin, other than proper nouns, that may not be accepted as English are shown in **bold italics.**

The unique list of world-wide tourist attractions remains. As before the attractions are referenced alphabetically and by country and are shown in a separate appendix.

Names of types or classes of people are now only included in the alphabetical listing where they are of special significance (for example, where the term has an additional meaning). This information, together with other important details, appears in the separate appendices. There is also an additional country-by-country appendix giving information on tourist arrivals, dialling codes and currencies.

We have also increased our coverage of key travel trade associations and have now included facsimile and E-mail details.

"A" clamp Device fitted to air hose, manifold or regulator so that they may be attached to a diving cylinder pillar valve.

"A" flag A small blue and white pennant used in the seafaring "international code of signalling" which represents the letter "A." When flown independently above any craft, this flag also denotes diving is in progress - translated as "*stand well clear I have divers down.*" Also called flag alpha.

à la carte **1.** A menu in a restaurant that contains a wide range of choices, individually priced. Usually more expensive than table d'hôte. **2.** A term often used by tour operators to denote a higher class of holiday, possibly one that can be varied to meet a customer's particular tastes. *See also tailor-made.*

a.m. Ante meridiem. The suffix used with the 12 hour clock to denote times between 12 midnight and noon.

a.s.a.p. As soon as possible.

AA Automobile Association. *See Appendix 7a.*

AAC Association of Airline Consolidators. *See Appendix 7a.*

Abacus The GDS owned by Cathay Pacific and others.

abaft The stern half of a ship

ABC **1.** Originally a publisher of rail timetables who expanded into other transport publication areas. Travel agents who talk about "the ABC" are usually referring to the Air ABC, now obsolete and published as the OAG. **2.** *See Advance Booking Charter.*

abeam On a line at right-angles to the length of a ship or aircraft.

ABLJ *See adjustable buoyancy life-jacket.*

aboard On or in a ship, aircraft, train, etc.

abode A person's usual residence.

aboriginal The original inhabitant of a place.

ABPCO Association of British Professional Conference Organisers. *See Appendix 7a.*

abroad A foreign country. From wherever a person happens to live, everywhere else is abroad.

absolute pressure The total pressure exerted at any depth (including atmospheric pressure).

A

ABTA Association of British Travel Agents. *See Appendix 7a.*

ABTA Travel Agents Certificate An examination-based qualification developed by ABTA and the Travel Training Company. It replaces the earlier COTAC and other examination-based qualifications run by ABTA's National Training Board and the City and Guilds of London. ABTAC was introduced following pressure from the industry that wanted an examination-based qualification to supplement the other methods of assessment used with NVQ's.

ABTAC *See ABTA Travel Agents Certificate.*

ABTOF Association of British Tour Operators to France. *See Appendix 7a.*

ABTOP The tour operating equivalent of ABTAC.

ABTOT Association of Bonded Travel Organisers Trust Ltd. *See Appendix 7a.*

abyss An exceptionally deep chasm.

AC 1. A vehicle rental abbreviation meaning air conditioning, an option with most companies operating in hot areas. Air conditioning has an additional benefit in that the vehicle windows can be kept closed in towns, a valuable security advantage in some parts of the world.
2. Alternating Current. An electrical supply that varies in voltage from zero to a peak and back to a peak in the opposite direction many times a second. In the UK the frequency of the change is 50 times per second. In the USA it is 60 and travellers need to take care that their appliances can work on the different frequencies.

acclimatise To become accustomed to new or changed conditions.

acclivity An upward slope.

accommodation In travel terms, anything that can "accommodate" a passenger. Thus, "sleeping accommodation" on a ferry could be a cabin, a berth in a cabin or a reclining seat. Generally, though, the expression is used to denote some form of hotel or other sleeping facility.

accommodation grading schemes Hotel and other accommodation is rated or classified according to many criteria, such as size, number of staff, facilities included, etc. No scheme is entirely satisfactory and it is always unwise to try to compare accommodation using the schemes of different organisations or even countries. Rating systems used include:
- Stars, * to ***** (AA and RAC)
- Crowns, one crown to five crowns (ETB)
- Percentages, up to 100% (Egon Ronay)
- Type name, third class to de luxe
Whereas it is might seem reasonable to assume that, say, a *** hotel will be similar to a three crown hotel, it would be unwise to make such a generalisation to a customer.

accommodation listing and grading organisations There are a number of organisations that operate classification schemes for hotels and other accommodation providers. The main ones are:

- **Government-run bodies.** Some governments (though not in the UK) operate an official registration scheme. The department responsible will allocate an official classification, and may well impose certain conditions on the establishment's operation. When government classifications exist, registration is normally obligatory.
- **Transport related organisations.** The most well known classifiers tend to be the motoring organisations - in the UK the AA and RAC. However, airlines and railways may also produce lists of recommended establishments. Not all establishments will be included, although the AA and RAC each has over 4000 hotels listed in the UK. Hotels listed in these sorts of guides will cater for the needs of travellers using the transport method that the compiler of the guide is interested in - motorists in the case of the AA and RAC.
- **Consumer organisations.** Consumer organisations such as Which? produce guides that give details of a wide range of establishments, although they tend to be fewer in number than in government or motorists' guides. The Which? guide has around 1000 entries and its slant is towards the needs of its members.
- **Commercial organisations.** Several organisations exist whose job it is simply to produce hotel guides. One of the most comprehensive is the "Hotel and Travel Index" published quarterly by Reed Elsevier. Such guides may use a grading system, possibly the "official" grade if such exists.

However, it is more likely that they will simply show details of the facilities offered and indicate a price range.

A

- **Holiday companies.** Most tour operators try to give their customers an indication of the quality of the accommodation they are considering and indeed, it is a requirement of the ABTA Code that the "official" classification (if such exists) is shown. However, many operators will also provide their own description and rating.

accommodations (US). Accommodation.

accredited agent An IATA term meaning a passenger sales agent that has met all its conditions for appointment and whose name appears on the IATA agency list.

ACE Association for Conferences and Events. *See Appendix 7a.*

acquirer An organisation that processes credit and charge card transactions on behalf of merchants.

acre An early measurement for an area of land equal to 4,840 square yards (approximately 0.405 hectare).

ACTA Association of Canadian Travel Agents. *See Appendix 7c.*

activity holiday A term used to describe any holiday that involves some type of structured or organised activity. There are many holidays produced by tour operators to meet the special needs of enthusiasts for the various different types of activity.

actual flying time The time an air journey actually takes, disregarding

A

local time differences. This expression is gradually replacing the earlier "EFT" meaning elapsed flying time, which has the same meaning.

AD Agent's discount. On air tickets the letters will appear with a secondary code to indicate the amount of discount allowed. E.g. AD75 = 75%.

ad hoc Anything that is arranged for a specific (usually exclusive) purpose. Typically ad hoc arrangements will be made at relatively short notice to suit the needs of an organisation or individual that has just decided on them.

ad hoc charter A flight added to an existing programme in order to meet an unforeseen demand.

ada room A room complying with the requirements of the Americans with Disabilities Act.

Adam The style of furniture, architecture, etc. created by the Adams brothers in the 18th century.

add-on An expression, more common in North America, that means anything that can be bought by a customer that is an extra to the basic cost of the holiday or other arrangement. Shore excursions for cruise passengers are an example. In the UK the term optional extra is more commonly used.

add-on fare An amount added to a gateway fare to construct a through fare to a destination. Add-on fares will usually differ from the normal advertised point-to-point fare from the gateway to the destination.

adjustable buoyancy life jacket An inflatable collar worn by divers underwater that can be partially inflated and then deflated to suit underwater buoyancy requirements. When fully inflated at the surface it also provides the function of a lifejacket.

administrative office An IATA term meaning the principal office of an accredited agent, that is not itself an approved location.

adult A person who will normally have to pay the full charge for a travel facility.

advance booking charter An obsolescent type of charter flight available to customers booking in advance. New charter regulations have virtually done away with ABC's.

AEA Association of European Airlines. *See Appendix 7d.*

AEADAVA Asociación Empresarial Agencias de Viajes Españolas. *See Appendix 7c.*

AEC Association of Exhibition Organisers. *See Appendix 7a.*

aeon A very long period.

aerodrome An obsolescent term for airport, still occasionally used in connection with a small airport, possibly one with a grass runway.

aero-engine (UK). An aircraft engine.

aerofoil Any one of the curved surfaces on an aircraft designed to give lift.

aeroplane Or airplane. A heavier than air flying machine.

A

aerostat An airship or balloon, especially tethered.

aerotrain A train supported on its track by a cushion of air.

affinity card A card that identifies members of an affinity group.

affinity charter Where a group, formed for purposes other than that of obtaining cheap travel, charters the entire aircraft. Such charters were once widely used to obtain cheap travel, especially across the Atlantic. However, the deregulation of air fares has virtually wiped out the practice.

affinity group A group of people linked by a common interest or purpose. Some principals offer special rates for affinity groups.

Africa The second largest of the continents with an area of some 30,097,000 square kilometres (11,620,451 square miles). Its estimated population (1984) is 537,000,000.

aft Towards the stern of a vessel. When a person moves toward the stern of a vessel he or she will be going aft.

AFTA Australian Federation of Travel Agents. *See Appendix 7c.*

after On a ship, nearer to the stern or aft.

agency administrator An IATA term meaning the official designated by IATA's Director General as the holder of that office, or his authorised representative. The administrator has overall responsibility for agency affairs.

agency list An IATA term meaning the list maintained by the agency administrator that gives the names and addresses of accredited agents, their approved locations and where applicable, their administrative offices.

agency services manager An IATA term for the official designated by the agency administrator to head the agency services office and to manage the accreditation programme in a particular country or area. The agency services manager may also be asked to act as the local representative of the Plan Management.

agent A person or organisation that acts for another. Technically an agent should be paid for the facilitation of the transaction regardless of its outcome. In practice, the term is often used to describe those, such as travel agents, who are paid on the basis of sales made.

agent's coupon The coupon of a ticket or voucher that is retained by the issuing agent.

agio The commission charged on the exchange of one currency into another. This term is less commonly used these days.

agonic line A line joining the north and south magnetic poles, along which a magnetic compass will point without deflection.

aground When a ship has run into the bottom of an area of water.

Agulhas current A very strong north/south current of the south-west coast of Africa.

AH&MA American Hotel & Motel

A

Association. *See Appendix 7b.*

ahead When used as a nautical term means to move forward, as in "full steam ahead".

AHTA Association of Hungarian Travel Agents. *See Appendix 7c.*

aiguille A sharp peak of rock, especially in the Alps.

aileron The hinged part of the wing of an aircraft used to control lateral balance.

air brake **1.** A brake operated by compressed air, commonly used on larger vehicles.
2. A movable flap or other surface used to reduce an aircraft's speed.

air bridge (UK). The portable walkway set against an aircraft for loading.

air corridor A route to which aircraft are restricted, especially when flying over a foreign country.

air hostess (UK). A female airline steward.

air mile A nautical mile when used as a measure of distance flown.

air pocket A region of low pressure that can cause an aircraft to lose height suddenly.

air sickness A feeling of nausea when flying, usually caused by a combination of nervousness and turbulence.

air taxi A small aircraft that can be chartered for one-off journeys. Most air taxis are relatively small and the journeys they undertake relatively short.

air terminal **1.** (UK). The building that serves as a town base to and from which passengers travel to the airport.
2. One of the passenger buildings at an airport.

air testing The analysis of an air sample to ascertain whether it conforms to the air purity standards laid down.

air traffic control The system or organisation responsible for the safe routeing of aircraft while in flight.

Air Travel Organiser's Licence In the UK it is a legal requirement for all operators of travel arrangements by air to obtain an ATOL from the CAA. Applicants must satisfy the CAA as to their financial viability before the licence can be granted.

air-boat A vessel propelled by an enclosed fan or propeller, used for travelling over shallow water and marshland.

Airbus Originally an aircraft designed to carry large numbers over relatively short routes. Now used to describe many types made by the Airbus Industrie consortium.

AIRC Association of International Rail Companies. *See Appendix 7a.*

aircraft Any machine that flies. Usually taken to mean a heavier-than-air machine but can be applied to lighter-than-air types, such as balloons and dirigibles.

airfield An area of land, possibly grass-covered, where aircraft can take off and land.

airfoil (US). Aerofoil.

airframe The body of an aircraft.

airline 1. A carrier providing regular public air transport.
2. An IATA term for any air carrier, operating scheduled air services, which is not a member of IATA but which has been admitted to participate in BSP.

airline code All airlines have a two-letter code, issued by IATA, that is used in ticketing and to designate their flights. Some are obvious, such as BA for British Airways; some are not, such as UM for Air Zimbabwe. In addition to their two-letter code, airlines also have a three-figure accounting code that appears before the number on their tickets. For BA the number is 125; for Air Zimbabwe it is 168. Since most of the possible two-letter combinations have now been taken up, three-letter codes are being introduced.

airliner A large passenger aircraft.

airmiss When two or more aircraft get closer to one another than safety regulations permit.

airplane (US). Aircraft.

airport The complete complex of buildings, runways, car parks, etc., that make up the overall facility for the handling of civil aircraft.

airport code All cities served by air have a unique three-letter designatory code. In the case of major cities this is often the first three letters of the city name, such as LON for London or PAR for Paris. This is not always the case, though, as codes such as YYZ (Toronto) and SXB (Strasbourg), readily demonstrate. In addition to their main code, cities with more than one airport may have secondary codes to denote which is which. Thus London, England (LON) has Heathrow (LHR), Gatwick (LGW), Stansted (STN), Luton (LTN) and London City (LCY).

airscrew An old-fashioned term for an aeroplane's propeller.

airship A powered aircraft that is lighter than air. The first ever passenger air service was operated by the German airline DELAG, before the first world war, using Zeppelin airships.

airside That part of an airport reached after passing through emigration and other controls.

airspace The sky available for aircraft to fly in, especially that part subject to the jurisdiction of a particular country.

airspeed An aircraft's speed relative to the air.

airstrip An area of land suitable for aircraft take off and landing but which has few of the facilities normally provided at airports, etc.

AITO Association of Independent Tour Operators. *See Appendix 7a.*

alehouse A tavern.

Algarve Portugal's southern coast and the country's premier resort area. Main towns include Lagos, Albufeira, Faro and Tavira.

alien A person from a foreign country.

all hands The entire crew of a ship.

alleyway A passageway or corridor on board a ship.

all-inclusive A package holiday that

A

includes more than just travel and accommodation. Typically an all-inclusive package will also include in its cost such things as all meals and refreshments, drinks, entertainment and sporting facilities.

allocation Sometimes known as an allotment. This refers to space or accommodation given in advance by a principal to an intermediary, such as a tour operator, for onward sale to a customer. Space held on allocation will not be sold directly by the principal without reference to the allocation holder.

aloft When used as a nautical term means at or near the top of the mast.

alongside When used as a nautical term means beside a pier or other vessel.

alp A high mountain. When used as a proper noun, the Alps refers to the range in and around Switzerland.

alpine Of or relating to mountains.

alpine skiing The main form of "modern" downhill skiing, invented in 1905 by Mathias Zdarsky in the village of Lilienfeld.

altimeter An instrument that shows a pilot the height of an aircraft.

altitude The height of an object or place, normally measured from sea level. The altitude of a place will directly affect its air pressure and this will have implications on any activities undertaken.

altitude sickness A sickness caused by the lack of air pressure at higher altitudes.

Amadeus A GDS operated by Air France and other carriers.

AMATUR Mexican Association of Tour Operators. *See Appendix 7c.*

AMAVE Asociación Mayoristas Agencias de Viajes Españolas. *See Appendix 7c.*

ambient Local, immediately surrounding. The term is usually used in relation to pressure and temperature.

amenity A pleasant or useful feature, often mentioned in sales literature to stimulate interest.

American plan A hotel rate that includes accommodation and all meals. Also known as full board.

Americas The land mass comprising North, Central and South America. It has an area of around 42,000,000 square kilometres (16,000,000 square miles). The Americas are usually regarded as two continents, North and South America. The estimated population of the entire region (1991) is 500,000,000.

amidships (US amidship) The longitudinal centre part of a boat or ship.

amphibian Of an aircraft, one that can operate from land or water.

amusement park *See theme park.*

anchor The heavy, fluked metal weight used to moor a ship to the sea bed.

anchor ball A black ball hoisted above the bow of a ship to show that it is at anchor.

anchorage A place where a ship may be anchored.

ancient monument (UK). An old building or similar, often preserved under government control.

ancillary services In travel, extra services provided such as visas and foreign exchange.

Andean **1.** The Aztec civilisation of ancient Peru that lasted from around 100 BC until AD 1783.
2. Of or relating to the Andes mountains of South America.

anemometer A wind speed gauge.

Anglo **1.** Used as a prefix to denote anything of English or British origin.
2. (US). A person of British or north-European origin.

Anglo-Saxon **1.** Of English descent.
2. (US). The modern English language.

annexe When referring to a hotel or similar, a separate or added building giving extra accommodation.

anoxia A critical lack of oxygen in the tissues of the body that can lead to severe damage or death.

Antarctic Circle The parallel of latitude at 66° 33' S. Any point south of this will experience at least one period of 24 hours without daylight and a similar period without sunset.

Antarctic circumpolar current The longest ocean current on earth runs around the entire continent of Antarctica at a speed of around half a mile an hour. It is driven by the constant blowing of the Westerlies.

Antarctica The continent at the southernmost point of the earth with a total area of 13,727,000 square kilometres (5,300,000 square miles). The only people living there are research scientists.

anticyclone A system of winds rotating outwards from an area of high pressure, usually producing fine weather.

antipasto The Italian equivalent of hors d'oeuvres.

antipodes The opposite point on the earth to where one is. From the UK, the antipodes is Australasia.

ANTOR Association of National Tourist Office Representatives in the UK. *See Appendix 7a.*

ANVR Algemene Nederland Vereniging Reisburo. *See Appendix 7c.*

AOA Airport Operators Association. *See Appendix 7a.*

aparthotel A hotel in which the accommodation is provided as self-catering apartments.

apartment A room or collection of rooms. When used as holiday accommodation it will normally be rented out on a self-catering basis.

APAVT Association of Portuguese Travel Agencies and Tourism. *See Appendix 7c.*

APEX Advance Purchase Excursion Fare. A type of advance booking fare.

Apollo The GDS owned by United Airlines.

appetiser A small amount of food or drink, taken before a main meal, to stimulate the appetite. *See also hors d'ouvres.*

A

A

appointment Apart from the normal meaning, a travel agent can be appointed by a principal to sell its products or services.

approved location An IATA term meaning a location for the sale of passenger tickets, including head offices, branch offices and satellite printer locations, that appear on IATA's agency list.

après ski The social activities taking place (usually in the evening) after a day's skiing.

apron The hard surfaced area of an airfield used for manoeuvring aircraft. Also known as a ramp.

APTG Association of Professional Tourist Guides. *See Appendix 7a.*

aqualung Portable breathing apparatus for underwater activities. (Jacques-Yves Cousteau 1911-1997). *See also SCUBA.*

aquarium A place where fish and other marine species are kept in captivity for the enjoyment of visitors

aqueduct A bridge, similar to a viaduct, but designed to carry water.

Arab Originally a member of the Semitic peoples inhabiting the area around what is now Saudi Arabia. The term is often used to refer to anyone from the Middle East of non-Jewish extraction.

Arabian peninsula The geographical region comprising Bahrain, Oman, Qatar, Saudi Arabia, United Arab Emirates, Yemen.

Arabic civilisation Started around AD 975 in the Arabian peninsula and lasted until AD 1525.

Arabic numerals The commonly used system of numbers from 0 to 9 and then combining from 10 onwards. The use of 0 (zero) to cause preceding numbers to increase by 10 makes the system very flexible when used for complex calculations. *See also Roman numerals.*

arc Part of the circumference of a circle or other curve. Since the Earth is a globe, a "straight line" journey between any two points is actually an arc.

archipelago A group of many islands.

Arctic Circle The parallel of latitude at 66° 33' N. Any point north of this will experience at least one period of 24 hours without daylight and a similar period without sunset.

Arctic ocean *See oceans.*

area 1. A region or tract of land. **2.** An IATA term used to describe any one of IATA's three geographical areas.

area 1 The IATA area covering North, Central and South America.

area 2 The IATA area covering Europe, the Middle East and Africa.

area 3 The IATA area covering the Far East, Australia, New Zealand and the Pacific Islands.

arête A sharp mountain ridge.

ARMTA Association of Regional Multiple Travel Agents. *See Appendix 7a.*

arrondissement An administrative division of a large French city.

ARTA Association of Retail Travel Agents. *See Appendix 7b.*

artificial respiration A means of resuscitation by re-oxygenating the blood of an unconscious person.

Aryan A member of the peoples speaking any one of the languages of the Indo-European family.

ASATA Association of South African Travel Agents. *See Appendix 7c.*

ascent The process of rising towards the water's surface from any depth.

ASEAN The Association of South East Asian Nations. A regional organisation comprising: Brunei/Darussalam, Laos, Malaysia, Myanmar, the Philippines, Singapore, Thailand, Vietnam.

ashore Towards or on the shore or land.

Asia The largest of the continents with an area of 44,391,162 square kilometres (17,139,445 square miles). Its population (1990) is 3,112,700,000.

Asian 1. Of or relating to the continent of Asia.
2. (UK). A person from the Indian subcontinent and its environs.
3. (US). A person from any part of Asia, including the Far East.

ASIRT The Association for Safe International Road Travel. *See Appendix 7b.*

ASTA American Society of Travel Agents. *See Appendix 7b.*

astern A nautical term meaning the rear of a vessel. When a ship goes astern it will go backwards.

ASVA Association of Scottish Visitor Attractions. *See Appendix 7a.*

asylum, political Protection given by a state to political refugees from another country.

ATA 1. Air Transport Association. *See Appendix 7b.*
2. Association of Travel Agencies. *See Appendix 7c.*

ATB *See Automated Ticket and Boarding pass.*

ATC *See air traffic control.*

Athens Convention An international agreement that limits the liability of shipping companies in respect of loss or damage to passengers and their luggage.

Athens of... Boston was nicknamed the "Athens of America" in the 19th century as a reflection of the city's cultural importance. Nashville, Tennessee is known as the "Athens of the South" (and has a full-size replica of the Parthenon) and Lexington, Kentucky the "Athens of the West".

ATII Association of Travel Insurance Intermediaries. *See Appendix 7a.*

Atlantic *See oceans.*

atlas The first compilations of maps (published in the 16th century) often had a picture of the mythological character Atlas on their frontispieces. In time these books became known as "atlases".

ATM Automated Teller Machine. A US term for an automatic cash dispensing machine. (UK cashpoint).

ATOC Association of Train Operating Companies. *See Appendix 7a.*

ATOL *See Air Travel Organiser's Licence.*

A

atoll A ring shaped island formed by a coral reef.

atrium A central open area in a hotel or similar. Usually there will be access to natural light, either through an opening or a transparent roof.

ATTC Association of Travel Trade Clubs. *See Appendix 7a.*

attraction In tourism terms, something that a tourist wants to see or visit. Attractions can be natural (such as Table Mountain in Cape Town) or man-made, such as Disneyland. *For a list of attractions, see the appendix.*

auberge A French inn.

AUC Air Transport Users Council. *See Appendix 7a.*

auditor's coupon The coupon of a ticket or voucher that is used for accounting purposes. Usually it will be submitted to the principal with the sales return.

Aurora Australis The southern hemisphere's equivalent to the Aurora Borealis that can be seen regularly below 70° south. Also known as the Southern Lights.

Aurora Borealis Spectacular luminous phenomena caused by electrical solar discharges. Visible every dark night in the higher latitudes above 70° north but less frequently the nearer an observer is to the equator. London can expect a maximum of 7 sightings a year. Also known as the Northern Lights.

Australasia The geographical region comprising Australia, New Caledonia, New Zealand, Solomon Islands, Vanatu and the island of New Guinea including all of Papua New Guinea. Usually considered to be the smallest continent with a total area of 7,686,884 square kilometres (2,967,283 square miles). The population (1991) is 17,335,000.

auto 1. A car rental term - automatic transmission. Standard in the USA; an extra in most other countries. 2. (US). An abbreviation for automobile - a car.

autobahn A German motorway.

autogiro An aircraft with rotating wings, somewhat similar to a helicopter, but where the rotors are turned by their motion through the air and not by an engine. Autogiros were the first successful type of rotating-wing aircraft.

automated ticket and boarding pass A document that contains both ticket and boarding pass. The older type of ticket, coupons of which were exchanged for a boarding pass on check in, is gradually being phased out.

auto-pilot A device that maintains the attitude of a vehicle, usually an aircraft, without the pilot's intervention.

autopista A Spanish motorway.

autoroute A French motorway.

autostrada An Italian motorway.

avalanche A rapid and uncontrolled fall of snow and ice down a mountain. Avalanches cause many deaths and injuries to skiers and others travelling in the mountains.

avalanche transceiver A radio transmitter, used by skiers travelling off-piste, which sends a signal that can help rescuers locate users in the event of their being buried in an avalanche.

average An insurance term for the process by which an insurance company assesses how much to pay out in the event of a claim from an under-insured claimant. If a claimant had baggage insured for £2,000, lost a quarter of it through theft and claimed £1,000, the company would consider that he or she was underinsured by an average of 50%, since a quarter of the baggage should have been worth no more than a quarter of the insured value, that is, £500. They could therefore reduce their payout by the same percentage by which the claimant is under-insured, in this case, 50%. So the claimant would only receive £500 for the £1000 loss. Although it is technically possibly to

implement, the difficulties and bad will created means that average is not often applied to baggage claims nowadays.

aviation The skill or practice of operating aircraft.

avionics The electronic systems involved in aircraft.

awning A cover, usually of canvas, set up to provide temporary protection against sun or rain. Often used over an open deck of a ship.

AWTE Association of Women Travel Executives. *See Appendix 7a.*

axis The centre around which something rotates. The earth rotates around an imaginary line joining the poles.

Aztec The native people dominant in Mexico before the Spanish conquest in the 16th century.

Aztec civilisation *See Mexic.*

A

B
b

B & B *See Bed and Breakfast.*

BAA British Airports Authority. *See Appendix 7a.*

Babylonic The ancient Babylonian civilisation that lasted from around 1500 BC until 538 BC.

BACD British Association of Conference Destinations. *See Appendix 7a.*

back to back **1.** The principle by which a charter series works. The flight taking a group out to a destination will return with those holidaymakers who have finished their holidays. They in turn will return on the return flight of a flight bringing out another batch of holidaymakers. The empty return flights necessary at the beginning of a season and the empty outward flights at the end are known as "empty legs". Since these simply cost money, operators will try to find various devices to fill them, maybe by combining two seasons.
2. The practice of using restricted validity excursion tickets in such a way as to circumvent the restrictions and obtain a fare which undercuts the correct fare for the journey undertaken.

backcountry (US). An area away from settled districts.

backdate The practice of issuing a ticket or voucher later than the date shown in the issuing stamp box. This is usually done to circumvent the regulations covering advance purchase restrictions.

backhaul An IATA fare construction rule that states that it is not possible to apply normal fare rules to journeys that double back on themselves. This rule prevents the undercutting of fares to a more distant point than that where the journey ends.

backing Change of wind direction in an anti-clockwise manner.

back-pack Harness attached to a diving cylinder, comprising shoulder and waist straps, that allows the diver to "wear" the cylinder.

backwash **1.** The wave of waters created by a vessel's passage.
2. A similar wave of air caused by the passage of an aircraft.

badlands Extensive, uncultivatable tracts of land, usually arid and bare of vegetation.

Baedecker Travel guide books published by the Baedecker firm. Sometimes used as a generic term for a guidebook.

baggage The normal apparel and personal effects that a traveller might reasonably carry on a journey.

baggage allowance All forms of public transport have a limit on the amount of baggage passengers may take with them without additional charge. Obviously this is to stop people from using a transport company's services as a cheap way of conveying large quantities of goods. On most means of transport the free allowance is so high that few passengers will approach it and even if it is exceeded, few officials are concerned. In the case of air travel, though, the limitations on space mean that airlines tend to be stricter about their allowances. The usual free baggage allowance on airlines is 20k (44lb) for economy class passengers and 30k (66lb) for first class.

baggage check That part of a passenger's ticket that acts as a receipt for checked baggage and, where necessary, identifies him or her as the owner of an item of baggage.

baggage tag An IATA term for the numbered document issued by a carrier solely for the identification of checked baggage. Baggage tags are in two parts; one part is fixed to the item of baggage and the other is retained by the traveller as identification.

BAHA British Activity Holiday Association Ltd. *See Appendix 7a.*

Bahama islands Group of islands comprising the Commonwealth of the Bahamas and the Turks and Caicos islands.

BAHREP British Association of Hotel Representatives. *See Appendix 7a.*

bail bond In some countries, notably Spain, drivers committing a serious road traffic offence can be arrested and imprisoned pending trial. They will only be released if bail is paid. Bail bond cover will pay the bail to ensure immediate release.

bailiwick The district or area of jurisdiction of a bailee or bailiff.

baksheesh A term of Middle Eastern origin meaning a tip or gratuity.

balcony A platform built out from the outside of a building, with access from a door or window in the room.

Balkans The geographical region of the Balkan Peninsula (bordered by the Adriatic Sea to the west; the Aegean and Black Seas to the east and the Mediterranean to the south). The countries in this region are generally known as the Balkan States and comprise Albania, Bosnia-Herzogovina, Bulgaria, Croatia, Greece, the former Yugoslav Republic of Macedonia, Romania, Slovenia, the Federal Republic of Yugoslavia and the European part of Turkey.

ball lightning A very rare natural phenomenon where a glowing mass of energised air moves around until it strikes an earthed object, whereupon it discharges and disappears.

ballast 1. Heavy weights put in the hold of a vessel to give stability. Often necessary when a voyage is being made without cargo or passengers.
2. The stone chippings on which railway lines are laid.

balloon A lighter-than-air vehicle that cannot be steered. Now often used for sightseeing trips in such places as game parks where their quietness and slow speed avoid disturbance to the fauna. The first ever passenger carrying flight was in a balloon.

BALPA British Airline Pilots Association. *See Appendix 7a.*

bamboo curtain A name given to the moral, ethical and cultural divide that exists between communist China and the rest of the world. *See also Iron Curtain.*

banana republic A derogatory term for a state, often in a deprived area, dependent on one type of trade (such as banana growing).

bangstick A long rod containing an explosive-charged head (normally a shotgun cartridge) which detonates on contact. Used by divers against sharks.

bank holiday (UK). A day when the banks are officially closed and which is generally designated a public holiday.

bank settlement plan The previous name for billing and settlement plan.

banqueting rooms Rooms set aside in a hotel or similar for private and public functions.

bar 1. A place that serves alcoholic drinks and simple food. In the UK the term is generally reserved for the drinking area in hotels or similar; elsewhere it can be more generally applied to any drinking establishment. 2. A barrier of sand or sediment, usually caused by tidal action, near to shore or in the mouth of a river. 3. Abbreviation for "barometric" used as a unit of pressure.

Barbary An old name given to the western part of North Africa, now preserved in the name of the monkeys living on the Rock of Gibraltar that are known as "Barbary Apes".

Barbary Coast The coast of northern Africa from Morocco to Egypt, infamous for the Barbary Corsairs who preyed on trading ships in the Mediterranean.

bareboat charter When a ship or other vessel is chartered without supplies or crew.

barge A cargo vessel, usually towed, that plies rivers and canals. The expression is often used incorrectly to describe the narrow boats common on British inland waterways.

barograph A barometer that records its readings.

barometer An instrument for measuring air pressure. Since changes in the weather are closely associated with variations in air pressure, barometers are commonly used to forecast the weather.

baroque A highly ornate and extravagant style, popular in the 17th and 18th centuries. Commonly used to describe architecture of that period.

barotrauma Internal physical damage to human body caused by expanding or contracting air. Divers are most at risk from such damage which can include burst ears, air embolism, emphysema and spontaneous pneumothorax.

barque A type of sailing ship, usually with four masts.

barrage A structure built across a tidal river or estuary to control the flow of water. In some countries the word is synonymous with dam although is not strictly correct.

basement A storey in a building that is below ground level.

basin A geographical term meaning a portion of land that is lower than the surrounding area. The term may also be applied to an area drained by a river.

bassinet A little-used term that describes a cot provided for a baby on an aircraft.

BATA British Air Transport Association. *See Appendix 7a.*

bathometer An instrument used to measure the depth of water.

bathroom In the UK a room containing a bath and other washing facilities; in the US, a euphemism for a lavatory.

batten down To secure the hatches of a ship against bad weather. The term derives from the original practice of using wooden battens to secure the tarpaulin covers over a ship's holds.

BAWTA British Association of Wholesale Tour Agents. *See Appendix 7a.*

bay A geographical term for the part of an ocean or sea that extends inland.

Bay Area The urban area surrounding San Francisco Bay. Includes San Francisco in the west, Oakland in the east and San Jose and Silicon Valley in the south.

bayou A name given to a marshy creek or tributary in the southern USA.

bazaar An oriental market.

BCH Bonded Coach Holiday Group. *See Appendix 7a.*

beach The area of rocks, sand or shingle that makes up the shore of a lake, sea or river.

beach buggy A small, wide-wheeled motor vehicle, originally derived from the Volkswagen Beetle, used mainly for recreation, for travelling on sand or similar.

beam The width of a vessel at its widest point.

beamy A ship that is broad in the beam.

beanery (US). A slang expression for a cheap restaurant.

bearing A direction relative to a point. Something that is at a bearing of 40° from you will be found in that direction relative to where you are.

beating the lung A diving term that means breathing at a rate faster than an aqualung is able to deliver air.

Beaufort scale The scale used to measure wind speed, shown below. Although the maximum reading on the scale is 10, hurricanes that would be equivalent to force 17 have occurred. The levels of the scale are:

0	Calm	Less than 1 knot
1	Light air	1 - 3 knots
2	Light breeze	4 - 6 knots
3	Gentle breeze	7 - 10 knots
4	Moderate breeze	11 - 16 knots
5	Fresh breeze	17 - 21 knots
6	Strong breeze	22 - 27 knots
7	Near gale	28 - 33 knots
8	Gale	24 - 40 knots
9	Strong gale	41 - 47 knots
10	Storm	48 - 55 knots
11	Violent storm	56 - 63 knots
12 or above	Hurricane	Over 64 knots

becalm To deprive a ship of wind.

B

bed and breakfast 1. A hotel rate including accommodation and breakfast.
2. Establishments providing this type of accommodation.

Bedouin A nomadic Arab people, usually living in the desert.

beerhouse (UK). A public house that is licensed to sell only beer and wine, not spirits.

bell boy (US). A page or porter in a hotel.

bell captain (US). The head porter of a hotel.

bell hop (US). A hotel porter.

bells On board ship bells are sounded to denote the passing of ship's time - one bell of each progressive half-hour to a total of eight. The series starts at half past the hours of 4, 8 and 12 and each 4 hour period makes up a watch.

belongings A person's movable possessions or luggage.

below In nautical terms, anything beneath the main deck of a ship.

beltway (US). A ring road.

bend 1. A knot used for joining two pieces of rope together.
2. (Usually plural "the bends"). Common term for decompression sickness, so named because the patient is often found bent over with pain.

benefit An insurance term describing the amount that will be paid to the insured in the event of a successful claim for a specific incident. A benefit will be paid regardless of the amount of loss actually incurred. For example, a company may pay a sum of £50 for the inconvenience caused by delayed baggage, but the claimant does not have to substantiate the claim, merely to prove that the baggage was delayed.

Benguela current A cold-water current running northwards up the west African coast and then westwards into the south Atlantic ocean. Its significance is the up-welling of nutrient-bearing water it brings from the seabed that supports vast numbers of fish in the area.

benign When describing the climate, it means mild or favourable.

berg A South African expression meaning mountain.

berg wind A hot dry wind blowing from the interior of Africa to coastal districts.

Berliner 1. A resident of Berlin.
2. A type of yeast bun with a jam filling.

berm A narrow path or earthwork beside a road, canal, etc.

Bermuda agreement An air travel agreement that was developed in the 1940's that restricted air travel between Britain and the USA to the services of the national carriers. The agreement was substantially modified in the 1970's and few such restrictions now exist.

Bermuda plan A hotel rate that includes accommodation and full breakfast.

Bermuda triangle Triangular area of the Atlantic Ocean stretching from Bermuda in the north-east, Puerto Rico in the south-east and South Florida in the south-west that is supposed to have had a number of unexplained disappearances of ships and aircraft. The area first gained its reputation following the mystery loss of several US warplanes in the 1940s.

berth **1.** A bed on a ship or train. Berths can usually be folded against the wall when not in use and can be situated one above another. Obviously an upper berth can be inconvenient to passengers who are not fully able. **2.** The name given to an area where a ship ties up when in port.

BH&HPA British Holiday & Home Parks Association Ltd. *See Appendix 7a.*

BHA British Hospitality Association. *See Appendix 7a.*

Bibby cabin A cabin that has a narrow corridor leading to a porthole, thus getting some natural light and fresh air. It also had the advantage of being away from the ship's side and was thus cooler when the plates were heated by the sun. The name came from the Bibby Line, who introduced the type. Now rarely used.

Bible Belt Parts of the United States where Fundamentalist Christianity exerts a dominating influence on local politics and culture. The term was first used in the 1920s to describe rural communities and small towns in the South. Parts of the Southwest and the Midwest are now often included in the term.

big foot A short fun-ski, shaped like a giant foot.

bight **1.** A curve or recess in a coastline or river. **2.** A loop in a rope.

bike An abbreviation for bicycle. The expression is derived from the vehicle's number of wheels and not its method of control. It should thus not be used to describe a vehicle with a similar control system but having other than two wheels. *See also cycle.*

bilateral agreement An agreement between two parties (for example, countries). Generally used in connection with airlines' agreements with each other regarding routes, frequency, fares, equipment, etc.

bilge The lowest part of the hull of a ship.

bilharzia A disease of the tropics caused by a parasitic flatworm.

bilingual Relating to the ability to speak two languages.

bill of fare *See menu.*

billabong An Australian term for a branch of a river forming a backwater.

billing and settlement plan (BSP) An IATA payment system whereby agents hold one type of ticket, rather than separate documents for each airline. Payment for all tickets sold is made through a bank in the agent's own country and BSP arranges for the airlines to be paid. Agents do not have to make individual payments to airlines participating in the scheme.

bin The enclosed luggage container situated above the seats of an aircraft.

binding The mechanism that attaches a ski or snowboard boot to the ski or snowboard.

binnacle The receptacle for a ship's compass.

B

bioinvasion The phenomenon whereby indigenous species of plants and animals are being invaded by other types carried in by travellers. Many fragile ecosystems, such as the Florida Everglades, are under threat from bioinvasion. The effects of this phenomenon are known as biopollution.

biopollution *See bioinvasion.*

biosphere That part of the earth in which life exists.

biplane An aeroplane with two pairs of wings. Biplanes can usually operate at lower speeds than monoplanes and are thus still used in regions where STOL capabilities are important.

bisque Fish soup.

bistro A small, often informal, restaurant.

BITOA British Incoming Tour Operators Association. *See Appendix 7a.*

bitumen An Australian expression meaning a tarred road.

black box *See flight recorder.*

black diamond run *See black run.*

black run The grading given by most ski areas to the most difficult of ski runs. In North America the toughest runs are called "black diamond runs" with the relative degree of difficulty being indicated by the number of diamonds - usually one, two or three.

black tie (UK). The name given to the mode of formal evening dress for men that involves the wearing of a dinner jacket and bow tie.

black-water rafting An extreme sport that involves rafting down underground streams in the dark. The name is taken from that of the organisation that invented the sport in 1987.

blimp A non-rigid airship.

blizzard A violent snowstorm with high winds.

bloc A combination of parties, governments or other groupings sharing a common purpose or ideology.

blue flag beach A beach that meets the strict environmental requirements set by FEEE.

Blue Peter A blue flag with a white square, raised on a ship when leaving port.

blue run The grading given to the gentlest ski runs in most German, Austrian and Swiss resorts. In most French and Italian resorts this designation is applied to the next steepest after the easiest.

blue water The open sea.

bluff A steep cliff or headland.

board 1. To get onto a vehicle. **2.** Food and lodging.

boarding house (UK). An old-fashioned term for a private home whose owner rents out rooms and may provide meals. The expression "guest house" is now more commonly used as it has overtones of slightly better "class".

boarding pass A document given to passengers in exchange for a ticket coupon, which proves their entitlement to board an aircraft or other vehicle.

boardwalk **1.** A wooden walkway across a sandy or marshy area. **2.** (US). A seaside promenade.

boat A small water-borne vessel. The borderline between a large boat and a small ship is vague but it is safe to say that any vessel that is large enough to have more than one lifeboat is probably a ship.

boat deck The deck of a ship on which the lifeboats are located. Not recommended for passengers wanting a view of the sea.

boat drill *See lifeboat drill.*

boat stations The designated meeting points for passengers prior to the lowering of the lifeboats.

boat train A train scheduled to meet a ship.

boatel Also botel. **1.** A waterside hotel with facilities for mooring boats. **2.** A floating vessel converted to a hotel.

boatswain Pronounced and sometimes spelt bosun. The ship's officer in charge of equipment and crew.

bodega A shop selling wine and food, especially in Spanish speaking countries.

bog An area of wet, spongy ground.

bogie A wheelset on a locomotive or other railway vehicle.

Bohemian A native of Bohemia, a former kingdom in central Europe, roughly corresponding to the area of Slovakia and the Czech Republic. Now used to denote a socially unconventional person.

boiler The tank fitted to a steam engine in which the water is boiled into steam.

bollard A stout post, either on shore or on board ship, used for fixing mooring lines.

bond A guarantee of repayment following financial failure of the bondholder. Most travel principals require a bond to protect themselves against loss through the financial failure of a travel agent. Many insurance companies will arrange a bond in consideration of an appropriate premium.

book To make a reservation of some kind. The name originated from the original way in which reservations were made, which was, of course, to write them into a book. From this, the expression "a booking" has come to mean a reservation.

booking form Originally an essential document, completed and signed by customers to show in writing the arrangements requested. These days most bookings are made on the telephone or electronically and booking forms are not usually needed by principals. However, it is good practice for agents to hold a written and signed copy of a customer's request, since, in the event of a later dispute, this may avoid arguments about what was actually said at the time.

booking reference A name, number, letter or combination of any

B

or all of these that identifies a specific booking. Ideally a booking reference should enable immediate access to the booking in question without there being any need for cross-referring.

Bora A strong, cold, dry north-easterly wind blowing in the Adriatic region.

Borneo An island in the Malay Archipelago divided between Brunei/Darussalam, Indonesia (the provinces of Central, East, South and West Kalimantan) and Malaysia (the states of Sabah and Sarawak).

borough In the UK, a town represented in the House of Commons.

botel *See boatel.*

bottom time The duration between commencing a dive (i.e. leaving the surface) and beginning the final ascent.

bow The front of a ship. Usually used as the plural, bows.

bow thruster A screw mounted at the front of a ship, facing sideways, that assists docking. Many car ferries use bow thrusters.

bow wave The wave set up by the bows of a moving ship or other vessel.

bowsprit A spar projecting from the bows of a boat or ship.

BR *See British Rail.*

BRA British Resorts Association. *See Appendix 7a.*

brae A Scottish term for a steep bank or hillside.

Brahman A member of the highest Hindu caste.

branch office location An IATA term meaning an accredited agent's place of business, other than its head office, listed on the IATA agency list as a branch office location.

break even point The number of sales required on a given service to cover the direct costs of its operation. Profit will not be made until sales in excess of the break even are made.

breakaway A short holiday.

breakwater A barrier built out into the sea to mitigate the force of waves and currents.

bridge **1.** A structure built to carry a road, railway, etc., across an obstruction.
2. The control point of a ship.

bridleway A route or track intended for the use of horse-riders.

brig A two-masted, square-rigged ship.

British Of or relating to the British Isles, its inhabitants and culture.

British Isles The geographical region comprising The United Kingdom, Republic of Ireland, Isle of Man and Channel Islands.

British Rail The name for the rail network of the United Kingdom prior to its break-up into several private train operating companies.

British Summer Time The daylight saving time used in the UK. The expression "British Standard Time" (used 1968-71) is now obsolete.

Britisher A term, used by races other than the British, to refer to a British subject or someone of British descent.

Briton 1. A member of the peoples that inhabited the southern part of Britain before the Roman conquest.
2. A native or inhabitant of Great Britain.

broad gauge A railway track gauge of more than the standard 4' 8½".

brochure In travel terms, the catalogue issued by tour operators and others that gives details of the products on offer.

BSP *See billing and settlement plan.*

BSP Committee An IATA term for a committee composed of representatives of IATA members, established in accordance with the Provisions for the Conduct of IATA Traffic Conferences and having general responsibilities with respect to Standard Bank Plans.

BSP Coordinator An IATA term. A person appointed by the plan management as required, to act in accordance with its rules on behalf of airlines and IATA members.

BSP Panel An IATA term for a panel composed of all IATA members who operate services, or issue traffic documents through agents, in the country or area of a Billing and Settlement Plan. The panel also includes non-IATA airlines who participate in Billing and Settlement Plans.

BSP Steering panel An IATA term for the panel which, in accordance with the instructions and directions of the BSP committee, is charged with the implementation and certain supervisory aspects of BSP.

BST *See British Summer Time.*

BTA British Tourist Authority. *See Appendix 7a.*

B

bubble car (US). *See observation car.*

bucket and spade A term used to describe a "traditional" type of family holiday, typically with young children, taken in relatively low price destinations.

bucket shop A travel retailer specialising in the sale of discounted air tickets. The term is beginning to fall from favour as more legitimate agents are now involved in the trade.

buckshee (UK). A slang expression meaning free of charge. A corruption of the Middle Eastern word baksheesh.

Buddhism The philosophy or belief observed by the followers of Guatama Buddha, who lived in India during the 5th century BC.

buddy In sub-aqua terms a fellow diving companion.

buffet 1. An eating establishment, often on a railway station, where customers serve themselves from a counter.
2. The food service system where customers help themselves from a counter or table.

buffeting An irregular oscillation of an aircraft, caused by air turbulence.

bulkhead A vertical partition or wall in a ship or aircraft.

bullet train A high-speed passenger train, originally in Japan.

bulletin An obsolete term that was once used to describe certain types of accommodation ticket, especially

B

those issued for Wagon-Lit sleepers.

bulwarks The sides of a ship above the top deck.

bumboat A small boat plying between ships and the shore with provisions, etc.

bump A passenger who has a confirmed booking but is refused carriage is said to have been bumped. This happens when more confirmed passengers turn up than expected for an overbooked service

bumps (US). Moguls.

bunk A sleeping berth, especially one projecting from a wall or partition.

bunkering The taking on of fuel by a ship.

bunkers The space on ship where the fuel is stored.

buoy A floating marker that indicates a channel or hazard.

buoyancy compensator An inflatable jacket worn by divers underwater which can be partially inflated or deflated to suit underwater buoyancy requirements.

bure A South Pacific term used to describe a thatched-roof bungalow, especially in Fiji.

bus Short for omnibus. A large passenger-carrying road vehicle. In the UK a distinction is made between buses, which are those that operate short distance scheduled services, and coaches, that operate longer distance and chartered services. This distinction is not applied in many other parts of the world. As an abbreviation, the word was originally written with an initial apostrophe, 'bus. However common usage has meant that the apostrophe is usually dropped these days.

busboy (US). A person who clears tables in an eating establishment.

business centre A room for business travellers, usually including telecommunications equipment, office facilities, secretarial facilities, etc.

business class An airline class of service aimed, as would be expected, at business travellers. Its standard is between first and economy.

business house An obsolescent term for business travel agent

business travel agent At one time, travel agents would undertake bookings for all classes of traveller, whether they were travelling on holiday or for business reasons. However, as business travellers' needs became more specialised, the work of the retail agent and the business travel agent began to diverge. Business travel agents usually receive commission on the products they sell, in the same way as retail agents. However, in many cases they will charge their customers a fee for the maintenance of the travel account. This fee will allow for the provision of large amounts of information on the customer's travel pattern and spend and will also enable the agent to spend time and effort in negotiating preferential customer travel deals. The business travel agent who charges such a fee is, in fact, acting as an agent for the customer, so in this case the term agent is accurate. *See management fee.*

business traveller Any traveller who needs to make a journey for the purpose of trade or commerce, rather than for leisure or other personal reasons.

button lift The simplest form of drag lift, popular in France and Italy. A plastic disk, attached to the drag cable by an elasticated cord, is caught by the skier who then "sits" on it and is pulled up the slope.

BVRLA British Vehicle Rental & Leasing Association. *See Appendix 7a.*

BW British Waterways. *See Appendix 7a.*

bwana A polite form of address used in many African countries. From the Swahili for "sir".

bypass A route, usually a road, that avoids a town centre or other congested area.

byway A minor road.

Byzantine Of the eastern Roman Empire. Often applied to the highly decorated style of architecture, etc. of that time, or originating in Byzantium (modern-day Istanbul).

B

C
c

CAA Civil Aviation Authority. *See Appendix 7a.*

cab An alternative name for a taxi.

cabaña A US and South American term for a beach hut.

cabin 1. A small hut or shelter.
2. A room for sleeping on a ship.
3. The interior of an aircraft.

cabin bag A small bag suitable for carriage in the passenger cabin of an aircraft.

cabin class An obsolescent expression denoting a class on ship that is between first and tourist.

cabin crew Those members of an aircraft's crew that are responsible for the comfort and well-being of the passengers and who do not have flying responsibilities.

cabin cruiser A large motor boat with living accommodation.

cable A nautical measure of length equal to 100 fathoms (600 feet).

cable car A large cabin attached to a cable along which it travels. Cable cars are common in mountainous areas since they are relatively quick and easy to build and can travel very steeply.

cable railway A railway along which a train is drawn by means of an endless cable. Examples can be found in Llandudno, Hong Kong and San Francisco.

cabotage Air travel between territories of the same sovereign state. This may be between points within the same country (e.g. London to Manchester) or between a country and its dependencies (e.g. London to Gibraltar). The air fares for cabotage journeys are not governed by the normal international fare agreements.

café 1. A small, relatively informal, eating establishment.
2. (US). A bar or night-club

cafeteria The full name for café, to which it is usually abbreviated.

caique A small rowing boat used on the Bosphorus.

cairn A mound of stones built as a monument or landmark.

Cajun Country Area of southern Louisiana settled by a group of people of French origin, expelled from Nova Scotia in the 18th century by the British. The word Cajun is a corruption of "Arcadian".

Caledonian Of or relating to Scotland. (Roman name, Caledonia).

calendar A system for measuring the time that has passed over a long period. All calendars divide the aeons into years, but the subdivisions vary. In travel and business the Gregorian calendar of twelve months and 365 days is used. However, there are several other systems, of which the Chinese, Jewish and Muslim are the most important.

California current A wide, cold and sluggish current that runs north to south off the west coast of the USA.

calm As related to weather, little or no wind.

campground *See campsite.*

camping holiday A holiday where holidaymakers stay in temporary accommodation such as tents, caravans, etc.

camping site *See campsite.*

campsite An area where campers can pitch their tents or where static tents can be rented. In the USA most sites will accept motorhomes and caravans, but in the UK this is not always the case.

Canadian Technology Triangle Area south-west of Toronto, Canada, famous for its concentration of high-tech industries.

canal An artificial waterway. Most canals were originally built for goods traffic, but many are now used by leisure travellers.

cancel To release, withdraw or revoke a reservation.

cancellation and curtailment insurance It is important for travellers to have cover against cancellation charges (which are those incurred when the entire arrangement is cancelled) and curtailment charges (which are those incurred when the arrangement is cut short or curtailed). Cover is usually provided for a range of circumstances, mainly medical. What is never covered, though, is a customer's "disinclination to travel". In other words, customers can't change their minds about the holiday and decide they can't afford it after all!

cancellation charge A fee charged to a customer who cancels a booking. Since it is always difficult to collect such charges, it is important for agents to collect in advance an amount sufficient to cover any likely charges. Since the scales of cancellation charges can be complex, it is important that travel staff do not refund any part of a pre-payment without having proper authority from the principal involved.

canoe A small, narrow boat usually propelled by paddling.

cantina A Spanish expression, especially common in Mexico, meaning a bar or wine-shop.

Canuck A Canadian, especially a French Canadian.

canx. A commonly used abbreviation that means cancelled.

canyon A deep valley or ravine with steep sides.

cap As applied to commission, to place a ceiling or limit on the maximum amount that can be earned.

c

capacity The maximum carrying capability of a vehicle or the maximum number that can occupy a hotel or other accommodation.

cape A point of land projecting into a body of water, usually a sea or ocean.

Cape doctor A strong south-easterly wind experienced in South Africa.

capital The most important town or city of a country, state or region. It is important not to confuse the different capitals. For example, the state capital of Tasmania is Hobart, but the capital of Australia (and therefore Tasmania) is Canberra. Most capitals are also the seats of government for their countries but this is not always the case. Furthermore, in some countries governmental functions may be split between two or more centres. For example, although the Dutch government sits in the Hague, the commercial capital is Amsterdam.

Capsian Of or relating to the Palaeolithic culture of North Africa and South Europe.

capsize Of a boat, to overturn or upset.

capstan A thick revolving spindle used for winding a rope or hawser. Commonly found on marine vessels to haul in mooring ropes, etc.

capsule hotel Accommodation, commonly used in Japan, that provides sleeping compartments in drawer-like capsules, large enough for one person only.

captain The person in charge of a waterborne vessel or aircraft.

car 1. (UK). A private motor vehicle having three or more wheels.

2. A railway carriage.

3. Any passenger compartment in a vehicle such as a lift.

car ferry A vessel, usually a ship, designed to carry vehicles as well as passengers.

car hire An alternative term for car rental. Car rental is becoming the preferred expression.

car rental Travellers wanting the convenience and flexibility of a self-drive or chauffeur-driven vehicle at their destination, but unable or unwilling to take their own, may hire a car or other vehicle when they arrive. Car rental is now a major and growing part of the travel industry.

caravan Originally a trailer vehicle, but now frequently applied to many types of semi-permanent accommodation on special sites.

caravan site An area where caravans may be parked. Sites may be semi-permanent, where the caravans may be parked for months or years, or short stay. Short stay sites are intended for the use of touring caravan users stopping for a few nights.

caravanette A motor-caravan.

cardboarding A method of falsifying the audit coupons of a manually issued ticket. It is, of course, fraud and thus a criminal offence.

cargo Goods, other than a passenger's personal effects, carried on board a ship or aircraft.

carhop (US). A colloquial expression for a waiter at a drive-in restaurant.

Caribbean A general tourist term used to describe the West Indies.

carnet 1. A term of French origin that describes an official document that allows the temporary importation of goods without payment of duty.
2. On some transport undertakings (including the London Underground and the Paris Metro) a book of tickets sold at a discount.

Caroline islands Archipelago in the west Pacific Ocean. The islands comprise the Federated States of Micronesia and Palau.

Carolingian Of or relating to the second Frankish dynasty.

carousel A rotating delivery system for arriving passengers' luggage, especially at an airport.

carriage 1. The usual UK term for a railway passenger vehicle.
2. Transportation between two points by a company existing for that purpose.

carriageway That part of a road intended for vehicles.

carrier A generic term for any transport operator.

carrier identification plate A small embossed plate that is fitted into a ticket validating machine and which endorses the name of the carrier onto the ticket or other document.

carsickness Nausea caused by travelling in a car or other road vehicle.

cartel An organisation or group that seeks to control prices and other aspects of its members' trading. It is common practice for cartels to fix prices at a high level, thus forcing customers to pay more than they need. Although cartels are now illegal in many countries, it is often difficult to detect and prevent their activities.

cartogram A map with statistical information in diagrammatic form.

cartography The art and practice of map-making.

carving skis A modern development that is affecting the design of most traditional skis. Carving skis have wider sections at their front and rear that enable them to turn more easily.

casbah *See kasbah.*

cascade A small waterfall.

cash basis When an agent defaults on its payments, the principal concerned may withdraw credit facilities and only allow the agent to issue documents against immediate cash payment.

casita A bungalow, especially in Mexico.

caste system The system practised in the Hindu culture whereby different personal levels of purity or pollution are said to be inherited. In a strict caste system, members of different levels will have no contact with each other.

cat's paw A very slight breeze that just ripples the surface of water.

catacomb An underground cemetery or resting place for bones, especially Roman.

catamaran A boat with twin parallel hulls.

cataract A large waterfall or cascade, often one with a relatively slight drop.

catchment area In tourism, the area from which an attraction or resort gets most of its customers.

Caucasian Of or relating to the white or light-skinned division of humankind.

causeway A raised road or tract across low or wet ground or shallow water.

cave A large hollow in the side of a hill or cliff or underground.

cave tubing *See black-water rafting.*

caveat emptor A Latin expression meaning "let the buyer beware". In other words, the buyer is responsible for his or her own satisfaction with a purchase.

cavern A cave, usually large.

cay A small island (sometimes spelled key, as in the Florida Keys).

CDW *See collision damage waiver.*

ceiling 1. The maximum height at which an aircraft can fly under a given set of conditions.
2. The inside planking of a ship's hull.

Celebes Island in the Malay Archipelago.

Celsius *See centigrade.*

Celt A member of the pre-Roman inhabitants of Britain and Gaul and their descendants.

centigrade Also known as Celsius. The temperature scale in which water freezes at 0° and boils at 100°. A quick way approximately to convert Centigrade to Fahrenheit is to double the Centigrade figure and add 30. Thus 25°C x 2 = 50. Plus 30 = 80°F.

Central America The geographical region comprising Belize, Costa Rica, El Salvador, Guatemala, Honduras, Nicaragua, Panama.

Certificate in Business Travel (CBT) The qualification run by the Guild of Business Travel Agents and validated by City and Guilds. It is an examination-based qualification at several levels designed for those working, or intending to work, in business travel.

chain 1. An obsolescent measurement of distance equal to 66 feet (one eightieth of a mile). The railways of Britain were surveyed using chains and certain measurements may still be referred to in these units.
2. A group of shops, restaurants, hotels, etc., owned by the same person or organisation.

chair lift Similar in principle to a cable car, but with a chair (not a cabin) for carrying passengers. Chair lifts can carry 1, 2, 3, 4, 6 or 8 passengers.

chalet A small, wooden house or bungalow, usually with an overhanging roof. Traditional in Switzerland and Austria and often used as accommodation for winter sports enthusiasts.

chambermaid A housemaid in a hotel.

champagne powder Very light powder snow, typically falling in Western North America. The name has been trademarked by Steamboat resort.

channel A length of water, wider than a strait, joining two larger areas of water. Often used as a proper noun (the Channel) to describe the English Channel.

Channel Islands A group of British islands off the north-west coast of France comprising: Alderney, Guernsey, Herm, Jersey, Sark and Jethou. Although they are Crown possessions, they are not part of the United Kingdom.

charabanc An obsolete term for a motor coach that is still used in some circles.

charge card Similar to a credit card, although the extended payment facility is not automatically offered.

chart An alternative name for map, usually applied to the very accurate navigational maps used on aircraft and ships.

charter Usually applied to aircraft but can apply to any form of transport, where a person or organisation pays for the exclusive use of a vehicle. An ad hoc charter is a one off arrangement; a series charter is several journeys between the same points; a time charter is when the vehicle is chartered for a period of time. Providing the charterer can fill the vehicle, the per person cost will be far less than the scheduled fare between the same points.

chasm A deep, wide fissure or opening in the earth or rock.

chauffeur The paid driver of a motor car.

chauffeur drive In car rental, a vehicle rented with a driver.

check digit A number, following a document number, that bears a mathematical relationship to that number. It is used to verify the accuracy of the number and thus identify any transcription errors. Also known as check sum.

check sum *See check digit.*

checked baggage Baggage that is registered to a traveller's destination and is conveyed separately.

check-in 1. The process of registering at a hotel or other accommodation. **2.** The process of completing formalities before boarding a flight or other transportation.

check-in time The time by which a person must have checked in for a flight or at a hotel.

check-out The process of finalising the bill, etc., when guests vacate a hotel or other accommodation.

chef A cook, usually male, in a restaurant or similar establishment.

cheque card (UK). A card that guarantees payment of a cheque up to a stated amount.

chersonese An expression of Greek origin meaning a peninsula, especially the Thracian peninsula west of the Hellespont.

Chicago Convention The convention that defined the Freedoms of the Air in 1944.

child In travel, a young person who will not have to pay the full fare. The age at which a child becomes an adult will vary according to the carrier, but for most airlines it is 12 years.

C

c

chill factor The perceived lowering of temperature caused by wind, etc. The chill factor is often more important in determining comfort than is the actual temperature.

chine A deep narrow ravine, especially in the Isle of Wight or Dorset.

Chinook 1. A warm dry wind that blows east of the Rocky Mountains. **2.** A warm wet southerly wind that blows west of the Rocky Mountains.

chit A familiar expression meaning a note, memorandum or similar document.

cholera An infectious intestinal disease transmitted by water and endemic in countries with poor standards of sanitation.

chondola The name for a modern ski lift that can carry either chairs or cabins.

chopper A familiar term for a helicopter.

Christian Believing in or following the teachings of Jesus Christ.

christian name The first or given name. This term is not always recognised in countries where Christianity is not the main religion and the expression "given name" may be better understood.

chronometer Simply, an instrument that measures time but actually a very accurate timepiece. Accurate navigation across meridians of longitude was not possible until the invention of the chronometer by the Englishman, John Harrison.

Chunnel A familiar term for the Channel Tunnel between England and France.

chute 1. A narrow, short, steep ski run, off-piste in Europe. **2.** An inflatable slide used as a means of emergency exit from an aircraft.

CIMTIG Chartered Institute of Marketing Travel Industry Group. *See Appendix 7a.*

Cinque Ports A group of ports on the south-east coast of England with certain ancient privileges. The name is probably derived from the Latin *quinque portus* (five ports) since there were originally that number.

CIP *See commercially important person.*

circle trip A return journey which is continuous back to its starting point and via two or more intermediate points, each of which carries a different fare.

circuitous A journey that is indirect and usually a long way around. Such routeings are often discouraged or prohibited by many carriers.

circumference The enclosing boundary of a circle. The equator goes around the circumference of the earth.

circumnavigate To sail around, especially around the world.

circumpolar Around or near to one of the earth's poles.

cirque A deep, bowl-shaped hollow at the head of a valley or on a mountain.

cirrus A form of white, wispy cloud found at high altitude. Often known as "mare's tails" because of its resemblance to a horse's tail.

CIS *See Commonwealth of Independent States.*

CITA Confederation of Independent Travel Agents. *See Appendix 7a.*

CITC Canadian Institute of Travel Counsellors. *See Appendix 7c.*

citizen 1. A member of a State or Commonwealth.
2. (US). A civilian.

city 1. (UK). A large town with a cathedral.
2. In most of the world, a large town.

city terminal A point in a town or city where airline passengers may check in for flights rather than at the airport. Also, passengers may be taken into a city terminal at the end of their journeys.

claim To submit a request for reimbursement under the terms of an insurance policy.

claimant A person making a claim.

clan A group of people with a common ancestor, especially in Scotland.

class In travel, the divisions in a vehicle that segregate passengers according to the fare paid. Once simply first, second and third, the demands of marketing have resulted in a plethora of special names for the different classes. Whereas these new terms may be less emotive, they are certainly more confusing.

clay pan An Australian term for a hollow in the soil that retains water after rain.

clearance 1. Special permission granted to proceed, for example to an aircraft waiting to take off.
2. The act of being allowed through customs.

clearing bank An IATA term meaning the bank or other organisation appointed under BSP to perform various functions including: receipt of sales transmittals; extraction and processing of data therefrom; rendering of billings to agents; receipt of payments from agents.

clearstory (US). *See clerestory.*

clearway (UK). A road on which vehicles are not allowed to stop.

cleat 1. A projecting piece on a spar or gangway to give secure footing.
2. A clip to which a rope may be secured.

clerestory (US clearstory). A raised roof section of a railway carriage that contains windows and ventilators. Rarely seen these days.

CLIA Cruise Lines International Association. *See Appendix 7b.*

cliff A steep rock face.

climate The general condition of an area in terms of its temperature, rainfall, humidity, etc. Unlike weather, variations in climate are relatively regular and predictable.

climatic zones The climatic types, in approximately ascending order of warmth, are:
- **Polar.** Extreme cold with vicious winds. Rainfall or snowfall is low, but as there is little evaporation, polar regions are snow-covered for much of the year.
- **Mountain.** Each rise in altitude of 15,000 feet (4,500 metres) has the same effect as a change in latitude towards a pole of around 15°. At sea level mountains support the

same vegetation as the countryside around them, but as the height increases the temperature drops and the vegetation becomes more suited to a cooler climate. At the tops of the tallest mountains, the climate is often as cold as at the poles, even in equatorial latitudes.

• **Taiga.** The cold, coniferous forests that stretch from Siberia across northern Asia, Europe and North America through to Alaska. Long, cold winters and brief, warm, summers. There is relatively little rainfall. Taiga only occurs in the northern hemisphere since there are no large land masses at the equivalent southern latitudes.

• **Temperate**. Temperature and rainfall are reasonably evenly distributed throughout the year and there are no extremes of either. Temperate regions are characterised by very changeable day to day weather. The UK is in a temperate region.

• **Mediterranean**. Hot, dry summers and warm wet winters characterise the climate of west facing coastal regions between the temperate and desert latitudes. Mediterranean climates can be found in every continent except Antarctica and all are popular with holidaymakers.

• **Dry grassland.** Areas such as the prairies of North America, the pampas of Argentina and the veldt of Southern Africa are all screened from the moisture-laden sea air. There is only enough rainfall to support grass and similar plants.

• **Hot desert.** Desert areas have high daytime temperatures and little rainfall. With irrigation, desert areas can be made fertile and attractive.

• **Subtropical**. High temperatures throughout the year but with marked seasonal variations in rainfall.

• **Tropical**. High 24-hour temperatures and high rainfall give rise to luxuriant growth of many types of vegetation. Where unchecked this results in a typical "rain forest".

clime An alternative name for a region or climate.

clip The act of removing a small piece from a ticket (usually one for rail travel) to show that it has been used.

clip-joint A slang expression for a night club or similar establishment that swindles its guests by overcharging.

clipper A large, fast sailing vessel.

cloakroom **1.** A room where outer garments and baggage can be left. **2.** A euphemism for a lavatory.

cloud The visible masses of condensed water vapour floating in the atmosphere.

club car (US). A railway carriage equipped with a lounge and other amenities.

club class The most common term given to the part of an aircraft reserved for business travellers. In comfort it is between first and economy. *(See also class)*.

coach **1.** (UK). A motor vehicle carrying a large number of passengers and used mainly for longer distance journeys and tours. **2.** (US). Economy class. **3.** A railway carriage.

coach class A US term for economy class.

coaming Small raised partitions at the doorways and around the hatches on a ship that prevent the access of water.

coast The border of the land near the sea.

coaster A ship that travels along the coast from port to port.

coastguard An organisation keeping watch on the coasts and on local shipping to maintain safety and prevent smuggling.

coastline The line of the seashore, especially as regards its shape and characteristics.

cockpit 1. The part of an aircraft where the controls are located. **2.** The control position of a yacht or motor launch.

code sharing The practice of airlines' using the code of another carrier in an advertised schedule. Thus, a flight might be shown as British Airways but actually be operated by another carrier on its behalf.

coffee shop A small informal restaurant in a hotel or similar.

cog railway A special form of railway used on steep gradients where the normal friction between wheels and track would give insufficient grip. An extra toothed wheel engages with a toothed rack on the track.

collection charge See delivery charge.

collision damage waiver Although rented vehicles will be insured, most companies will charge hirers who sustain loss or damage an excess amount, which may be substantial, although limited. To avoid having to pay this excess, hirers can pay a "nominal" sum and the hire company will then waive its right to collect it. The expression "CDW" is being replaced by the more general "LDW" which stands for loss damage waiver. LDW usually covers a greater range of circumstances than CDW.

colonial Of or relating to a colony or colonies, especially of the former British colonies.

colony A group of settlers in a country, subject to a mother country.

colours The national flag or emblem flown by a ship.

commercially important person Similar to VIP but where the traveller's importance derives from commercial or business activities rather than status.

commis A junior waiter or chef.

commission The amount paid by a principal to its agents. Commission percentages can vary widely although there are "official" levels. (For international air, for example, it is supposed to be 9%). In general, for most services 5% would be considered low and 15% high, although there are products with commission levels outside even these extremes.

common carrier A carrier that undertakes to carry any person or goods in a specified category or categories.

common-rated The name given to two or more destinations to which the fare is the same.

commonwealth An independent State or community, especially democratic.

Commonwealth of Independent States The countries of the former Soviet Union with the exception of Estonia, Latvia and Lithuania.

Commonwealth, The (In full, the British Commonwealth of Nations). A free association of independent states comprising: Antigua and Barbuda, Australia, Bahamas, Bangladesh, Barbados, Belize, Botswana, Brunei/Darussalam, Cameroon, Canada, Cyprus, Dominica, Fiji, The Gambia, Ghana, Grenada, Guyana, India, Jamaica, Kenya, Kiribati, Lesotho, Malawi, Maldives, Malta, Mauritius, Mozambique, Namibia, Nauru, New Zealand, Pakistan, Papua New Guinea, St. Kitts and Nevis, St. Lucia, St. Vincent and the Grenadines, Seychelles, Sierra Leone, Singapore, Solomon Islands, South Africa, Sri Lanka, Swaziland, Tanzania, Togo, Trinidad and Tobago, Tuvalu, United Kingdom, Vanuatu, Western Samoa, Zambia, Zimbabwe. Dependencies and associated states of Australia, New Zealand and the UK are also members.

communicating cabins The shipboard equivalent of connecting rooms.

communism The political philosophy that started in Western Europe in 1848 and survives in a few states today. Its guiding principle is that there is no such thing as private property.

commuter Originally one who travelled regularly, usually daily, between the same points using a season ticket. Now used to refer to anyone who travels regularly on a route, usually from home to work and vice versa.

commuter aircraft An aircraft, usually with fewer than 30 seats, that operates on relatively short routes.

comp. *See complimentary ticket.*

companionway A staircase on a ship, properly to a cabin, but often used loosely to refer to any stairway on board.

compartment 1. In a railway carriage, a small separate section. On the railways of Britain, these days compartments tend to be restricted to use by holders of first class (or equivalent) tickets. 2. A watertight division in a ship.

compass An instrument used to determine direction. Magnetic compasses point to the magnetic north, other types of compass, such as a giro compass, can give a true north reading.

compatriot A fellow countryman.

compensate To make restitution for loss or damage.

compensation An amount of money or other reimbursement made as restitution.

complement Or full complement. The number of persons required to fill or crew a ship or other conveyance.

complimentary ticket A free ticket given as thanks for a service provided or to be provided, or possibly as compensation.

complimentary upgrade When a carrier agrees to upgrade a passenger without collecting additional

C

payment. It is common for well-known or titled people to make reservations in the cheapest class available, secure in the knowledge that they will be given complimentary upgrades on checking in for their service. Although this is almost a form of blackmail, one could not imagine an airline refusing a famous actor or film star, for example, a complimentary upgrade.

comprehensive Complete or all inclusive. Often used to describe insurance cover.

compressor A pump used to compress air to the high pressure necessary to charge diving cylinders.

computerised reservation system (CRS) The generic name given to a whole range of systems that enable agents to make bookings with principals. The expression GDS, standing for Global Distribution System, is now taking over from CRS.

concierge A term of French origin that refers to a person in a hotel who gives information and attends to similar needs of guests.

concourse An open area in a large building, station or airport, where people can wait for a short while before moving on.

conditions of carriage All principals have special terms and conditions under which they will carry passengers and their baggage. Purchase of a ticket is deemed to indicate acceptance of these terms and conditions, even if the passenger is not familiar with them. Many conditions

of carriage exclude the rights that people have under normal law.

condominium 1. (US). A block of flats or apartments, often rented out on a long term or timeshare basis. Often abbreviated to "condo". 2. A region administered by two or more powers.

conducted tour A tour led by a guide on a predetermined and fixed itinerary.

confederation A union or alliance of states.

conference The generic name for any sort of medium to large gathering for discussion, especially one held annually.

conference rooms Rooms set aside for business and similar meetings.

confidential tariff The rates published by principals, such as hotels and excursion companies, for agents' use when constructing travel arrangements.

configuration The way in which the seats and other parts of an aircraft's interior are laid out.

confirmation A written or printed document that verifies the existence and details of a booking. Most travel bookings are no longer confirmed in writing but under CAA regulations, package holidays must be.

confluence A place where two rivers meet and join.

conjunction tickets An air journey that exceeds 4 sectors cannot be fitted onto one ticket. In such instances, two or more tickets will be issued "in conjunction" to cover the entire itinerary and the entire batch treated as one document.

connecting rooms Two or more rooms in a hotel that have a private connecting door, so that occupants can move from one room to another without using the public corridor.

connecting service A flight or other service that is timed to meet an arriving service.

consequential loss An insurance term meaning a loss arising from an original loss. Consequential losses are often excluded from cover in travel policies.

conservation area A region protected against damage or undesirable change. Many tourist destinations such as safari parks are also conservation areas.

consol. fare *See consolidation (2).*

consolidation **1.** Charter flights. If a charter flight or holiday has too few passengers, the operator may decide to combine two or more departures, thus maximising the passenger load. **2.** Scheduled air. Various regulations prohibit the public sale of "official" air fares at a discount, but airlines often wish to maximise their profits by selling surplus seats cheaply. They circumvent the various rules by selling their surplus seats, at heavily discounted rates, to a "consolidator". The consolidator then sells the seats on to agents or travellers at a price that includes his profit, but which is far lower than the official fare. These fares are colloquially known as "consolidation" or "consol." fares.

consolidator A person or organisation dealing in discounted airfares, especially those made available by scheduled carriers.

consortium An association of companies.

constellation A group of stars whose outline or appearance in the sky is considered to represent the outline of a figure or mythical being.

consul The government official, stationed in a foreign country, who represents the interests of the nationals of the represented country when they are in that foreign country. Consuls can render considerable assistance to travellers who find themselves in difficulty.

consulate The office where the consul works.

contents gauge A gauge which indicates the pressure of air inside a diving cylinder.

contents, table of A list, in order of appearance, of the items appearing in a book or manual.

continent The Earth is divided into 6 (some say 7) continents and one of the stranger facts about their names is that every continent's name begins and ends with a vowel, each one's name ends with the same vowel that it starts with and with only one exception (Europe) every one starts and finishes with the letter A. Alphabetically they are:
- Africa
- America (or the Americas)
- Antarctica
- Asia
- Australasia (Australia is only part

of Australasia)
• Europe

The land mass of the Americas is nowadays often divided into North America and South America, thus making 7 continents and spoiling the symmetry of the initial and final letters.

continental breakfast A light breakfast of rolls, coffee, toast, etc.

continental plan A hotel rate that includes accommodation and continental breakfast.

contour lines Lines drawn on a map to connect points of equal height.

contour map A map that shows heights and depths by means of contour lines.

contraband Items that are prohibited or illegal for export or import.

contrail An abbreviation of **con**densation **trail**. The visible trail of condensation left by a high-flying aircraft.

contremarque A term of French origin meaning a simple document issued to identify passengers, usually those travelling by rail, on a group ticket. This avoids the necessity for issuing separate tickets to each passenger.

contribution An insurance term for the principle that any liability is shared between all insurers involved.

control tower The building at an airport from which aircraft movements are controlled.

conurbation An extended urban area, often when several towns and their suburbs merge.

convenience A lavatory, especially public.

convention 1. Agreement about standards of behaviour, dress, etc.
2. A formal meeting or conference.
3. A formal agreement about standards and practices (such as the Warsaw Convention that relates to air travel).

convertible 1. A car with a roof that can be folded down.
2. An aircraft whose layout can be changed rapidly from cargo to passenger configuration and vice-versa.

Coordinated Universal Time *See UTC.*

co-pilot The second pilot of an aircraft.

coracle A small boat made of wickerwork and covered with watertight material. Used on Welsh and Irish lakes and rivers.

coral The shells of various marine animals. When laid down over aeons, these form reefs, islands and atolls.

Coral Coast The northern coast of Tunisia, main town Bizerte.

cordillera A chain of mountains, especially one (such as the Andes) that forms the axis of a large land mass.

cordon bleu Cookery of the highest possible standard of preparation and presentation.

corduroy road A road made of tree trunks and laid across an unsound area such as a swamp.

Corinthian Relating to ancient Corinth, in southern Greece.

C

corkage The amount a restaurateur may charge customers who wish to bring their own drinks into a restaurant.

corked Of wine. When the contents of the bottle have reacted with the cork and spoiled. Nothing to do with any small fragments of cork that may have broken from the stopper and fall into the glass.

Corniche Three roads in the French Riviera running parallel to the coast between Nice and Menton and cutting through spectacular cliffs. The Grande Corniche was built by Napoleon in 1806.

corniche A road cut into the face of a cliff.

Coromandel Coast Coast of south-east India, main ports include Nellore, Madras, Pondicherry, Cuddalore and Nagappattinam.

corona A ring of light that appears closely around the moon or sun under certain meteorological conditions. *See also halo.*

corporate rate Specially discounted rates offered to major purchasers of travel products. These rates are usually offered by hotels and car rental operators, although other principals are now adopting the principle. Business travellers are probably the main users of corporate rates.

corridor (UK). The passage in a railway carriage from which compartments can be accessed. *See also korridorzuge.*

cosmopolitan Of, or knowing, many parts of the world.

Cossack One of the people of southern Imperial Russia, originally famous for their military skill.

Costa Blanca 'White coast': resort area on the eastern coast of Spain from Denia to Torrevieja. Main town is Alicante, other resorts include Calpe and Benidorm.

Costa Brava 'Wild coast': the coast of the province of Gerona, north of Barcelona, with many popular tourist resorts. The coast south of Blanes is strictly speaking the Costa del Maresme.

Costa de Almería The eastern part of the Costa del Sol in southern Spain, main town Almería.

Costa de la Luz 'Coast of light': the Atlantic coast of southern Spain, principal towns are Huelva and Cádiz. More popular with the Spanish than with foreign tourists, the main resorts are Sanlúcar de Barrameda, Rota and Chipiona.

Costa de Lisboa The resort coast around Lisbon, Portugal. Also known as the Costa do Sol. Principal resorts are Cascais and Estoril.

Costa de Prata 'Silver coast': Portuguese coast stretching from Oporto in the north to the Costa de Lisboa in the south. Main resorts include Figuera da Foz and Nazaré.

Costa del Azahar 'Orange-blossom coast': Spanish resort area on the Mediterranean coast between the Costa Dorada in the north and the Costa Blanca in the south. The main town is Castellón de la Plana.

Costa del Sol 'Coast of the sun': resort

region of southern Spain, stretching along the Mediterranean coast from Tarifa in the west to Cabo de Gata in the east, with the main concentration of resorts between Marbella and Motril. The main town is Málaga and resorts include Marbella, Fuengirola, Torremolinos, Nerja, Almuñécar, Salobreña and Almería.

Costa Dorada 'Golden coast': the coastal resort area in Catalonia south of the Costa Brava. Main towns are Barcelona and Tarragona.

Costa Dourada 'Golden coast': Portuguese coastal region between Lisbon and the Algarve. Main towns are Sines and Vila Nova de Milfontes. Also known as the Costa de Ouro.

Costa Verde 'Green coast': resort coast in Portugal north of Oporto. Also the Spanish coast of the Asturias region, principal town Gijón.

cot A small bed, usually only suitable for a child, that may be put into a room to supplement the sleeping arrangements.

COTAC The Certificate of Travel Agency Competence. Now obsolete. *See ABTAC.*

COTAM The Certificate of Travel Agency Management. Now obsolete. *See ABTAC.*

Côte d'Argent Section of coast in south-west France, running from the Gironde estuary to the Spanish border with the resorts of Bayonne and Biarritz in the south.

Côte d'Azur The coast of south-east France, also known as the French Riviera. Main towns include St Tropez, St Raphaël, Cannes, Antibes, Nice and Monte Carlo.

COTICC The Certificate of Tourist Information Centre Competence. Now obsolete.

co-tidal line A line on a map connecting points at which tidal levels (such as high or low tide) appear simultaneously.

COTOP The Certificate of Tour Operating Practice. Now obsolete. *See ABTOP.*

COTOR The Certificate for Tour Operators' Representatives. Now obsolete.

couchette A type of sleeping accommodation offered on European trains, which provides 6 berths to each standard class compartment. No proper bedding is supplied and there is no segregation of the sexes. Couchettes are not used on UK rail services.

couloir *See chute (1).*

counterfoil Part of a receipt, ticket or other document retained by the issuer.

country The territory of a nation with its own government. Alternatively a territory possessing its own language and/or culture, etc. The distinction is important, since the UK and the USA, for example, both use the same language, but are different countries since they have their own governments. England and Wales, on the other hand, have the same government but are considered as separate countries because of their different cultures. *See the separate appendix for a full list of countries and the names of their inhabitants.*

C

county Any of the territorial divisions of a country (or in the USA, a state), forming the main unit of local administration.

coupé (US coupe). A car with a sloping roofline and frequently with limited seating accommodation in the rear.

coupon **1.** A page of a multi-part ticket. Such tickets will have at least four types of coupon. Exchange coupon(s) that are presented in exchange for the service; passenger coupon(s), that are the passenger's record and details of conditions of carriage; agency coupon(s) which are for the agent's records and audit coupon(s) which are used for accounting purposes.
2. A marketing term that refers to that part of an advertisement which is designed to be returned to the advertiser as a request for further information, etc.

courier An escort responsible for a group of travellers who travels with them throughout their journey. Sometimes used as an alternative name for a tour operator's resort representative.

courier flight A journey undertaken by a messenger carrying documents, samples, etc.

course The direction in which a vehicle is heading.

court cabin A ship's cabin that has a window opening onto a naturally lit area.

courtyard An area, enclosed by walls or buildings, often with access to a street.

cove An inlet from a sea or other body of water, smaller than a bay.

cover charge An extra charge levied in some restaurants and night-clubs.

coxswain **1.** Usually pronounced cox'n. The person who steers a boat. **2.** (UK). The senior petty officer in a small ship.

CPT Confederation of Passenger Transport UK. *See Appendix 7a.*

CRAC Continental Rail Agents Consortium. *See Appendix 7a.*

craft A general term for any boat or aeroplane.

crag A steep or rugged rock.

crater The mouth of a volcano.

credit card A small plastic card that identifies a customer and allows him or her to buy goods or services without payment at the time of purchase. Payment for the goods or services is made to the credit card company after a period of days or weeks. Credit card companies allow the debt to be discharged over a period if required and then charge interest for this facility.

creek A small bay or harbour.

Creole **1.** A descendent of European settlers in the West Indies or Central or South America.
2. A white descendent of French settlers in the Southern United States.
3. A person of mixed European and Black descent.
4. A language formed by contact with European and African languages.

crevasse A deep crack, especially in a glacier.

crew Those who work on board a ship, aircraft or similar vehicle.

cross trees A pair of horizontal timbers at the top of a lower mast of a ship, supporting the topmast.

cross-border ticketing The practice of issuing a ticket to start from a country other than that of the passenger's real origin. This is done to take advantage of a more favourable fare structure or exchange rate and is obviously discouraged by carriers.

crossroad 1. (UK). An intersection between two roads.
2. (US). A road that joins or crosses a main road.

crow's nest A small lookout position, near the top of the mast of a ship.

Crown Colony A British colony controlled by the government of the UK.

CRS *See Computerised Reservation System.*

cruise A voyage taken for its intrinsic pleasure, not for the purposes of transport. Most cruises will depart from and return to the same port

CTA China Tourism Association. *See Appendix 7c.*

CTC Coach Tourism Council. *See Appendix 7a.*

CTO Caribbean Tourism Organisation. *See Appendix 7a.*

CTT Council for Travel & Tourism. *See Appendix 7a.*

cultural attraction An attraction that capitalises on its importance as a

centre for artistic or similar intellectual pursuits.

culture The characteristics and behaviour shared by a group or nation.

C

cumulus A type of cloud, generally dense and with sharp outlines, looking rather as if it were made of cotton wool.

curfew A restriction on the public movement of people, typically during the hours of darkness. Curfews are usually imposed during periods of conflict or civil unrest.

currency The instruments of exchange of a country. Money.

currency restrictions Controls put in place by governments to restrict the flow of money in and out of their countries. Experience seems to show that tough controls do not benefit the countries imposing them and vice versa. For example, there are very few currency restrictions in the United Kingdom, whereas the controls applied by most of the old communist regimes were draconian.

current 1. A flow of water.
2. The measure of flow of electricity usually rated in amperes (generally abbreviated to amps). UK appliances are usually protected by a fuse in the plug rated at 3, 5 or 13 amps. Travellers should be aware that, if they adjust an appliance to run on a lower voltage, the fuse may need to be upgraded. This is because a halving of the voltage will lead to a doubling of the current drawn.

customer profile Information stored by business travel agents and similar

C

organisations about their clients. (E.g. class of travel, passport details, credit card details).

customs 1. The manners, morals and behavioural patterns of a country or society.
2. The government agency that seeks to control the movement of goods into and out of a country.

customs duty A tax levied on goods being imported.

cut-off date The last date by which an arrangement must be confirmed or completed.

cutter A small boat, other than a lifeboat, carried by a ship.

cutting An excavated channel through high ground for a railway or road.

cycle Technically any wheeled vehicle, but usually used to refer to lightweight vehicles such as bicycles, tricycles, etc.

cycle route A track or path reserved for the use of those on pedal cycles.

cyclone 1. A circular storm revolving around a relatively calm centre.
2. An area of winds rotating inwards towards an area of low pressure, usually causing bad weather.

cylinder A metal container designed to hold air at high pressures and used by scuba divers underwater. Also called bottle or tank.

Cyrillic The alphabet used by the Slavonic people of the Orthodox Church, especially in Russia and Bulgaria. *See Appendix 8 for a transliteration from English to Cyrillic alphabets.*

D
d

d.w.t. Dead-weight tonnage.

daily delegate rate A rate offered by a hotel to organisers of conferences, training events, etc. The rate usually includes room hire and refreshments. A 24-hour delegate rate will include all the daytime facilities, plus overnight accommodation.

Dalmatia The Adriatic coast of most of former Yugoslavia, stretching from Zadar, Croatia in the north to Montenegro in the south, generally barren but with some excellent harbours. Principal towns are Zadar, Split and Dubrovnik.

dam An artificial barrier built across a river or other watercourse to hold back water and create a reservoir.

Danelaw That part of Northern England administered by the Danes in the 9th and 10th centuries.

Dark Continent, The The continent of Africa. This term was commonly used when Africa was largely unexplored by Europeans.

data Information of any kind. These days the term is commonly used in connection with information stored on a computer. The word data is actually plural, the singular being datum. However common usage is tending to treat it as a singular uncountable noun.

davit A special crane built into a ship. A good example of davits are those used for lowering the lifeboats.

Davy Jones's locker Nautical slang for the bottom of the sea. Often used to describe the fate of someone who has drowned at sea.

day out (UK). A short trip or excursion completed in a single day.

day rate A rate offered by a hotel or similar to a guest wishing to stay for a short time and not overnight.

day return A fare, often discounted, that is valid for travel out and back during the same day only.

day trip *See day out.*

daylight saving The way in which an hour of extra daylight may be achieved in the evening by setting the clocks an hour ahead of standard time.

daylight time (US). Time adjusted for daylight saving.

DC *See direct current.*

DCA *See deposit collection advice.*

de luxe The term usually applied to the very best accommodation or facility. It has no official meaning unless it is related to other terms

D

within the classification to which it belongs.

dead calm No measurable wind.

dead reckoning A method of calculating a vessel's position from existing data when fresh observations are not possible.

dead-and-alive (UK). A dull or boring place or destination.

deadheading (US). When a vehicle is operating without passengers or payload.

deadlight 1. A cover for a ship's porthole fixed to prevent the entry of light or sunlight. Deadlights may also be fitted to the portholes of the lowest decks in stormy weather conditions. **2.** (US). A skylight that cannot be opened

debark To land from a ship.

debit card A card, similar in size and shape to a credit card, but which takes money directly from its holder's bank account.

deck A horizontal division of a ship. The upper decks are often named: sun deck; boat deck; lido deck; etc. Lower decks tend to be numbered or lettered. There is, however, no standard system.

deck plan A diagram showing the layout of cabins and public rooms on a ship.

deckhand A person employed to do jobs on the deck of a ship.

decompression 1. In aircraft, the sudden loss of cabin pressure. **2.** The reduction in pressure experienced by divers when ascending, during which dissolved gases such as nitrogen escape from the body tissues.

decompression sickness A physical condition caused by the reduction in pressure in a diver's body being too fast thus allowing dissolved gases such as nitrogen to form bubbles within the body tissues.

decompression tables A published list of stages at various depths of water at which a diver must pause and wait in order to allow for decompression to occur safely within the body.

Deep South The south-eastern states of the USA. Often considered as an area embodying traditional southern culture and values.

deep-sea Used to describe activities, such as diving or fishing. in the deeper parts of a sea or other body of water.

degree A measurement of angle denoted by the symbol °. There are 360 degrees in a circle and all bearings are based on the angular measurement as a part of this. Each degree is subdivided into 60 minutes (symbol ') and each minute into 60 seconds (symbol ").

delivery charge A car rental term, which is not the same as a drop off charge. A delivery or collection charge is the charge for delivering a vehicle to, or collecting a vehicle from, an address requested by the renter.

delta An area of land, usually roughly triangular, at the mouth of a river. This will have been formed from the sediment deposited from the river and its flatness will allow the river to create a large number of small channels.

delta wing An aircraft wing of triangular shape.

demand valve A regulator. So called because it supplies air as demanded by the diver.

demesne Land belonging to a state or sovereign.

demi-pension Also known as half-board. A hotel rate which includes room, breakfast and one other meal.

democracy A country or state that is governed by the elected representatives of the people.

demographics Factors concerning the characteristics of a population. Demographics can include aspects such as age, income, family size, employment, etc.

demurrage An amount payable to the operator of a cargo vessel because of failure to load or unload a cargo in the agreed time.

dengue A tropical viral disease, transmitted by mosquitoes.

denied boarding compensation Compensation to which passengers have a statutory right if they are not allowed to travel on a booked flight, for which they have checked in on time, simply because the airline has overbooked.

denizen An inhabitant or occupant of a place.

departure **1.** To leave.
2. A start. (As in "the departure of the service")

departure delay insurance The insurance cover in respect of delays to a booked means of transport. The cover is of two types. Firstly there is an agreed sum paid simply to help compensate for the inconvenience. Secondly there are payments made to reimburse certain losses, including cancellation fees if the journey has to be abandoned and additional transport and/or accommodation costs necessary to complete the journey.

departure tax Travel is a heavily taxed commodity, the more so since travellers are usually unaware of how much of their fare is being swallowed up by governments. There are two main types of tax. Ticket taxes, which are levied at the time of purchase of the ticket and departure taxes, which are collected, as one would imagine, on departure.

dependency A country or province that is controlled by another.

deplane To get off an aircraft.

deportation The lawful forced removal of an alien from a country or state.

deportee A person who is being deported.

deposit A partial payment made to hold space or show good will.

deposit collection advice A document issued by travel agents to confirm collection of a customer's deposit. Agents will be billed at agreed periods for the total value of deposits collected. DCA's are becoming less common as electronic payment systems take over.

D

D

depot 1. (UK). A storage place.
2. (US). An alternative name for a terminal or station.

depression A low pressure air circulation in temperate latitudes. The condition is usually associated with wet weather.

depressurisation *See decompression.*

depth gauge An instrument which recognises changes in pressure and calibrates these in terms of depth for a diver to read.

derail When a railway locomotive and/or its train leave the tracks.

deregulation The term given to the gradual removal of government controls over transport competition that has resulted in a plethora of new and different fares and special deals.

desert A dry and barren area, often sandy, and characterised by its lack of water and vegetation. The ten largest deserts, in order of size, are:
• Sahara
• Australian
• Arabian
• Gobi
• Kalahari
• Takla Makan
• Sonoran
• Namib
• Turkestan
• Thar

desolate Of a place, abandoned, uninhabited or neglected.

destination Simply the end point of a journey, regardless of its purpose.

detour A deviation from a planned or intended route.

detrain To alight from a train.

developing country A poor or underdeveloped country that is trying to become more advanced.

dhow A lateen-rigged ship used on the Arabian sea.

dialect A form of speech peculiar to a particular region or group.

diarchy A region governed by two independent authorities.

diarise From the noun "diary". The act of recording an item in a diary or other scheduling system.

dictatorship A state ruled by a dictator.

diesel engine An internal combustion engine in which the heat of compression of the air in the cylinders ignites the fuel.

diesel-electric A vehicle propelled by electricity generated by a diesel powered generator, carried on the same vehicle.

diesel-hauled A railway expression indicating that a train is hauled by a diesel-powered locomotive.

diligence A historical term meaning a public stagecoach. Still sometimes used to denote a horse-drawn vehicle.

diner 1. (US). An informal roadside restaurant.
2. A restaurant car on a train.

dinghy A small boat, often carried by a ship.

dining car *See diner (2).*

dinner jacket (UK). British formal evening wear for men comprising a jacket (usually black) and trousers, worn with a frilled shirt and bow tie (which is usually black but can be of any colour). The expression dinner jacket does not refer simply to the jacket but to the whole ensemble.

direct current An electrical supply whose direction does not alter. Battery operated appliances run on DC, whereas most mains appliances run on AC. Travellers must take care in countries where DC supplies still exist as AC equipment will usually be damaged if it is used on such supplies.

direct service A flight or other journey that does not require a passenger to change services. A direct service is not necessarily non-stop.

directional fare A fare that only applies in one direction of travel. Few fares now have a close relationship with the distance travelled, most being determined by "market forces". Such forces often mean that there is a greater demand for travel originating in one of a pair of cities than the other. Directional pricing can help restore the balance of supply and demand.

Director General An IATA term meaning IATA's Director General or his authorised representative.

dirigible A steerable, lighter than air, aircraft. Also known as an airship.

discount A reduction given from the published fare, price or tariff.

disembark To get off an aircraft, ship, train or other method of transport.

disintermediation This expression means "cutting out the middle man".

Thus, in travel, large providers of services are disintermediating by cutting out the retail agent and dealing directly with their customers, using new distributive systems such as the Internet.

displaced person A person who has been forced to leave his or her home country because of persecution, war, etc.

displacement effect A tourism term given to the phenomenon where workers move from primary jobs (such as agriculture) to tourism-related jobs, such as hotel work.

distant signal (UK). The early warning signal on a railway.

distribution channel A means by which a product or service is made available to customers. Tour operators, for example, can choose either to use travel agents as their distribution channel, or maybe to sell via the Internet. In this example, they have the choice of two distribution channels.

distributory A branch of a stream that does not return to the main channel once having left it.

district 1. A territory or region marked off for special administrative purposes.
2. A part of a town or city.

ditch 1. A long, narrow gully that provides drainage.
2. To bring an aircraft down in the sea.

dock An area designed for the safe mooring of ships and the handling of their passengers and cargoes.

D

D

document Any item of printed or written material that gives details of an arrangement, agreement or ownership.

dogwatch Nautical. A split watch of 2 hours. *See bells.*

doldrums A region of unpredictable weather near the equator. In the days of sail the doldrums were feared because of the possibility of long periods of completely calm weather.

Dolphin Coast Stretch of coast in South Africa from Durban in the south to the Tugela river in the north.

domain Territory of one sovereign or government.

dome car (US). *See observation car.*

domestic Within one's own country. Domestic tourism is tourism within the country where a person lives; domestic flights are those within the airline's own country.

domicile A person's own home or dwelling place.

dominion *See domain.*

dory A small flat-bottomed fishing boat with high sides

douane A name, most recently from the French, commonly given to a customs post

double An abbreviation for a double room.

double booking When two or more reservations are made for the same accommodation or service. Sometimes done deliberately to protect space by ensuring that others cannot use it. When done in an attempt to maximise load factors, it is usually known as over-booking. *See over-booking.*

double chair A two-seater chairlift.

double double A room with two double (large) beds.

double room A room with one double (large) bed. The term is sometimes used casually to describe any room that can accommodate two people, even if it has two small beds, but this is not strictly correct. *See twin.*

double-decker A bus with an upper and lower deck. Common in the UK; less so elsewhere in the world.

double-headed A train hauled by two locomotives.

down under (UK). A colloquial expression meaning Australia and/or New Zealand.

downgrade To move to a lower grade of accommodation or service.

downriver At or towards the mouth of a river.

downtown (US). The lower or more central part of a town or city.

downwind In the direction in which the wind is blowing.

drag The air resistance a vehicle is subjected to when in motion. Most important to, and generally applied to, aircraft.

drag lift The commonest form of ski lift which "drags" skiers up the slope using a continually moving cable that has shorter cables attached to it that skiers catch. Also known as surface lift, tow or ski lift.

draught The depth of water a ship draws. That is, the minimum depth that is required for it to float clear of the bottom.

dress code Some higher category hotels and restaurants insist on the wearing of certain types of clothes. Typically they will insist on the wearing of jackets and ties by men and dresses or skirts by women. On board ship, especially the more expensive vessels operating from the UK, it is still common to wear evening dress. In general, black tie is adequate. *See dinner jacket, black tie, white tie.*

drift Deviation from the set course, due to the effect of sidewinds or currents.

drift diving A dive where divers allows the current to move them along.

drive-in (Also drive-through). Mainly US. Of an establishment, such as a bank, into which customers may drive and transact business without leaving their vehicles.

drive-on A ferry or similar, onto which vehicles are loaded by their own drivers, rather than by a crane or other method.

drop off charge The name given to the charge levied by a car rental company in connection with a one-way rental.

drophead (UK). A car with a collapsible fabric roof.

droshky A Russian small four-wheel open horse-drawn carriage.

DRV Deutscher Reiseburo Verband. *See Appendix 7c.*

dry dock A structure large enough to contain a ship and from which the water can be emptied. Dry docks allow work to be undertaken on those parts of the hull of a vessel that would normally be submerged.

D

dry lease The rental of a vehicle, such as an aircraft, without supplies or crew. *See also wet lease.*

dry suit A diving suit which keeps its wearer dry by means of neck, wrist and possibly ankle seals.

duchy The territory of a duke or duchess.

dude ranch (US). A ranch converted to a holiday centre.

dumb terminal A VDU connected to a mainframe computer, that has no intelligence of its own.

dune A hillock or mound formed of sand. Sand dunes can move with the wind and have been known to engulf large features.

dune-buggy *See beach-buggy.*

duplex A hotel suite with two floors.

Dutch 1. Of or relating to Holland or the Netherlands.
2. (US). The region of Pennsylvania, mainly Lancaster County, settled by Amish people and others originally from Germany. "Dutch" is, in this case, a corruption of Deutsch.

duty The tax levied on certain goods especially alcohol and tobacco.

duty-free Goods bought in a place where duties are not levied, such as aircraft or ships in transit in international waters or airspace.

D

duty-free allowance The number, amount or value of goods, bought duty-free, that may be brought into a country without payment of duty.

duty-free shop A retail outlet, usually at a port, selling goods free of its country's duties and taxes.

DVW Damage-to-vehicle waiver. Similar to CDW.

dyke (Also dike). A long wall or bank built to prevent flooding.

E
e

E

ear clearing The process of equalising the pressure outside the ear - caused by increased depths, by using the Valsalva manoeuvre.

earlybird Originally a proprietary term used to describe advance booking discounts offered by certain principals. Now often used as any form of advance purchase product attracting a discount.

easement **1.** A right of passage over another's land.
2. A relaxation in routeing restrictions, especially on local rail journeys.

East Greenland Current A cold current running down the east coast of Greenland, bringing Arctic waters in the Atlantic.

East Indies A general geographical term used for the area comprising India and the Malay Archipelago. Not commonly used these days.

eastern hemisphere The half of the earth containing Europe, Africa and Asia.

eatery A colloquial expression for a restaurant or other eating place, often an informal one.

ebb The movement of the tide back out to sea.

Ebonics (US). A relatively new expression for the separate linguistic style used by African-Americans. The word is created from a combination of *ebony* and *phonics*.

EC *See European Community.*

echo-sounder An apparatus for measuring the depth of water below a ship.

ecology The study of the interaction of people with their environment.

economy class Usually the cheapest available class on a service.

economy of scale A business expression that refers to the savings that might be made when larger quantities of a product or service are supplied. For example, a 12-coach train will only incur the same driver costs as a 2-coach unit.

ecotourism Tourism that considers or encourages the preservation of the environment.

ECTAA Group of National Travel Agents' and Tour Operators' Associations within the EU. *See Appendix 7d.*

eddy A small circular movement of air or water.

educational trip *See familiarisation trip.*

EEC European Economic Community. One of the original constituent parts of the EU.

effendi A man of standing and respect in many eastern Mediterranean and Middle Eastern countries, occasionally used as a term of respect to a visitor.

efficiency An American term for accommodation, such as a small apartment, with some cooking facilities

EFT Elapsed Flying Time. *See actual flying time.*

EFTPOS *See Electronic Funds Transfer at Point Of Sale.*

Egyptiac The civilisation of the ancient Egyptians that lasted from before 4000 BC to AD 280.

El Niño A change in the ocean-atmosphere system in the eastern Pacific that contributes to significant weather changes throughout the world. El Niño is characterised by an increase in water temperatures in the equatorial regions of the central and eastern Pacific. El Niño is a recurrent phenomenon, first recorded in 1567 and the most recent occurrence prior to the 1990s was in the early 1940s.

elapsed time The actual time taken to travel between two points, taking local time changes into account.

electric storm A thunderstorm.

electrified A railway expression indicating that the line has electrical conductors, using either overhead lines or an extra rail. Electrified railways usually provide a faster and more reliable service than those operated by steam or diesel locomotives.

electronic funds transfer at point of sale A payment system whereby funds are drawn electronically from a customer's bank account as soon as a transaction has been authorised.

electronic ticketing The system by which passengers can travel without their holding a conventional ticket. Their details are stored on a computer system and on reaching their departure point and identifying themselves, passengers will be given authority to board.

elevator 1. The moveable part of an aircraft's tailplane that controls vertical motion.
2. (US). A lift.

Elsan A British proprietary brand of portable chemical lavatory, now used often generically to describe any such appliance. Chemical lavatories are often used on safaris or similar types of "adventure" holiday.

embankment An earth or stone bank for carrying a railway or road over a depression. Embankments and other earthworks are necessary for railways since they lose efficiency very rapidly if faced with gradients.

embargo 1. A prohibition preventing suppliers from dealing with a country or organisation.
2. A period during which, or for which, bookings may not be taken.

embark To get on board.

embassy The residence and offices of an ambassador. Embassy staff can often provide assistance to travellers, especially those who find themselves in trouble with a country's legal system.

Emerald Coast Stretch of coast in north-west Florida; main resorts are Destin and Fort Walton Beach.

Emerald Isle Ireland.

emigrant A person who leaves his or her native country permanently.

emigrate To leave one's native country permanently.

émigré An emigrant.

emirate A domain of an emir.

empire An extensive group of states or countries under the control of one supreme power (an emperor). The Empire, as a proper name, is usually taken to mean the British Empire. Historically it meant the Holy Roman Empire.

emplane *See enplane.*

empty leg *See back to back.*

en bloc All together. Sometimes used in travel to denote an action taken for a group. (E.g. cancelled en bloc).

en fête Holding or getting ready for a holiday or celebration.

en route Literally the French for "on the way". Actually travelling on a journey.

en suite Forming a single unit. For example, bedroom and bathroom en suite.

endemic A region or population where something is regularly found. In travel this usually applies to a disease. Thus, a malarial endemic zone is one where malaria is commonly found.

end-on construction A fare construction method whereby a fare from point A to point B is added to the fare from point B to point C. Since this type of construction is usually resorted to by those wishing to undercut an advertised through fare, there are many ways by which its use is restricted. *See also split ticketing.*

endorsement 1. A signature or other entry on a document to indicate that it has in some manner changed. 2. (UK). A record of a driving conviction entered into a driving licence.

engine A colloquial term for a railway locomotive.

engineer (US). The driver of a railway locomotive.

English breakfast Full cooked breakfast in the English style.

English Riviera The resort coast of south Devon centred on Torquay and Paignton.

enplane To get onto an aircraft.

ensign 1. A banner or flag, especially one used on a ship. 2. A junior naval officer.

entente cordiale A friendly understanding between nations or states.

entrain To get onto a train.

entrée (UK). A dish served before the main course. (US). The main course.

entremets Any light dish served between two courses.

E

E

entrepôt A warehouse for the temporary storage of goods in transit.

entresol A mezzanine floor.

entry permit A form, often needing completion immediately prior to arrival, that gives details of a traveller and thus allows entry.

envelope The covering of a balloon or airship.

environment The physical surroundings and conditions of an area, especially as they relate to people's lives.

environs The vicinity; the local area.

EP 1. *See European plan.*
2. *See extended protection.*

epidemic A widespread occurrence of a disease.

equator An imaginary line dividing the earth into its two hemispheres, northern and southern.

equatorial At or near the equator.

Equatorial Counter-current The force of the trade winds carries water to the western sides of the oceans and the Equatorial Counter-current flows in the reverse direction to restore the balance.

equinox The times of the year when the sun is directly over the equator (around 21 March and 23 September). On these dates the nights and days are of equal length.

ERA European Regional Airlines Association. *See Appendix 7d.*

escalator A moving staircase.

escape road (UK). A road on a dangerous bend or other hazard that allows a driver to leave the road in safety should an emergency arise.

escarpment A steep slope at the edge of a plateau.

escort A person travelling with, and responsible for, the well-being of a group. *See also courier.*

escorted tour A tour, often on a coach, that is accompanied by an escort. Escorted tours were once the main type of holiday for those few who could afford such luxuries. Now, however, they are of more specialised interest.

escrow account Where customers' money is placed in a special account, only to be released when the services paid for have been performed.

ESITO Events Sector Industry Training Organisation. *See Appendix 7a.*

Eskimo A member of the peoples inhabiting North Canada, Alaska, Greenland and Siberia. The name Inuit is now becoming the preferred term. *See also Nunavut.*

Eskimo civilisation (Also referred to as Inuit). The civilisation that started in the Aleutian Islands in 1100 BC and lasted until AD 1850. *See also Nunavut.*

esplanade A long level area for walking, usually between the beach and road.

estaminet A French term for a small café selling alcoholic drinks.

estate car (UK). A car with an extended rear luggage area.

estuary The mouth of a river that is

relatively long and wide. Estuaries are considered to begin at the upstream point where the tidal effect can be detected.

ETA Estimated Time of Arrival.

ETB English Tourist Board. *See Appendix 7a.*

ETC European Travel Commission. *See Appendix 7d.*

ETD Estimated Time of Departure.

Etesian Northwest winds that blow each summer in the eastern Mediterranean.

ethnic Belonging to a group having a special cultural or national tradition.

ethnic minority An ethnic group living in a country or area where they are significantly outnumbered by the majority of the population. In many countries ethnic minorities are disadvantaged.

ethnocentric The evaluation of the culture and traditions of other races by criteria relating to one's own. For example, those holidaymakers who complain that Mediterranean food is too oily could be considered to be guilty of mild ethnocentricity.

e-ticket *See electronic ticketing.*

ETOA European Tour Operators Association. *See Appendix 7a.*

Etruscan Of or relating to ancient Etruria in Italy, especially its pre-Roman civilisation.

EU *See European Union.*

Eurasian Of mixed European and Asian parentage.

Euroland An informal term for the group of EU countries that adopted the single currency in 1999. By this definition, the UK is not in Euroland.

Europe The second smallest continent with an area of 10,400,000 square kilometres (4,000,000 square miles). Its population (1990) is 498,000,000.

E

European Community The original name for the grouping of European countries for the purpose of common trade, etc. The expression is now obsolete as the EC is now known as the European Union (EU).

European Plan A hotel rate including accommodation only and no meals.

European Union An economic and political association comprising the countries of Austria, Belgium, Denmark, Finland, France, Germany, Greece, Ireland, Italy, Luxembourg, The Netherlands, Portugal, Spain, Sweden and the United Kingdom.

EVA Exhibition Venues Association. *See Appendix 7a.*

even keel When a ship is in an upright position.

ex gratia A payment or reimbursement made as a favour, rather than by legal obligation.

exceptions and exclusions An insurance term that means anything connected with a type of risk that an insurance policy does not cover. Certain exclusions are common to most policies - radioactive contamination is one such. Others will depend on the insurance company's business decisions - for example, some cover motorcycling,

E

some do not. Yet others will depend on the premium paid - many companies will cover sports such as scuba diving and skiing only if an additional premium is paid.

excess (insurance) An amount that may be deducted from an insurance claim prior to payment. For example, if a baggage cover section had an excess of £35, then a claim for £100 would be reduced to £65 on settlement. One of the reasons for this practice is to discourage policyholders from making very small claims, since these involve insurance companies in administrative costs which can be very high in relation to the amount claimed.

excess baggage All carriers have a limitation on the amount of baggage a traveller may take free of charge. This is rarely a problem except in the case of air travel, where space is at a premium and passengers carrying baggage in excess of the free allowance may be asked to pay extra. Traditionally the standard charge was set at 1% of the first class one way fare for each kilo of excess, and although some carriers have now changed their charging system, the amount can still be considerable.

exchange coupon The coupon or coupons of a ticket or voucher that are exchanged for the service provided.

exchange order *See voucher.*

exchange rate The rate at which money can be converted from one currency to another.

excise duty The tax payable on certain goods, typically alcohol and tobacco.

exclusive Originally accommodation or other facility the use of which is restricted to a select few. Now frequently used as a marketing term to try to imply that a particular offer is special and restricted, even though this may not be true.

excursion 1. A special trip taken as an extra while on holiday, often to a place of special interest.
2. A short trip away, usually for a day or less.

excursion fare A discounted fare with restrictions designed to discourage its use by business travellers.

excursionist A day tripper. The term is more usually used in the US.

executive floor A hotel floor reserved for business travellers, usually at a premium rate.

executive lounge The general name given to a room, especially at an airport, that provides extra facilities to those passengers who have paid a premium fare.

exit permit A form similar to an entry permit but which allows a traveller to leave a country.

exit visa A visa that allows a traveller to leave a country.

exotic In travel, a destination that is strange but attractive. Often implies that the destination is also far away.

expatriate A person living in a country other than that of his or her origin.

expedition A journey made for a specific purpose, such as exploration, scientific research, etc.

exploration A journey made with the intention of discovery.

expo An abbreviation for exposition.

export To take or send items out of a country.

exposition A large international exhibition.

express A faster than normal method of transport or delivery. Usually applied to railways.

express train A train stopping at few intermediate stations and thus affording a faster journey.

expressway (US). An urban motorway.

extended protection A car rental term providing an extension to SLI that improves its cover.

extras In hotel terms, these are items, such as telephone calls, that are not included in the terms agreed.

extreme sport A generic name given to any sport or activity that involves more than the normal amount of hazard and/or discomfort.

exurb The district outside a town or city, especially a prosperous area beyond the suburbs.

E

F
f

f.o.b. Free on board. Delivered without charge to a carrier's vehicle (typically a ship or railway wagon).

f.o.c. Free of charge. Issued or provided without charge.

face-mask A mask with a glass port that fits over the eyes and nose of a diver to facilitate underwater operation.

Fahrenheit The temperature scale in which water freezes at 32° and boils at 212°. A quick way to convert approximately Fahrenheit to centigrade is to deduct 30 and halve the remainder. Thus, 70°F - 30 = 40. Divide by 2 = 20°C.

fairway A navigable channel.

fall (US). Autumn.

familiarisation trip Colloquially known as a "fam trip". A trip arranged by a principal, tourist board or operator to familiarise travel staff with a destination or service and the facilities offered.

family cabin A cabin on a ship with sufficient accommodation for a family, usually assumed to be two adults and two children.

family fare A special fare offered to families travelling together.

family plan A special rate for family groups.

family room A hotel room with sufficient accommodation for a family, usually assumed to be two adults and two children.

fan jet A type of jet aircraft engine where the incoming air is compressed by a fan.

fantail The overhang at the stern of a ship.

Fantasia The GDS used by airlines including JAL and Qantas.

Far East A general geographic term describing East and Southeast Asia and including: Brunei/Darussalam, Cambodia, China, Indonesia, Japan, Democratic People's Republic of Korea (North Korea), Republic of Korea (South Korea), Laos, Malaysia, Myanmar, the Philippines, Singapore, Taiwan, Thailand, Vietnam. Sometimes the definition is taken to include Mongolia and the eastern Siberian region of the Russian Federation.

Far Eastern civilisation The civilisation of Japan and Korea that has lasted from AD 645 to date.

fare **1.** The amount that a passenger must pay to be conveyed on a vehicle

providing public transport.
2. The range of food, etc., provided in a restaurant.

fare basis The type of fare used for a particular ticket. The code that indicates this.

fare construction point The point where a fare ends. That is, where the journey can be said to be returning. This is usually, but not always, the most distant point on the journey.

fare construction unit An artificial airline currency, now replaced by the neutral unit of construction.

fast-food outlet An imprecise term given to any eating establishment that concentrates on providing simple meals, on demand, without delay.

fast-track An imprecise expression given to any system that allows a more rapid completion of a task. Typically used to describe special airline and hotel check-in and checkout systems that allow more rapid processing.

Fatherland One's native country.

fathom A measure of water depth. A fathom is 6 feet (**1.82** metres).

fathometer A type of depth gauge; an echo sounder.

fauna The indigenous animal life of a region.

favela A Brazilian shack or shanty town.

FB *See full board.*

FCU *See fare construction unit.*

FE *See foreign exchange.*

federal A system of government in which several states form a unity but remain independent in their internal affairs.

fee-based pricing *See management fee.*

feeder service A service that carries passengers from a smaller originating point to a main hub, and back.

fell A stretch of hills or moorland, especially in northern England.

felucca A small Mediterranean coastal vessel with oars and/or lateen sails.

fen A low, marshy or flooded area of land.

fender **1.** A piece of rubber or other resilient substance hung over the side of a ship or boat to prevent damage when against another vessel or a wall. **2.** (US). A wing or mudguard of a motor vehicle.

ferry A boat, ship or aircraft used for conveying passengers and goods on a regular and relatively short journey.

ferry mileage The distance that a vehicle has to travel, without passengers, in order to position itself for its intended passenger service. Various devices are used to avoid ferry mileage, one of the best known being the "W" pattern.

FHA Family Holiday Association. *See Appendix 7a.*

FIAVET Federazione Italiano Agenti di Viaggio e Turismo. *See Appendix 7c.*

fictitious construction point *See Hypothetical Construction Point.*

fiesta A public holiday, usually in

F

F

Latin countries, often associated with a particular saint or other religious figure.

fifth freedom *See freedoms of the air.*

fin The vertical control surface of an aircraft, usually at the rear, that controls its side to side motion.

fire-box The fuel chamber of a steam engine or boiler. Sometimes referred to as the furnace.

firm up To make definite.

first class One of the best categories for transport or accommodation, exceeded in comfort only by de luxe.

first floor 1. (UK). The floor above the ground floor.
2. (US). The ground floor.

first sitting The earlier of two meal sittings on a cruise.

firth A narrow inlet or estuary.

fixed wing aircraft The traditional type of heavier-than-air aircraft, where the wings project from the fuselage and don't move.

fjord A narrow sea inlet, usually bounded by high cliffs. Fjords were formed by glaciers which is why they are found mainly in the northerly regions.

flag carrier The name given to the national airline of a country or state.

flag of convenience All ships must be registered in a particular country. However, the standards, wage rates and taxes in many countries are high and to save money, some ship owners will register their vessels in a country other than their home country, where the standards, and consequently costs, are lower.

flagpole *See flagstaff.*

flagstaff 1. Any pole set up to fly a flag.
2. On a ship, the pole at the stern that flies the flag of the ship's country of registry.

flaps Extendible, hinged surfaces on an aircraft's wings that control the amount of lift generated.

flat light A condition common in skiing resorts after the sun has gone down. At this time it is difficult to make out the conditions of a run because the various shades all blur to grey.

flight attendant A member of an aircraft's cabin crew.

flight code Every flight is allocated a unique code that identifies it thoughout the duration of the journey. Flight codes are made up an airline identifier (such as BA for British Airways) and a number that denotes the route of the journey.

flight coupon An exchange coupon valid for a flight.

flight deck The name usually used for the cockpit on larger aircraft.

flight path The planned course of an aircraft.

flight recorder An automatic device fitted to all commercial passenger aircraft that records technical data monitored during a flight. In the event of an accident this data can help to find the cause. Popularly known as a "black box" although they are usually painted orange.

float plane *See seaplane.*

floatel A floating hotel.

flood tide An exceptionally high tide.

floodplain A low lying flat area of land around a river that is subject to flooding.

flora The indigenous plant life of a region.

flotilla A collection of boats sailing together. Holidays based on flotillas of yachts are very popular in the Mediterranean.

flotsam Floating rubbish or wreckage, usually from a ship.

fly-cruise A cruise starting at an overseas port with a connecting flight from the customer's home country.

fly-drive A package holiday by air in which one of the integral components is car rental.

flying boat A large aircraft designed to operate from water. Prior to the construction of large numbers of airports, flying boats maintained many of the longer distance services. The largest aircraft ever flown was the "Spruce Goose", a flying boat with a wingspan considerably greater than that of a Boeing 747.

flying wing An aircraft with little or no fuselage and containing its passenger and cargo accommodation within the wing. Although aircraft of this configuration have flown, none has yet entered regular service.

fo'c'sle *See forecastle.*

fog Any cloud of moisture touching the ground that reduces visibility to less than one kilometre (1,100 yards).

Föhn 1. A hot, southerly wind on the northern slopes of the Alps.
2. A warm dry wind on the lee side of a mountain.

foot passenger A passenger travelling on a car carrying service without a vehicle.

footfall A marketing expression that refers to the number of people entering a shop or other location. It does not indicate the numbers who spend, only those who enter.

foothill A small hill or range of hills around the bottom of a mountain.

footpath 1. (UK). A path for pedestrians, especially between buildings.
2. A track though woods, etc.

footplate (UK). The cab of a railway locomotive.

ford A shallow point in a river or stream where it may be crossed by wading or by driving through.

fore Towards the front of an aircraft or ship.

forecastle Pronounced "foke-sul".
1. The forward part of a ship where the crew has its quarters.
2. A raised deck at the bow of a ship.

foreign Of, from or situated in a country other than one's own.

foreign exchange A term used to refer to any commercial transaction relating to the supply, exchange or purchase of currency other than that of one's own country.

F

F

foreshore That part of the shore that lies between high and low water.

forest A large area covered with trees and undergrowth. In tropical areas forests can be extremely dense and inhospitable.

form of indemnity An airline form which a passenger must complete to indemnify a carrier against loss. It is often used in the case of a lost ticket, where the carrier may replace the ticket without charge providing the passenger agrees to repay any loss incurred by the airline should the lost ticket later be fraudulently used.

formal dress 1. Clothing appropriate to an occasion bound by set, usually traditional, rules and standards. **2.** (US). Evening dress.

former Soviet Union The countries of: Armenia, Azerbaijan, Belarus, Estonia, Georgia, Kazakhstan, Kyrgyzstan, Latvia, Lithuania, Moldova, Russian Federation, Tajikistan, Turkmenistan, Ukraine and Uzbekistan.

fortnight (UK). Two weeks.

foyer The main lobby or entrance hall of a hotel or theatre (or sometimes a cruise ship).

FP Full pension. *See full board.*

Franc Zone Those countries whose currencies are linked to the French Franc at a fixed exchange rate. Each country has its own issuing band and its currency is freely convertible into French Francs. The member countries are: Benin, Burkina Faso, Cameroon, Central African Republic, Chad, Comoros, Congo, Côte d'Ivoire, Equatorial Guinea, Gabon, Guinea-Bissau, Mali, Niger, Senegal and Togo.

franchise An authorisation granted to an individual or organisation, by another, that gives the right to sell the other's products or services and to use its brand name. Many catering outlets, especially those in fast food, are franchises.

Frank A member of the Germanic nation that captured Gaul in the 6th century.

free ascent When a diver ascends towards the water's surface without the use of additional air supply.

free house (UK). A drinking establishment, usually a pub, not owned by a brewery which is thus free to sell beers from several suppliers. The opposite to a tied house.

free port A port where goods in transit are not subject to taxes or duties.

free trade The philosophy of allowing trade between nations without governmental regulations, controls or duties. Rarely seen.

freeboard The space between the lowest open deck and the waterline of a vessel.

freedoms of the air In the Chicago Convention on Civil Aviation of 1944, it was agreed that airlines would have five "levels" of freedom under which they could operate. The higher the level of freedom afforded, the greater the level of flexibility the airline will enjoy. Since then a sixth

freedom has been added and the levels now are:
1. The right to fly over a country.
2. The right to land in a country for technical reasons such as refuelling.
3. The right to off-load freight, mail or passengers from an aircraft of the country from which they originated.
4. The right to load freight, mail or passengers onto an aircraft of the country from which they originated or for which they are destined.
5. The right to load or off-load freight, mail or passengers onto or from an aircraft other than that of the country for which they are destined.
6. The right of an airline of one country to carry passengers between two other countries, providing it travels via its home country.

freesale A system whereby an agent can sell a facility without reference in advance to the principal. Reservations made in this way will have to be reported to the principal in accordance with specified procedures.

freeway An express highway, the US equivalent of a motorway.

freighter In shipping, a vessel operating line services for freight. Some of these vessels carry a limited number of passengers, rarely more than 12.

frequent flyer programmes Incentive programmes operated by airlines on behalf of customers who use their services regularly. Travellers accumulate points in proportion to the number and value of their journeys and these can be exchanged for gifts of various types.

frogman An archaic term, coined during World War 2, to describe a scuba diver. The term is still sometimes used by lay persons.

front of house The reception area of a hotel.

frontier The border between two countries.

FTO Federation of Tour Operators. *See Appendix 7a.*

full board A hotel rate including three meals daily. Also called American Plan.

full face mask A face-mask that covers the whole face, including the mouth, eyes and nose.

full foliage (US). The time in the fall when the colours of leaves of trees, especially in New England, are at their most vivid.

full house Originally from the theatre and meaning that all seats are taken. Now often applied in a casual manner to any other accommodation that is fully taken up.

full pension *See full board.*

fumarole An opening in or near a volcano from which hot gases emerge.

funicular A mountain railway, usually one operated by cable.

funnel The smokestack on a ship. Originally it carried the large quantities of smoke and steam from the engines but these days is more likely to carry diesel exhaust.

furlong An archaic measure of length equal to one eighth of a mile.

F

F

furlough Leave of absence granted to a member of the services, etc.

fuselage The main body or an aircraft to which the wings and tailplane are fitted.

FX An abbreviation for foreign exchange. *See foreign exchange.*

G
g

g.r.t. *See gross registered tonnage.*

Gaelic Any of the Celtic languages spoken in Ireland, Scotland and the Isle of Man.

gale A very strong wind measuring between 24 and 40 knots (force 8) on the Beaufort scale.

Galileo A multi-national GDS owned by a number of European airlines.

galley A ship's or aircraft's kitchen.

game lodge Accommodation in a game reserve or safari park.

game reserve An area in which "game animals" (especially large ones) are kept in protected but natural environments. Usually they may be viewed by visitors under controlled conditions.

gangplank A movable plank, often with cleats, used to board a vessel.

gangway 1. (UK). A passage between rows of seats.
2. A bridge laid from ship to shore to enable embarkation and disembarkation.

Garden Route Scenic stretch of South African coast stretching from Mossel Bay in the west to Storms River in the east. Main resorts are Knysna and Plettenberg Bay. Other attractions include Tsitsikamma National Park and the Wilderness Lakes.

gasthaus A small German hotel or inn.

gasthof A hotel or inn in German-speaking countries, larger than a gasthaus.

gate The exit from an airport that leads to an aircraft.

gateway A point of access to a country or region. A gateway will usually be an airport or seaport, although certain frontier points and railway stations can be given the designation. In general a gateway is the point served most directly from the originating point, which usually implies that it accepts international traffic. For example, the gateway to the Whitsunday Islands on Australia's Great Barrier Reef would probably be Mackay or even Brisbane, even though there are nearer airports such as Proserpine.

gauge 1. The distance between the rails of a railway track. In most countries of the world this is the British-invented gauge of 4'8½" (167 cm).
2. The "loading" gauge of a railway that relates to the physical size of the vehicles. This is important insofar as

clearances in tunnels and at platforms are concerned. The loading gauge in mainland Europe is larger than that in the UK and normal continental rail vehicles cannot work UK rail routes.

gazetteer A geographical index or dictionary.

gazpacho A Spanish vegetable soup, served cold.

GB Great Britain.

GBCO Guild of British Coach Operators. *See Appendix 7a.*

GBTA Guild of Business Travel Agents. *See Appendix 7a.*

GDS *See Global Distribution System.*

Gemini A GDS owned by Air Canada and Canadian Airlines.

general sales agent When a principal does not have its own office in a country it may appoint a GSA to handle its promotion, sales and enquiries. A GSA may represent several principals.

geographical mile A distance equal to one minute of longitude. Approximately 1,850 metres (2,024 yards)

geography The study of the earth's physical features, resources and climate as well as the physical aspects of its population.

geology The study of the earth's structure and composition.

George A familiar term for an automatic pilot.

geyser A volcanic phenomenon causing the eruption of hot water and steam, often at regular intervals.

ghetto Part of a town or city (usually a rundown area) occupied by a minority or deprived group.

ghost town A deserted town or settlement, usually found in areas that have experienced a short-lived boom. (E.g. from mining).

gig A light, two-wheeled horse-drawn carriage.

gimbals A device to keep something horizontal on a ship, regardless of any pitch or roll.

GIT *See group inclusive tour.*

gîte A French expression meaning a holiday dwelling, usually situated in the countryside and rented on a self-catering basis.

glacier A slowly moving "river" of ice. In higher mountain regions glaciers remain frozen all through the year and thus allow summer skiing.

glasnost A Russian expression meaning openness. The practice has lead to a far greater exchange of ideas and people within and between the former communist countries and the rest of the world.

Glass Country Area in south-east Småland, Sweden, famous for glass-making.

glen A narrow valley.

glider An engineless heavier-than-air aircraft, often one that is towed by a powered aeroplane.

global distillation The phenomenon whereby cold areas, such as the Arctic, are polluted by emissions produced far away. Such emissions can be carried far from their source and not be deposited until they condense in the colder atmosphere.

global distribution system The term that is taking over from the expression Computerised Reservation System

global indicator A code shown against the fare on an air ticket that indicates the general route of a long distance flight.

global price tickets Tickets, often rail, that include a package of facilities. For example, travel, sleeping accommodation and a meal.

globe The planet earth or a representation thereof.

glühwein Mulled wine popular in Switzerland, Austria and Germany. Often served in ski resorts.

GMT *See Greenwich Mean Time.*

goggles 1. Used as an aid to seeing in water. Unlike the face mask, goggles cover the eyes only and are for use by surface swimmers.
2. Used by skiers to protect their eyes against the effect of wind, sun and snow.

Gold Coast 1. Australia's largest resort area. 30 kilometres of coast in south-east Queensland with Brisbane just to the north. Main resorts include Southport, Surfers Paradise and Coolangatta.
2. Section of Florida coastline around Palm Beach and Miami with numerous exclusive resorts.
3. The coastal strip of Ghana, originally named after the gold mined in the area.

Golden Coast Coastal region in south-west Sweden stretching from Strömstad in the north to Laholm in the south. Main towns are Gothenburg and Halmstad.

Golden Horseshoe Area around the western end of Lake Ontario containing over 20% of Canada's population. Main towns are Oshawa, Toronto, Hamilton and St Catharines.

Golden Ring Area to the north-east of Moscow with many towns of great historical, architectural and spiritual significance, including Suzdal, Vladimir and Yaroslavl.

golden rivet A mythical term describing a supposed rivet made of solid gold, usually said to be installed in an isolated part of a ship. Used as a device to persuade a gullible person (usually female) to accompany a male crew member to a spot where they will be undisturbed.

Golden Triangle 1. Area with many ancient sites and important monuments in northern India with Delhi to the north, Agra to the south-east and Jaipur to the south-west.
2. Region in south-east Asia on the borders of Laos, Myanmar and Thailand. Notorious for the production of opium.

gondola 1. A traditional vessel used on canals, especially in Venice.
2. A type of cable car with an enclosed cabin.
3. The passenger-carrying cabin on an airship or balloon.

gondolier The oarsman of a gondola.

gorge A deep narrow canyon.

gorge-walking An extreme sport that involves following a stream or small

G

G

river from near its source. The actual stream is walked, not its general route, even when this involves wading in a considerable depth of water.

Goth A member of the Germanic tribe that invaded the Roman Empire in the 3rd to the 5th centuries

Gothic An architectural style common in Europe in the 12th to 16th centuries.

gourmand A glutton. Not to be confused with a gourmet.

gourmet A person who appreciates the finest things, especially food and drink.

gourmet meal Food and drink prepared to the exacting standards expected by the most discerning.

GPCA Guild of Professional Cruise Agents. *See Appendix 7a.*

GPU *See ground power unit.*

grade crossing (US). A level crossing.

gradient The slope of a road or railway. Gradients can be measured in percentages or as a ratio. A slope of 10% is equivalent to a ratio of 1 in 10. That is to say, for every ten feet of progress forward a vehicle would gain one foot in height.

Grain Coast Coastal strip of west Africa now situated in Liberia.

Grand Tour A historical term given to the practice of sending wealthy young aristocrats on a circuit of the major cultural centres of Europe. The fashion for taking the Grand Tour started in the 17th century and is one of the foundations of modern travel.

gratis Free of charge.

gratuity A tip for service. Theoretically for service over and above that expected but now often demanded as a right by many providers.

greasy spoon A slang expression meaning a cheap, often inferior, restaurant.

Great Britain A geographical region comprising England, Scotland and Wales.

great circle The shortest distance between two points on the Earth. A piece of string stretched between two points on a model globe will follow the great circle route and this route will often be significantly different from a straight line on a flat map projection.

Greater Antilles A group of Caribbean islands comprising the Cayman Islands, Cuba, Hispaniola, Jamaica and Puerto Rico.

green card 1. A certificate issued by an insurance company that provides evidence of cover (especially of motor insurance) outside the UK. 2. A work permit issued to residents of the USA who are not citizens.

green run The grading given to the easiest ski run in most French and Italian ski resorts.

Greenwich Mean Time The time at the zero meridian of longitude, from which all other times are calculated. Although still in general use, the term will eventually be replaced by UTC (Universal Time Co-ordinate).

Greenwich meridian The meridian

of longitude that passes through Greenwich (London) and from which all the meridians are numbered. Also known as the prime meridian or the zero meridian.

gringo A slang expression in common use in Spanish-speaking countries, meaning a foreigner, especially one from North America.

gross registered tonnage Used mainly for merchantmen. A measure of the capacity of a ship. One GRT is equivalent to 100 cubic feet of enclosed space. The expression derives from the word Tun (a type of barrel) and has nothing to do with weight. *(See also tonnage)*.

grotto A cave, often one part filled with water.

ground arrangements The additional facilities required by air travellers when they arrive at their destinations, such as accommodation, excursions, etc.

ground floor (UK). The lowest floor of a building.

ground handling agent A provider of ground arrangements.

ground power unit A small engine, separate from the main engines, that maintains an aircraft's air conditioning and other services while it is on the ground.

ground speed An aircraft's speed relative to the ground.

ground staff Members of the staff of an airline who are responsible for ground duties such as check-in and ticketing.

group inclusive tour Travel arrangements made in bulk for a group.

groyne A low wall built out into the sea to help prevent erosion of the beach.

GRTG The Guild of Registered Tourist Guides. *See Appendix 7a.*

GSA *See general sales agent.*

GTOA Group Travel Organisers Association. *See Appendix 7a.*

GTT The Guild of Travel and Tourism. *See Appendix 7a.*

guarantee An agreement by a principal to provide accommodation, even though the exact type, reference or category cannot be advised at the time.

guaranteed reservation Usually applicable to hotels, where a client or agent will guarantee payment for the accommodation booked, even if the client is a no show.

guaranteed upgrade Members of airlines' frequent traveller clubs are often given the guarantee of a complimentary upgrade to higher grade of accommodation than that paid for.

guard (UK). The person who rides on, and is in charge of, a train.

guard's van (UK). The coach or compartment on a train occupied by the guard.

guest A person resident in a hotel or other accommodation.

guest beer (UK). A beer available in a pub owned by a brewery, that is not

G

brewed by that brewery. It is now a statutory right of pub landlords in the UK to have a guest beer.

guest house A more modern term for boarding house.

guide 1. A person who guides or escorts groups. The duties of the various types of guide vary considerably and the official definitions, where they exist, are shown under their respective headings. *For further definitions see under tour and tourist.*
2. A book or other reference manual that gives details of an attraction, resort, country or other place or area.

Guinea Current An extension of the Equatorial Counter-current that flows southwards down the north-west coast of central Africa.

gulch (US). A ravine.

gulet Also *gulett* or *gullette*. A beamy Turkish sailing vessel built mainly of wood on traditional lines. Commonly used for flotilla type holidays.

gulf Similar to a bay, but generally larger.

Gulf Coast Stretch of coastline on Florida's west coast between Cedar Key in the north and Marco Island in the south. Developed as a resort area separately from Miami's Gold Coast.

Gulf Stream A warm water current that moves from the Gulf of Mexico to the North Atlantic. The warmth of the Gulf Stream is said to have a moderating effect on British winters.

gunwale Pronounced (and sometimes spelt) "gunnel". The very top of a ship's sides. Thus, "full to the gunwales" means there's no more space whatsoever.

Gypsy A member of the nomadic people of central Europe, of Hindu origin, speaking a language related to Hindi.

gyrocompass A non-magnetic compass working by the action of a gyroscope. A gyrocompass can be set to indicate true north.

gyroplane An aeroplane deriving its lift from a freely spinning overhead rotor. *See also autogiro.*

gyrostabiliser A stabiliser using the steadying effect of a gyroscope to maintain the stability of a ship or other vessel..

H
h

habitat The natural or traditional location of a plant or animal species. Destruction or modification of habitats is a frequent consequence of tourism development.

habitué A regular visitor or resident (of a hotel or resort, etc.).

hachures Parallel lines shown on better maps to indicate the steepness of gradients on hills, etc.

hacienda In Spanish-speaking countries, an estate or plantation with accommodation.

hackney carriage The original term for a taxi. No longer in common use but still the official term for a licensed taxi in the UK.

ha-ha (UK). A dry ditch, usually with a wall on its inner side, used as a boundary that does not spoil the view.

hajj The Islamic pilgrimage to Mecca.

hajji A Muslim who has been on the pilgrimage to Mecca.

half board *See demi-pension.*

half round trip A fare construction based on the sum of half the two return fares to a destination. This type of construction is useful when, for example, a passenger travels outward on a peak date and returns off peak.

half pension *See demi-pension.*

hall porter (UK). The member of hotel staff in charge of messages, passing of information, etc. *See also concierge.*

halo A ring of light that appears around the sun or moon under very particular meteorological conditions. Haloes differ from coronæ, appearing very much further away from the object they surround. *See also corona.*

halocline Boundary between waters of differing salinity.

halt (UK). A minor station on a railway line.

hamburger junction (UK). A type of road junction that includes a short extra section of road within a roundabout, protected by signing.

hamlet (UK). A small village, usually one without a church.

hand baggage Baggage, usually that of airline passengers, that is carried rather than being registered to a passenger's destination. All carriers have strict limits on hand baggage that must usually be capable of being stored under a seat or on a rack. Sometimes referred to as "carry-on" baggage.

H

hand spear A spear, used for catching fish, which does not include any form of propulsive gun.

handle tow A simple form of ski lift comprising a continually moving cable that skiers simply catch hold of.

handling agent An organisation that provides services to incoming visitors on behalf of a travel agent or tour operator. The rates for such services are contained in a confidential tariff.

handling fee A fee paid to an agent for working on a ticket that was sold by another and on which no further commission can be earned.

hangar A large building used to house aircraft.

Hanseatic League A medieval political and commercial league of Germanic towns

hansom A two-wheeled, horse-drawn cab. The term is still in use in some areas to denote a horse-drawn sightseeing vehicle.

harbour A bay or other protected area where ships can anchor in safety.

hard currency A currency that is sought after and has a relatively high rate of exchange is said to be hard. The currencies of most western European countries are relatively hard; those of many Third World countries are not.

hard shoulder (UK). An emergency stopping area along the edge of a motorway.

hard-top A car with a hard but detachable roof.

Harmattan A dry, dusty land wind of the west African coast, occurring from December to February.

HATA Hellenic Association of Travel & Tourism Agents. *See Appendix 7c.*

hatch An opening, usually covered when at sea, on a ship's deck that gives access to the holds.

haute cuisine A French expression meaning food of the highest quality, usually, but not invariably, served in expensive and elegant surroundings.

haven A harbour or port, often considered a refuge.

Hawaiian Sling A hand-held divers' spear with an additional tube-like device and rubber band which enables the user to propel the spear in a catapult fashion.

hawse That part of a ship's side where the hawse holes are situated.

hawse hole The opening in a ship's side through which the anchor chain passes.

hawser A cable used to tow or secure a ship.

HCA Holiday Centres Association. *See Appendix 7a.*

head The correct name for a ship's lavatory. Common in nautical circles, this expression is rarely used by passengers.

head office location An IATA term for an accredited agent's place of business that is also an approved location.

heading A direction or bearing.

headland A promontory.

headline city The main city of entry in a timetable, beneath and following which services to other destinations are listed.

headwaters Streams flowing from the source of a river.

headway The rate of progress of a ship. ("To make headway").

health requirements Travellers need to be aware of the possible dangers of disease or other health hazards. Details of risks are published by several organisations, and under the terms of the E.C. Directive on Package Travel, travel agents are obliged to inform their customer of them.

heartland The central or most important part of an area.

heat-stroke A feverish sickness caused by over-exposure to high temperatures.

heave The up and down motion of a vessel at sea.

heave to Shipping term - meaning to stop in the water without anchoring or mooring.

heavier-than-air Of an aircraft, one that weighs more than the air it displaces. Such aircraft can only remain in the air through the power of their engines.

Hebrew Of the Semitic people originally from ancient Palestine.

hectare An area equal to 10,000 square metres (2.47 acres).

HEDNA Hotel Electronic Distribution Network Association. *See Appendix 7b.*

heel When a vessel at sea tilts to port or starboard.

helicopter An aircraft with rotating wings. Helicopters can take off and land vertically and are thus often used for flights to destinations where there are no runways. Helicopters have a physical limitation on their top speed and for this reason are mainly used for short distance journeys.

heliport The equivalent of an airport, but used for helicopters. As they need no runways, heliports are much smaller than ordinary airports.

heli-skiing A holiday arrangement where skiers are taken to the skiing area, frequently on a mountaintop, by helicopter. This has obvious advantages for those who wish to ski in areas not served by lifts.

helium An inert, light gas used these days to give buoyancy to lighter-than-air aircraft.

Hellenic The civilisation of ancient Greece that lasted from 1300 BC to AD 558.

helm The mechanism by which a ship is steered. Originally a rudder, then a directly connected wheel. Nowadays often a small computer-linked wheel.

hemisphere In geography, one half of the earth's surface, each separated from the other by the equator.

hepatitis An infection of the liver causing jaundice. It can be fatal. There are two main types of infectious hepatitis, A and B. A is caused eating contaminated food or drink; B by contaminated blood products or sexual contact. Apart from the obvious precautions, short term immunity can be obtained by a pre-journey injection.

H

heritage A very broad expression that describes anything that has a link with some past event or person. Cultural heritage, for example, refers to past customs and traditions with the unspoken implication that these are worthwhile or creditable.

heritage attraction An attraction that capitalises on its connection with heritage.

Hibernian Of or concerning Ireland.

H

Hibiscus Coast Coastal area in South Africa near Port Shepstone, main resort Margate.

hidden city ticketing The practice of issuing a ticket to a more distant point with a lower fare than an intermediate change point and suggesting that the passenger ends his or her journey at the change point. This contravenes ticketing regulations, since the fare to the distant point should be raised to that of the higher intermediate point if the passenger intends to stop there.

high latitudes The areas of the earth near the poles.

high road A main road.

high seas The open seas, not within the jurisdiction of any state or country.

high season The busiest time for the use of a travel facility.

high tide *See high water.*

high water The tide at its fullest.

high water mark An indicator showing the level reached at high water.

higher rated intermediate points Often abbreviated to higher intermediate point. Usually applicable to air travel but can apply to other journeys. If a multi-sector journey passes through a point en route to its turnaround destination, to which the fare is higher than that applicable to the journey from the origin to the turnaround destination, then the fare for the whole journey must be raised to the fare for the highest rated point.

highway A public road.

hijacking The taking control by force of a vehicle, usually an aircraft.

hill A raised area of ground, less high than a mountain.

hill station A government settlement, originally used for officials' holidays during the summer, in the higher elevations in India, Malaysia and Ceylon (Sri Lanka)

Hindu civilisation Started in Jumna-Ganges around AD 775 and survives today.

hinterland **1.** In geography the area beyond a coast or river banks.
2. An area served by a port or other centre.

historical attraction Any attraction that derives its interest from something that could be considered famous or important in the past.

hitchhike To travel by soliciting lifts in passing vehicles. Against the law in some places and often dangerous.

Hittite The civilisation of ancient Turkey that lasted from before 2000 BC until 1200 BC.

HMA Hotel Marketing Association. *See Appendix 7a.*

HMS When placed in front of a ship's name means Her or His Majesty's Ship. A vessel in the Royal Navy.

hold The area in a ship or aircraft where the baggage or cargo is stored.

hold baggage Baggage that is not required by a passenger on a voyage is often placed in the hold. Obviously this would only apply if the passenger were on a line service.

holiday This expression originally meant a "holy day". That is, one where time would be taken off to worship. However, common usage now applies this to any time away from the normal working environment and by extension, to a trip taken away during such time.

holiday camp Now usually referred to as holiday centres. Mainly a UK phenomenon which arose from the 1935 Holiday Pay Act. Billy Butlin saw a sales opportunity and started his first camp with the slogan "a week's holiday for a week's pay". Holiday camps or centres now offer a high grade product, with many entertainment and other facilities included.

holiday centre *See holiday camp.*

holiday complex *See holiday camp.*

holidaymaker A person on holiday.

home port The port from which a ship originates.

home town The town of one's birth, early life or fixed residence.

home zone (UK). A residential street or area in which motor vehicles are actively discouraged in favour of people. Common in some parts of continental Europe for a quarter of a century, but only now being introduced in the UK.

homecare An emergency service insurance that will ensure that, should an accident happen to an insured group's home during their absence, emergency repairs will be put in hand immediately.

homeland A person's native land.

horizon The point at which the earth and sky appear to meet.

horizontal integration The terminology used to describe the expansion of an organisation by moving into associated areas of activity, but not those areas connected with the work done by its suppliers or distributors. In travel, for example, an airline might decide to buy a hotel chain.

hors d'oeuvres An expression of French origin (pronounced "orderv") meaning the appetisers or small snacks eaten before a meal.

horse latitudes A geographical expression that refers to two regions of calm, located at 30° north and 30° south of the equator.

hospitality In tourism a term that describes those people and organisations that are involved in the accommodation and catering sectors. Commercially it can mean the business of entertaining others, hopefully for commercial gain.

hospitality suite A hotel room used for entertainment or meetings, rather than sleeping.

H

host location An IATA term meaning a head office or branch office to which a satellite ticket printer is connected and controlled.

hostal A Spanish term for a small hotel or guest house.

hostel Originally low priced residential accommodation at a university or similar institution, the term now has several meanings. For holidaymakers the facilities provided by the Youth Hostels Association and its associated bodies can offer very cheap accommodation throughout the world. The sleeping arrangements are usually in dormitory style and there may also be self-catering facilities on site.

hostelry (UK). A pub (US). A small inn.

hotel 1. An establishment providing accommodation and meals. A hotel would be expected to provide a greater and/or superior range of facilities than establishments such as guest houses.
2. In Australia and New Zealand, a public house.

hotel register The list of guests who are staying or have stayed at a hotel. These days it is usually computerised, although written ledgers still exist.

hotel representative An organisation that represents a number of hotels. This enables travel agents to obtain information and make bookings more easily.

hotelier A hotel manager, operator or owner.

houseboat A boat fitted out as living accommodation.

house-flag The flag indicating to which company a ship belongs.

hovercraft Otherwise known as an air cushion vehicle (ACV). A vehicle that travels on a cushion of air, constrained by a flexible skirt, rather than being in contact with ground or water. Although hovercraft are considered to be flying vehicles, they are only able to travel at a maximum height of a few feet, as determined by the skirt depth.

hoverport A port for hovercraft.

hovertrain A tracked air cushion vehicle.

hub and spoke The usual way in which transport services develop. As the name implies, the carrier establishes operations at a suitable base (the hub) and operates out to various destinations along the "spokes". Passengers wishing to travel between destinations on different spokes will have to travel to the hub and change. (*See also interchange point*).

hull The body or frame of a ship or aircraft.

human geography The branch of geography that deals with the effects of human activity on the earth's surface and vice versa.

Humboldt Current A current flowing northward along the coast of Peru and Chile.

humidity The concentration of moisture in the atmosphere. Higher levels of humidity are uncomfortable since sweat is less able to evaporate from the surface of our bodies and its cooling effect is therefore reduced.

Hun A member of the nomadic warlike people who invaded Europe in the 4th and 5th centuries. Nowadays sometimes used offensively to refer to a German.

hurricane A storm with winds in excess of 64 knots. Hurricanes usually occur in tropical areas, since they need plenty of sun to provide their power.

hydraulic test The process of pressure-testing a diving cylinder in order to assess its suitability for further use as a container of high pressure gas.

hydrofoils 1. Foils or wings attached to the hull of a specially designed vessel. Once sufficient speed has been attained, the vessel rises until its hull is clear of the water and it is supported on the wings.
2. The name given to a ship or boat fitted with hydrofoils. Such vessels can travel at much higher speeds than conventional ships.

hydrogen A highly inflammable, light gas that was originally the first choice for giving buoyancy to lighter-than-air aircraft. Accidents caused by fire were common and hydrogen is no longer used for this purpose.

hydroplane A light, fast motorboat designed to skim over the water.

hypersonic Over five times the speed of sound.

hyperventilation A dangerous process of deliberate deep breathing resulting in carbon dioxide being flushed from the lungs. This removes the desire to breathe and allows those practising the technique to hold their breath for extended periods. The process can result in hypoxia.

hypothermia Reduced body core temperature.

hypothetical fare construction point *See fictitious fare construction point.*

hypoxia Reduced levels of oxygen within the body. A risk to travellers at extreme altitudes or in certain diving situations. Severe hypoxia can lead to anoxia.

H

I
i

IATA International Air Transport Association. *See Appendix 7d.*

IATAN International Airlines Travel Agent Network. *See Appendix 7b.*

Iberian Of or relating to the peninsula that contains Andorra, Gibraltar, Portugal and Spain.

IBTA International Business Travel Association. *See Appendix 7a.*

ICCA International Congress and Conference Association. *See Appendix 7d.*

ice-boat A boat-like vessel mounted on runners and able to travel on ice.

idyllic Blissfully peaceful or happy. Often used to describe an exceptionally pleasant place.

IFTO International Federation of Tour Operators. *See Appendix 7a.*

IFTTA International Forum of Travel and Tourism Advocates. *See Appendix 7b.*

IFWTO International Federation of Women's Travel Organisations. *See Appendix 7b.*

igloo A dome-shaped house made of ice, as built by the Inuit (Eskimo) peoples.

IIT Independent Inclusive Tour. A "tailor-made" arrangement put together to meet the specific needs of a customer that cannot be met by a standard package.

ILAM Institute of Leisure and Amenity Management. *See Appendix 7a.*

immigrant A person living or working in a country other than his or her own.

immigration Entering a country with the intention of settling there permanently.

imperial Of or relating to an empire or similar state.

implant A business travel agency employee working in the customer's own location, usually to undertake that customer's business travel only. Sometimes referred to as "in-plant" but this is probably a misunderstanding of the origins of the expression.

import To bring items or commodities into a country.

inaugural The first time of use of a new aircraft, route or similar introduction.

inboard Within the sides or towards the middle of a ship, aircraft or other vehicle.

inbound Returning to the point of origin of a journey.

Inca *See Andean.*

incentive commission An extra amount of commission paid to an agent in order to encourage extra sales. Usually such commission will be paid once an agreed sales target is reached

incidentals Minor items of expenditure that are too small to be worth detailing.

inclusive resort A large-scale accommodation and leisure complex which aims to satisfy as many of the requirements of its visitors as possible on the one site

inclusive tour **1.** Another name for a package holiday.
2. A specific IATA term meaning "A pre-arranged combination of air transportation and surface arrangements other than solely public transportation which is designed to encourage air travel and which conforms to certain minimum standards as defined in the applicable resolution."

inclusive tour excursion fare Although the term ITX refers to a specific type of tour basing fare, the expression is often used to denote any type of fare used to construct inclusive arrangements.

incoming tour operator A tour operator that specialises in supplying services for visitors to a country.

incoming tourism Tourism coming into a country from another country.

Indaba A Zulu word for a gathering. Now also used as the name for an annual tourism marketplace held in South Africa.

indemnify To make good a loss.

indemnity Compensation for a loss. One of the types of cover provided by insurance. For example, if a policy gives indemnity against loss by theft, then it is saying that it will make good the loss if the goods are stolen, but not necessarily if they are burned.

index An alphabetical list or names, subjects, etc. In an atlas or similar, it would be a list of places.

Indian ocean *See oceans.*

Indic **1.** The civilisation of the region around the Indus and Ganges rivers that lasted from before 3000 BC to AD 500.
2. The language of this group.

indicator *See global indicator.*

indigenous Belonging to or originating from a country or region.

indirect routeing A routeing going via a point or points that it need not necessarily take in. Indirect routeings may be made necessary through lack of suitable services or through passenger inclination.

Indochina The geographical region comprising Cambodia, Laos, Malaysia (peninsula), Myanmar, Singapore, Thailand and Vietnam.

industrial attraction A tourist attraction that capitalises on its connection with industry, usually historical.

ineligible Not entitled or allowed. For example, a 17 year old is ineligible for a child fare.

infant In travel, a child who has not yet reached the age at which child fares will be charged. This will vary according to the carrier, but for most airlines it is up to 2 years.

inflatable Or inflatable dinghy. A small boat made from rubber or a similar material that can be easily carried and is inflated when needed for use.

in-flight catering The food and beverage services provided on board an aircraft. On most airlines the cost is included in the fare, but on some of the so called "no-frills" airlines an extra charge is made.

in-flight entertainment Those services, such as films, music and magazines provided to keep passengers occupied during a flight.

informal Without ceremony or formality. When referring to an event it usually refers to the style of dress expected.

information display Any system for making information available to an audience. Information displays can be manual (such as a noticeboard) or automated (such as a VDU).

information technology The use of computers for manipulating information.

infrastructure An underlying framework. For example, the infrastructure of a tourist resort would include such things as roads and railways; water and electricity supplies; shops and catering establishments, etc.

inhabit To dwell in or occupy a region or house, etc.

inhospitable Uninviting or otherwise unwelcoming. An inhospitable

climate is one that is unpleasant for visitors.

in-house Done or existing within an institution. E.g. in-house entertainment in a hotel is that provided by the hotel itself.

inland Situated in the interior of a country or state.

inlet A small arm of water penetrating the land.

inn Historically a house providing food and accommodation for travellers. Nowadays the term may be applied to establishments, such as pubs, which provide only refreshment. Also, confusingly, it is sometimes also used by establishments (such as Holiday Inns) who actually operate hotels.

innkeeper A person who keeps or runs an inn.

inoculation An alternative name for vaccination that is nowadays less commonly used.

insalubrious Of a climate or place, unhealthy.

inshore At sea, but close to the shore.

inside cabin A ship's cabin that has no window or porthole and thus no natural light.

insular Like or relating to an island.

insurable interest The rule that states that a person cannot insure against a risk in which he or she has no direct interest.

insurance premium The sum taken by an insurance company from a proposer in order to accept the risk.

As a rule, the higher the risk the greater the sum required.

interchange point Theoretically any point on a public transport network where passengers may change services. In practice, transport undertakings will encourage passengers to use specifically designated interchange points by showing them in timetables and ensuring that the timings work well. *See also hub and spoke.*

inter-city Existing or travelling between cities. Sometimes used as a generic term for transport or services offering rapid conveyance between major points.

intercontinental Literally, between continents. Thus intercontinental travel is travel between continents.

interior Inland. Remote from the coast or frontier.

interline The official IATA term for anything involving two or more of its members. Thus, if an "interline agreement" exists between two members, they will agree to accept each other's documents.

internal combustion engine An engine, using petrol or diesel fuel, that develops its power by means of controlled burning of the fuel in enclosed cylinders. Most cars and motorcycles are driven by internal combustion engines.

international Existing, involving or carried on between two or more nations. International travel is considered to be that between two countries in the same continent.

international dateline When a traveller goes westward, the local time goes back 1 hour relative to GMT for each 15° of longitude traversed. When a traveller goes eastward the local time goes forward. Halfway round the world, at approximately 180°, there is a difference of 24 hours, or 1 day. This is the International dateline. When a traveller crosses the dateline from East to West, the date goes forward by a whole day; when travelling from West to East, the date reverts to the previous day.

interoceanic Between or connecting two oceans.

interprovincial Situated or carried on between provinces.

interstate **1.** (US). A motorway crossing a state boundary. **2.** Existing or carried on between states.

Inuit Of or relating to the peoples who inhabit North Canada, Alaska and Greenland. This term is replacing the former term, "Eskimo".

Inupiaq **1.** Of or relating to the Inuit peoples. **2.** Their language.

invalid **1.** Not valid for use. **2.** A person who is enfeebled through disease or injury and will need special help or care when travelling.

invalidate To make a document invalid for use.

invisible exports Items, such as services, that require the transfer of funds into a country but that do not involve the actual movement of goods. Incoming tourism is an example of an invisible export since such tourists bring funds into the country.

invisible imports Items, such as services, that require the transfer of funds out of a country but that do not involve the actual movement of goods. Outgoing tourism is an example of an invisible import since such tourists take funds out of the country.

involuntary change In airline terms, an alteration to a passenger's journey that has been brought about by circumstances beyond his or her control. The passenger will not lose the benefit of any special fares or concessions granted, even if the involuntary change takes the ticket out of validity.

IPA International phonetic alphabet. *See phonetic alphabet.*

Iranic (Islamic) civilisation Started around AD 1320 in the Oxus-Jaxartes basin and survives today.

Irminger Current The northernmost arm of the Gulf Stream.

Iron Curtain The name given to the barrier that existed between countries with different ideologies and which prevented the free interchange of communication and goods. This was most evident between those countries allied to the old Soviet Union and the western nations. There are now few such barriers left.

Islam The religion of the Muslims.

island A piece of land, other than a continent, entirely surrounded by water. Excluding the continents, the largest island is Greenland with an area of 2,200,000 square kilometres (840,000 square miles).

island-hop To travel from island to island, especially in places such as Greece, where there are many small islands in a limited area.

islet A small island.

isobar A line drawn on a weather map that joins points of equal barometric pressure.

isolated Remote or cut off. Lonely.

isopleth A line on a weather map joining points that have an equal incidence of a particular meteorological feature.

isotherm A line drawn on a weather map that joins points of equal temperature.

Israeli Of or relating to the modern state of Israel.

issue Of documents, to prepare by writing or printing, ready for handing over to a customer.

isthmus A narrow strip of land joining two larger land masses.

IT 1. *See inclusive tour.*
2. *See information technology.*

ITAA Irish Travel Agents Association. *See Appendix 7c.*

itinerary The written details of a customer's travel arrangements, in the form of dates, times and destinations.

ITM Institute of Travel Management. *See Appendix 7a.*

ITMA Incentive Travel & Meetings Association Ltd. *See Appendix 7a.*

ITT Institute of Travel & Tourism. *See Appendix 7a.*

ITX *See inclusive tour excursion fare.*

Ivory Coast The Atlantic coast of Côte d'Ivoire, formerly popular with traders in ivory.

I

J
j

jack A ship's flag, especially one flown from the bow.

jackstaff The staff at the bow of a ship that carries the jack.

jamboree Originally celebration or merrymaking but now usually applied to a large international gathering of Scouts or Guides.

Japan Current A warm-water current in the Pacific Ocean, the equivalent of the Atlantic's Gulf Stream.

JATA Japan Association of Travel Agents. *See Appendix 7c.*

jato *See jet assisted take off.*

jeepney A small bus especially common in the Philippines. Many were originally built from old US Jeeps.

jet aircraft An aircraft powered by jet engines. The first jet airliner was the De Havilland Comet, introduced in the 1950's, but it was the adoption of larger jets like the Boeing 707, and the rapid increase in runway length and airport facilities to accommodate them, that created a dramatic increase in world wide air travel.

jet assisted take off When a supplementary jet engine is installed to provide extra thrust at an aircraft's take-off. Rarely used these days.

jet engine An engine that relies on the continuous burning of fuel to provide thrust and/or power to drive a propeller. The jet turbine engine was invented in the 1930's but the first jet aircraft did not fly until the end of the Second World War.

jet lag The disturbance to a person's bodily rhythms caused by crossing time zones too quickly.

jet set A term applied, sometimes pejoratively, to groups of wealthy and socially prominent people who supposedly travel from place to place by jet in search of enjoyment.

jet ski A water vehicle designed to carry one or two persons and propelled by a jet of water. These are usually controlled by handlebars similar to those on a motorcycle, and are thus often referred to as "wet bikes". Since they have no wheels, this expression is obviously nonsensical.

jet stream A high speed air current. Pilots often take advantage of jet streams to increase the speed of their aircraft without having to use extra power and thus save fuel.

jetfoil A hydrofoil vessel, powered by water jets.

jetsam Discarded materials, rubbish, washed ashore.

jetty **1.** A pier or breakwater. A landing jetty is one that passengers can use for embarkation and disembarkation.
2. Part of a building that projects. Thus the extensions at airports where aircraft park and load are sometimes called jetties.

Jew A person of the Jewish faith. The expression does not mean someone from the Jewish state of Israel.

jib A triangular sail extending from the outer end of the bowsprit to the top of the mast of a boat or ship.

jolly-boat A type of ship's boat, smaller than a cutter.

journey To travel from one place to another. The act of so travelling.

joystick A colloquial name for the control column of an aircraft.

Judaic Of or relating to Jews or Judaism.

jumbo jet The familiar term applied to large, wide-bodied aircraft, in particular the Boeing 747.

jump jet A jet aircraft that can take off vertically.

jump seat An extra seat, often foldaway, usually used to accommodate crew members on a full flight.

junction Of a road or railway, a point where they meet, join or cross.

jungle An area of very dense vegetation, especially in tropical areas.

jungle fever Severe malaria.

junior suite A large hotel room with a partition separating the bed and sitting areas

junk A flat-bottomed sailing vessel typically used in the China sea.

J

junk food Food of low nutritional value The term is often used to refer to the various types of fast food, even though this may not always be correct.

junket A slang expression for a trip offered at the expense of a principal to thank its customers and hopefully gain new business.

junta A political or military group or faction that takes power after a revolution or coup d'état.

K
k

kala-azar A tropical parasitic disease transmitted by sandflies.

Karoo Or Karroo. An elevated, semi-desert, plateau in South Africa.

kasbah The Arab quarter of a North African city.

kayak Originally an Eskimo canoe, but now used to describe any similar type of vessel.

keel A horizontal structure, usually of steel, that runs the length of the bottom of a ship. It could be considered the ship's backbone and is the base from which all other parts are built.

keelboat 1. A yacht with a permanent keel.
2. (US). A large flat riverboat

keelson A line of timber fastening a ship's floor-timbers to the keel.

Kelvin A scale of temperature with the same graduations as those used in centigrade, but with absolute zero (-273°C) used as its starting point. Freezing water is 273°K.

kerosene The North American term for paraffin. The fuel used for all jet aircraft.

key *See cay.*

key card A small card, similar to a credit card, used instead of a room key in some hotels.

Khamsin An oppressive, hot, south or south-easterly wind occurring in Egypt in March, April, and May.

Khmer 1. The civilisation of ancient Cambodia that lasted from AD 100 to AD 1432.
2. A native of modern Cambodia.

kibbutz Plural *kibbutzim*. A communal settlement in Israel.

kilometre A length of 1000 metres or approximately .62 of a statute mile.

king room A hotel room with a king-sized bed.

King's highway *See Queen's highway.*

kingdom A country ruled by a king or queen.

klong A canal in Thailand.

kloof A steep-sided ravine in South Africa.

knap The summit of a hill.

knock-for-knock An insurance term relating to an agreement whereby each company pays for the losses of its own policyholder, regardless of blame.

knoll A small hill.

knot When used as a measure of speed, means nautical miles per hour. 20 knots is approximately 23 mph

Kona Coast Part of the south-west coast of the island of Hawaii, also known as the Gold Coast.

korridorzuge An Austrian expression meaning "corridor train". This is not, however, a description of the type of carriage. A korridorzuge is a train that travels through another country in a special "corridor" of track, within which it may not stop to pick up or set down passengers. This type of routing will avoid the circuitous journey that would otherwise be necessary, such as that from Innsbruck to Salzburg

kosher Food and drink prepared in accordance with the strict Jewish hygiene laws. The term is often used loosely to describe anything that is true or genuine.

kremlin A citadel within a Russian town. When written as a proper noun (the Kremlin) refers to the seat of the Russian government in Moscow.

Kurds The Aryan peoples living in Kurdistan and some neighbouring countries.

Kuroshio A warm current that brings tropical waters northward past Japan. Almost the equivalent of the Atlantic's Gulf Stream.

kyle A Scottish name for a narrow channel between an island and another island or the mainland.

K

L
l

La Niña The opposite phenomenon to El Niño that also causes significant global climatic changes. La Niña is characterised by unusually cool water temperatures on the equatorial regions of the central and eastern Pacific.

Labrador Current A current bringing cold water and icebergs down from Baffin Bay. Where it meets the Gulf Stream of Newfoundland, the mixing of the waters gives rise to the fogs that affect the Grand Banks for around 120 days each year.

ladder The form of fare construction box on airline tickets in which the calculations are shown vertically.

lagoon An enclosed body of water, usually sea, such as the centre of an atoll.

lake A large body of fresh water surrounded by land. The ten largest lakes, in order of area, are:
• Caspian Sea
• Superior
• Victoria Nyanza
• Ar'skoye More (Aral Sea)
• Huron
• Michigan
• Tanganyika
• Great Bear
• Ozeri Bakal
• Malawi

lanai A room with a balcony or patio, usually overlooking water or gardens. The term is commonly used in Hawaii.

land arrangements Another name for ground arrangements.

land breeze A breeze blowing off the land onto the sea.

land bridge A neck of land joining two land masses.

land mass A single large body of land, such as a continent.

land yacht A vehicle with wheels and a sail used for racing, etc. on a beach, etc. Sometimes called a sand yacht.

landau A four-wheeled enclosed horse-drawn carriage with a rear hood that can be lowered.

landfall The first sighting of land after a journey across an ocean or sea.

landing card A pre-printed questionnaire filled in by passengers before arrival at a foreign destination to facilitate progress through immigration.

landing gear The wheels of an aircraft. Also known as the undercarriage.

landing stage A platform, often floating, onto which passengers may disembark from a vessel.

landing strip An aircraft runway, often small and away from an airport and possibly unsurfaced.

landlocked A destination surrounded by land.

landlubber A derogatory expression used to describe a person aboard a ship who is new to the experience.

landmark A conspicuous building or topographical feature that is easily recognised from a distance.

landscape The natural scenery or view of an area.

landside That part of an airport open to any legitimate visitor; the area before customs and other controls.

landward Towards the land.

lane A narrow, often rural road, street or path.

langlauf Cross-country skiing.

Lapp A member of the nomadic Mongol peoples of northern Scandinavia. The term Sami is now the preferred name.

larboard An obsolete name for the port side of a vessel.

Lassa fever A serious viral disease of tropical Africa.

last seat availability The facility available on some GDS's to give information about the up-to-date availability of airline seats.

late booking A vague term that means any booking that is made only a short while before travel. The period will vary according to the service booked. For example, an inclusive holiday booked a week before departure would

probably be considered late; an air ticket to Paris booked by a business traveller over the same time scale would probably not.

lateen sail A triangular sail on a long yard at an angle of 45° to the mast. Used on Arab dhows.

Latin 1. The language of the Roman Empire.
2. A general description of anything relating to the peoples or countries using languages developed from Latin (such as Spain or Mexico).

Latin America Those parts of Central and South America where the Latin-derived languages of Portuguese or Spanish are the main languages. In other words, most of that area.

latitude To assist navigation, the Earth has, for many years, been divided by imaginary lines. The main "horizontal" division is the Equator, which runs around the globe at its widest point, at right angles to its axis. The Equator is approximately 40,076 kilometres (24,902 miles) in length and is said to be at 0 degrees (0°). The other lines of latitude run parallel to the equator and are numbered in degrees north or south. Both the northern and southern parallels end at the poles at 90° north and 90° south respectively. The parallels are approximately 100 kilometres (63 miles) apart and diminish in length as they approach the poles. At the poles, of course, they have no length at all.

launch A motor boat, sometimes used to carry passengers from ship to shore.

lavatory Another name for a toilet or rest-room.

L

lay-by (UK). An area, usually by a road but also on canals or railways, where vehicles may stop.

layover A period of rest or waiting time between one part of a journey and the next.

LDW Loss damage waiver. *See CDW.*

le surf A French expression for snowboarding.

league **1.** A group of people, nations, etc., combining for a particular purpose.
2. An old-fashioned measure of distance equal to three miles.

lee The direction away from the wind. Sometimes referred to as leeward.

leeward *See lee.*

Leeward Islands The group of Caribbean Islands that includes: Anguilla, Antigua and Barbuda, Dominica, Guadeloupe, Monserrat, Saba, St. Eustatius, St. Kitts and Nevis, St. Maarten/St Martin.

leeway **1.** The sideways drift of a ship to the lee of its desired course.
2. An allowable deviation or freedom of action.

left luggage (UK). Luggage temporarily deposited in a storeroom specially designated for that purpose.

leg The official IATA term for the journey between two consecutive scheduled stops on a flight.

legal advice and expenses insurance Insurance cover offered to travellers who have to undertake legal action against a person or corporate body in respect of death or serious illness. Usually the insurance company will advance funds to cover the costs of legal and associated expenses, and will expect repayment of the loan from the compensation received from the court. However, should no compensation be forthcoming, then the costs incurred will be covered by the policy.

lei A Polynesian garland of flowers, traditionally placed around the necks of visitors to these Pacific islands.

leishmaniasis Any one of a number of parasitic diseases cause by the bite of sandflies.

leisure Free time or time at one's disposal.

leisure travel agent A travel agent dealing mainly with holidaymakers, rather than business travellers.

leisure traveller A traveller who is not travelling on business or for some other obligatory reason.

leprosy A slightly contagious disease that affects the nerves causing loss of sensation and consequent damage and disfigurement through unfelt injury. Still common in some Third World countries although easily treatable.

Lesser Antilles A group of Caribbean Islands comprising the Leeward Islands, the Virgin Islands, the Windward Islands and the small chain of Venezuelan islands east of Bonaire. Also the islands of Aruba, Barbados, Curaçao and Trinidad and Tobago.

level crossing An intersection where a railway crosses a road on the level. Railways usually have the right of way.

levy A tax or toll.

lido deck The deck of a ship that contains the pool and sunbathing area.

lien A right over another's property to protect a debt. Most commonly used in travel to refer to the innkeeper's lien, which is the right of an innkeeper or hotelier to keep a guest's goods to defray the cost of an unpaid bill.

life jacket A buoyant outer garment that keeps the wearer afloat in water.

lifebelt (UK). *See lifebuoy.*

lifeboat A small boat carried on board a ship to evacuate passengers in the case of serious emergency. It is a maritime regulation that all ships must carry enough lifeboats to accommodate all those aboard.

lifeboat drill An obligatory demonstration of the safety procedures on board a ship.

lifebuoy A buoyant support, often a ring, that will keep a person afloat in water.

lifeline A line which connects a diver to a point on the surface.

life-raft A raft carried on board a ship to provide an alternative or additional safety measure.

life-support systems The systems of air-conditioning, pressurisation, heating, etc. that allow passengers to survive in a hostile environment, such as at a high altitude.

lift 1. The force generated by an aircraft's wings that enables it to fly. 2. The UK term for an elevator.

lift pass A ticket giving users access to all the lifts in a given ski area or areas.

light railway A railway, often narrow gauge, constructed to less demanding standards than normal and designed to cope only with light traffic.

lighter A small boat used to transfer goods between ships or to the shore.

lighter than air Of an aircraft, one that weighs less than the air it displaces, in other words, one that can float in the air. Such aircraft can remain in the air indefinitely without the need for engine power.

lightning A high-voltage, naturally occurring electrical discharge between clouds and other clouds or the earth.

limited 1. Of accommodation generally, when only a small amount of space remains available for sale. 2. A service, often rail, where the number of passengers is restricted to the amount of seating or other accommodation available. Usually such services require advance reservation. In the US the name is sometimes given to any long-distance luxury rail service.

limo *See limousine.*

limousine An enclosed motor car, originally one with a division between driver and passengers, but the term is now often used casually to refer to any luxurious vehicle.

liner Originally the name given to ships belonging to the famous shipping lines, such as Cunard, Union Castle or P & O, that travelled on scheduled "line" voyages between ports. Line service shipping is now almost obsolete but the term is still used for most large ships, including those on cruise itineraries.

L

link span Many ports, including those on the English Channel, are affected by high tidal movements. In order to allow embarkation at all times, a complex loading bridge is employed which can be adjusted to allow for tidal height variations. The name given to this type of bridge is link span.

lithosphere The scientific name for the earth's crust or surface.

livery The distinctive colour scheme used by a carrier to identify its vehicles.

llano A treeless plain, especially in South America.

load factor The percentage of occupancy of seats or other accommodation. 100% load factor is full, 50% load factor half full, etc.

load line *See Plimsoll Line.*

lobby An entrance or reception area of a hotel, typically of a hotel.

local 1. Belonging to a particular place of region.
2. Of or belonging to the neighbourhood.
3. (UK). A pub.

local service A transport service operating in and around the local area.

local time The time as reckoned in a particular destination. Local times can vary from GMT by as much as 12 hours. Most timetables use local times.

locality A district or neighbourhood.

location The place or position where something is situated.

locator A unique reference given by a computer at the completion of a reservation. The booking is accessed using this reference.

loch A Scottish expression for a lake or arm of the sea.

lock A separate section of a canal or river fitted with gates to control the flow of water, thus allowing vessels to change levels.

locomotive A vehicle designed to haul a trailer or a train. The expression is usually used in connection with railways although road locomotives do exist, as do road trains. It is incorrect to refer to a locomotive as a "train".

lodge card A charge card "lodged" in the care of an agent (usually a business travel agent) against which travel facilities may be charged. This system allows the cardholder a credit facility without the necessity for opening an account directly with the agent.

log The official record of the progress and happenings on board a ship or aircraft.

log cabin A hut or similar dwelling built from tree trunks.

loggia An open-sided extension to a building.

long vacation (UK). The extended summer holiday taken by students at British universities.

longboat The largest boat used on a sailing ship.

long-haul An inexact term that is usually applied to journeys between continents.

longitude These divisions of the globe are half great circles passing through both poles. The meridians of longitude are numbered from the "zero meridian" which runs through Greenwich, London, UK. The numbering is done in degrees east or west of Greenwich. At 180° in either direction the meridians meet and this is the approximate position of the international date line. Meridians of longitude are not parallel and so the distance between each will vary. At the equator it is about 112 kilometres (70 miles) and at the poles, zero.

loo (UK). Colloquial. A lavatory.

lounge A seating area designed to accommodate people for a short period while they are waiting to move to another area or facility.

Low Countries The geographical region comprising Belgium, Luxembourg and the Netherlands.

low latitudes Regions at or near the equator.

low season The period during which there is the least demand for a product or service.

low tide *See low water.*

low water The tide at its lowest.

lower deck Generally the lowest deck of a ship, immediately above the hold.

luau A Hawaiian outdoor feast with entertainment.

lubber line A line marked on a compass showing a ship's forward direction.

luggage Another term for baggage.

lugger A small ship with two or three masts with a lugsail on each.

lugsail A four-sided sail.

Lutine bell A bell kept at Lloyd's of London, originally rung to announce a shipwreck but now to make any important announcement to the underwriters. The bell is from the wreck of the ship "Lutine".

luxurious With choice or costly surroundings.

L

M
m

Mach number A measure of speed as compared to the speed of sound. Mach 1 is the speed of sound; Mach 2 is twice the speed of sound and so on.

Mae West A type of inflatable life-jacket. So called because of its supposed resemblance to the ample bust of the actress of that name.

magic carpet A simple ski lift in the form of a moving walkway. Often used on beginners' and children's ski slopes.

maglev From **mag**netic **lev**itation. A train supported slightly clear of its track by magnetic repulsion.

magnetic compass A compass that indicates direction by means of a magnetised pointer.

magnetic north pole The point indicated by a magnetic compass needle.

magnetic poles *See poles.*

Magyar The Ural-Altaic peoples now predominant in Hungary.

main course The chief course of a meal.

main deck The upper deck between the forecastle and the poop of a merchantman.

main line A primary railway line.

main road A major highway.

mainland A large continuous piece of land, excluding its associated islands.

mainplane The main wing of an aircraft.

maître d'hotel A French expression meaning the head waiter in a restaurant. Used world-wide and often abbreviated to "maître d".

mal de mer Seasickness.

Malabar Coast Coast of Karnataka and Kerala states, south-west India. Main ports are Cochin and Trivandrum.

malaria One of the common diseases to which travellers are exposed. It is caused by parasites that live inside the anopheles mosquito. It is difficult to cure and travellers should protect themselves by avoiding mosquito bites and by taking suitable anti-malarial drugs.

Malay Archipelago The largest island group in the world, off the south-east coast of Asia. Major islands in the group include: Borneo, Sulawesi (Celebes), Jawa (Java), New Guinea and Sumatera (Sumatra). Major countries within the archipelago include:

Brunei/Darussalam, Indonesia, Malaysia (East), Papua New Guinea and the Philippines.

malecón A Spanish term for a seafront promenade, especially in Mexico and Cuba.

management fees An amount paid by a corporate customer to a business travel agent to look after its business. There are two main ways of charging. A simple management fee would be an agreed amount charged over a specified period, regardless of the number of transactions taking place. A transaction fee is an amount charged per transaction, regardless of the period over which they were completed. It is, of course, possible to combine the two systems. Management fees seem increasingly likely to become the normal way of trading.

management information system In travel the term used to denote the statistical and other data supplied by business travel agents to their customers.

mañana An expression of Spanish origin meaning literally tomorrow, but implying later or possibly never.

manifest The official list of passengers (or cargo) being carried on a vehicle.

manifold A connecting pipe between two high pressure diving cylinders.

manual issue When a document is written out by hand, rather than being printed by computer.

Manx Of, or relating to the Isle of Man.

map A diagram or representation of an area. There is a vast range of maps available, ranging from those that show the whole world down to those that show an area of only a few square metres. Specialised maps exist to show every significant aspect of an area, literally from archaeological to zoological.

MAP *See modified American plan.*

map projection *See projection.*

map reference A set of numbers and/or letters specifying a particular location on a map.

march with, upon A geographical term denoting a common boundary or frontier. For example, the border of Spain marches with that of Portugal.

Mardi Gras 1. Shrove Tuesday in certain Catholic countries. **2.** The celebration often associated with this.

marina A port designed for small boats or yachts.

marine Of or relating to the sea or shipping.

mariner A seaman.

mark-up The amount added to a net price to arrive at the selling price. Gross profit.

Marlin Coast Area of coast in northern Queensland, Australia, centred on Cairns.

maroon To leave a person isolated in a place, often an island.

marsh Low land flooded for much of the time.

marsh fever *See malaria.*

M

mask clearing An underwater process whereby the mask is held firmly to the forehead whilst the diver exhales through the nose. The exhaled air rises to the top of the mask and forces water out at the bottom thus clearing the mask.

massif A compact group of mountains.

mast A tall pole, usually fixed to the hull of a ship, rising vertically though all the decks. On sailing vessels masts will be high and substantial to take the weight and thrust of the sails. On powered vessels, they may carry little more than the ensigns and wireless aerials.

masthead The highest point of a mast.

maximum permitted mileage The maximum number of miles that may be flown in each IATA fare component without surcharge or penalty for a given journey. The MPM is usually about 20% greater than the actual ticketed point mileage. For example, the ticket point (or flown) mileage from London to New York is 3,458 but the MPM is 4,149. A passenger may, if he or she wishes, travel up to 4,149 miles and still only pay the London/New York fare.

Mayan The civilisation of ancient Mexico and Guatemala that lasted from before 2500 BC to AD 1550. At over 45 centuries this is the longest surviving civilisation in history.

mayday From the French "M'aidez" (help me). The standard international radio distress call.

MCO *See miscellaneous charges order.*

MDR-TB Multiple Drug Resistant Tuberculosis. An increasingly common and very serious disease with mortality rates in excess of 50%.

meadow An area of grass and small flowers.

mean sea level The level of the sea midway between high and low tides.

meander A section of a river that has a series of bends.

medical expenses insurance Not to be confused with personal accident insurance. Although an accident may give rise to claims under both sections of a policy, the two covers are different. Medical expenses cover is intended to reimburse a claimant for the costs of medical and associated expenses, caused through accident or illness. The term medical expenses usually covers a wide range of items, usually including hospital accommodation costs, additional travel costs and funeral or repatriation costs, as well as the cost of medical treatment.

medina The old Arab quarter of a north African town.

Mediterranean 1. A general tourist term that describes the islands of the Mediterranean Sea and the countries bordering it.
2. A type of climate. *See climate.*

meet and greet The provision of a service to meet and assist passengers on arrival at their destination port, station or airport.

Megalopolis Densely populated continuous urban area in the north-east United States stretching from Boston through New York,

Philadelphia and Baltimore to Washington DC. The region is also called the Boston-Washington Corridor and the Northeast Corridor. The term, from the name for an Ancient Greek city, was first used in the 1960s and is now used generically to describe similar urbanised regions.

Melanesia The collective name given to the group of islands in the south-west Pacific Ocean, south of the equator and north-east of Australia. It includes Fiji, Nauru, New Caledonia, Papua New Guinea (excluding New Guinea mainland), Solomon Islands, Vanuatu.

melt water Water formed from the melting of ices especially from a glacier.

Member An IATA term meaning an airline belonging to IATA.

menagerie A collection of wild animals for exhibition.

menu 1. A list of food, drinks, etc. available in a restaurant.
2. A list, on a computer screen, of alternative actions that may be taken.

merchant marine (US). *See merchant navy.*

merchant navy (UK). A nation's commercial shipping fleet.

merchantman A ship used for merchant (or passenger and mixed cargo) purposes, as opposed to military or tanker use.

meridian A line of longitude.

mesa A high, steep-sided plateau. (From the Spanish "table".)

mestizo A Spanish expression meaning a person of mixed parentage, especially Spanish or Portuguese and Native American (Indian).

meteograph An instrument that records a number of different meteorological phenomena simultaneously.

meteorology The science of the study of weather. Meteorology is important in travel since weather conditions can easily upset the operation of most forms of transport.

metro A name used in some parts of the world to describe an underground railway. Although it is most popularly associated with the Paris Metro, the term is probably derived from the Metropolitan Railway, one of London's pioneering underground systems.

M

Metroplex The metropolitan area of Dallas-Fort Worth in Texas. The cities between Dallas and Fort Forth are described as the Mid-Cities: the largest of these is Arlington.

metropolis A US expression for the main town or city in a region.

Mexic The civilisation of the Aztecs that started on the Mexican plateau around AD 1075 and lasted until AD 1821.

mezzanine A low storey between the first and ground floors.

Micronesia Collective name for the islands in the west Pacific Ocean, north of the equator and east of the Philippines. It includes Guam, Kiribati (west), the Marshall Islands, Federated States of Micronesia, northern Mariana Islands and Palau.

Middle America Mexico and Central America.

Middle East A general geographic term that describes an area comprising the countries of the Arabian Peninsula, Egypt, Iran, Iraq, Israel, Jordan, Lebanon and Syria. These days it is often extended to include Cyprus, Libya and Turkey.

midnight sun In extreme northern or southern latitudes, the sun is visible for 24 hours each day at the height of summer.

Midnight Sun Coast The eastern coast of Sweden from Gavle to the Finnish border.

midships *See amidships.*

midtown (US). That part of a town or city midway between the uptown and downtown areas.

migration The mass movement of people or animals from one place to another place some considerable distance away.

mile *See statute mile, geographical mile.*

mini-bar A self-service bar placed in a hotel room for the use of guests.

minibus A small bus, usually for fewer than twelve passengers.

minicab (UK). A taxi that has not been licensed to ply for hire.

minimum connecting time The minimum time that a passenger can allow between connecting services.

minimum rated package A UK term for an inclusive tour by air that provides "nominal" accommodation

in order to comply with regulations. *See also "seat only".*

minimum stay The shortest time a passenger can stay before using the return portion of a ticket. Return before this time will involve a surcharge.

Minoan The civilisation of ancient Crete and the Cyclades that lasted from before 2000 BC until 1400 BC.

minute **1.** One sixtieth of an hour. **2.** One sixtieth of a degree of arc.

mirage An image of an object that does not exist at the point where it appears to be. Mirages are caused by the refraction of light where layers of the atmosphere have sharply different densities (caused by significant temperature differences).

MIS *See management information system.*

miscellaneous charges order An airline voucher that can be used for almost any type of service. For example, a passenger might choose to have an MCO issued to cover excess baggage charges. MCO's are being phased out and will eventually be replaced by MPD's (Multi-Purpose Document).

mist Water vapour near the ground limiting visibility.

mistral A cold, northerly wind that blows down the Rhone valley and southern France into the Mediterranean.

mobile home **1.** A large caravan permanently parked and used as a residence. **2.** (US). A recreational vehicle (RV).

modified American plan *See demi-pension.*

mogul A skiing term referring to a bump on a ski slope.

momentarily 1. Lasting for a very short time.
2. (US). Shortly.

monarchy A country or state with a sovereign at its head.

Mongol The Far Eastern civilisation that began in AD 589 and still survives today.

monitor A screen, similar to a televison, that displays data.

mono-hull A vessel with a single hull. (That is, the usual construction).

monolingual Speaking only one language.

monoplane An aeroplane with one pair of wings. The conventional arrangement for modern aircraft.

monorail A railway whose track consists of a single rail.

monoski A single, straight ski, used with both feet locked to it in a parallel position.

monsoon A wind in Southern Asia blowing from the south-west in summer and from the north-east in winter. The wind gives rise to the summer rainy season.

moor 1. To secure a vessel to the land.
2. A tract of open, uncultivated land.

Moor A member of the Muslim peoples of mixed Berber and Arab descent.

mooring A place where a vessel can be moored.

moraine An area of rocks and other debris deposited by a glacier.

more distant point Originally a hypothetical air fare construction point that is further from the originating point than is the actual point of turnaround. The principle is no longer used.

Moresque Architecture in the Moorish style.

Morse code An early communications system using a combination of dots and dashes to represent the different letters of the alphabet. The increasing power and sophistication of modern communication systems has rendered it obsolete. (Invented by the American, Samuel Morse).

motel Originally a hotel designed for overnight stays by car travellers, often with limited facilities. The name is now sometimes given to more traditional types of hotel, whose visitors may well arrive by other means.

motion sickness Nausea caused by the movement of any form of transport.

motor bike *See motor cycle.*

motor boat A boat with an engine, usually internal combustion.

motor coach A large passenger-carrying road vehicle.

motor cycle A cycle, usually with two wheels, driven by an engine.

motor scooter A small motorcycle with additional weather protection.

motor ship A ship powered by internal combustion engines, usually diesel. Usually denoted by the abbreviation MS in front of its name.

M

M

motor yacht A yacht driven by a motor.

motorail Originally a proprietary term for the vehicle-carrying services operated by British Rail. Now often used to denote any such service generally.

motorman The driver of an underground train, tram, etc.

motorway A high speed multi-carriageway road designed for rapid end-to-end journeys.

motu A South Pacific term for a very small island or islet.

mountain A large elevation of the earth's surface, larger than a hill. Traditionally a mountain had to be over 1,000 feet (305 metres) in height to be considered as such. The ten largest mountains are all in the Himalayas and, in order of height, are:
- Everest
- K2
- Langchenjunga
- Lhotse
- Yalung Kang
- Kangchenjunga
- Lhotse Shah
- Dhaulagiri I
- Manusli I
- Cho Oyu

The highest mountain in Europe is Mont Blanc.

mountain sickness *See altitude sickness.*

mouth 1. The opening of a cave. 2. The point where a river enters the sea.

mouthpiece That part of the aqualung or snorkel which enters the mouth and through which the wearer may breathe.

MPD Multi-Purpose Document. *See MCO.*

MPM *See maximum permitted mileage.*

MS When placed in front of a ship's name means Motor Ship.

MTAA Multiple Travel Agents' Association. *See Appendix 7a.*

mudéjar A Spanish expression meaning a fusion of Romanesque and Gothic with Arabic architectural style.

mull Scottish. A promontory.

multi-hull A vessel with several hulls.

multi-lateral agreement An agreement between three or more parties.

multi-lingual In or using several languages.

multiple In the UK this term is used to describe a travel agency group with a large number of branches, generally accepted to be 10 or more.

multiple dives More than one dive taken within a relatively short space of time.

multiple entry visa A visa valid for several visits.

multiplier effect In tourism, the term used to describe the way in which expenditure by tourists affects the local economy by a greater amount than the value of the initial expenditure might suggest. For example, a meal bought in a restaurant will make a profit for the restaurateur, who will spend some of that profit in other local enterprises. In turn they will themselves create expenditure, and so the initial expenditure will be multiplied many times over. The effect is made even greater by the increase in consumption of supplies (such as food or fuel) necessary to support the tourist infrastructure.

multi-sector When applied to a journey, one that involves several separate legs.

municipality A town or area having its own local government.

Muslim Also Moslem. Of or relating to the Islamic religion or its followers.

MV When placed in front of the name of a boat or ship means Motor Vessel.

MY When placed in front of the name of a boat or ship means Motor Yacht.

Mycenaean Of or relating to the late Bronze Age civilisation of ancient Greece.

mystery tour (UK). A coach excursion to an unknown destination.

M

N
n

n.r.t. *See net registered tonnage.*

n/a Not available or not applicable.

NACOA National Association of Cruise Oriented Agencies.

NACTA. National Association of Commissioned Travel Agents. *See Appendix 7b.*

nadir The lowest point. Typically used to describe the fortunes of a person or organisation.

NAITA National Association of Independent Travel Agents. *See Appendix 7a.*

narks Slang term for nitrogen narcosis.

narrow boat A vessel used on a canal, mainly in Great Britain, these days for leisure although there are a few commercial services. Often incorrectly referred to as a barge.

narrow gauge A railway track gauge of less than the standard 4' 8$\frac{1}{2}$".

narrow seas The English Channel and the Irish Sea.

narrow-bodied When applied to aircraft, means the traditional design with a single centre aisle

nation A community of people of mainly common descent, history, language, etc.

nation state A sovereign state in which most of whose subjects are united by factors such as language, descent, etc.

national 1. A person who has the citizenship of a country or state. **2.** Generally of or belonging to a nation.

national park An area of natural beauty or interest protected by a state for the use and enjoyment of the general public.

national vocational qualification (NVQ) A series of competence-based qualifications, not restricted to the travel industry but taken up by its training lead body with some enthusiasm in the early 1990's.

nationality The status of belonging to a particular nation.

native A person born in a particular place, a local inhabitant.

natural attraction A tourist attraction that has not been made or created by man.

naturalise To admit a person to the citizenship of a country.

nature reserve A tract of land left in its natural state to preserve its fauna and flora.

nature trail A signposted track through an area of countryside, whose natural attractions it is designed to show off.

nautical Of or relating to sailors or navigation.

nautical mile Officially the length of one minute of arc of a great circle round the Earth. More usefully, about 1.15 statute miles.

navigable Of a river or other stretch of water, one that allows the passage of vessels.

navigation 1. The act of plotting the course of a vehicle and ensuring that it keeps to it.
2. A river artificially modified to improve its ability to convey commercial traffic such as barges or narrow boats.

NEA National Exhibitors Association. *See Appendix 7a.*

neap tide A tide occurring just after the first and third quarters of the moon, when there is the least difference between high and low water.

Near East A general geographical term, now rarely used, that describes an area of south-west Asia that includes the Arabian Peninsula, Cyprus, Israel, Jordan, Lebanon, Syria and Turkey. Often extended to include Egypt and the Sudan.

negative buoyancy The state of being heavier than water and, therefore, sinking.

neighbourhood 1. The region in or near to a place.
2. A district in a city.

net fare Any non-commissionable fare to which an agency must add its own mark-up.

net rate A wholesale rate to holiday organisers who would be expected to add their own mark up.

net registered tonnage A measure of the capacity of a ship. As with g.r.t., it is the measure of the enclosed space in a ship, but the calculation is made after spaces such as crew quarters, engine room, etc. have been deducted. In other words, it a measure of the space that can be used for paying passengers' accommodation.

Netherlands Antilles Those islands of the West Indies administered by the Netherlands. They comprise: Bonaire, Curaçao, Saba, St. Eustatius and St Maarten.

neutral buoyancy The state of being the same weight as water and, therefore, neither sinking nor floating.

neutral unit of construction An artificial "currency" used to construct IATA air fares. With the volatility of currency exchange rates between countries, it would be impossible for air travel to work if every part of a journey had to be calculated in the local currency for that sector and converted at whatever the government or market forces had decided the exchange rate would be at that time. The use of the NUC is one part of the IATA system of fare construction which seeks to get around such problems

new tourist A recent term that refers to tourists who exhibit a number of characteristics including:

N

- greater independence in their travel habits
- greater experience
- greater environmental awareness
- greater flexibility
- more health consciousness
- more consciousness of quality

New World North and South America collectively, as regarded by Europe.

nimbostratus Low, dense, grey cloud from which rain often falls.

NITB Northern Ireland Tourist Board. *See Appendix 7a.*

nitrogen narcosis A condition sometimes experienced by divers where sufferers become insensible, in a manner similar to being drunk. It is caused by the effects on the body of nitrogen when under pressure. Symptoms vary with each individual.

no man's land An area assigned to no particular owner. Often used to describe the stretch of land between the frontiers of adjoining territories.

no show The failure to use a confirmed reservation without having cancelled. On many short flights the proportion of no-shows can reach 20%, which explains why all airlines overbook. No shows can be reduced or eliminated by charging cancellation fees but for airlines to do so would require concerted action (unlikely with the present international trend towards legislation designed to prevent just such action).

no-frills A basic service or product providing the minimum to meet a customer's requirements.

no-go area (UK). An area to which access by unauthorised people is forbidden.

non-aligned Of a state. One that does not side with any other particular state or country.

non-commissionable A product or service that carries no agent's commission.

non-op Non-operational. Not operating.

nonref An airline code that officially means "refund restricted" but that is usually assumed (incorrectly) to mean non-refundable.

non-resident Not resident, not a guest. When applied to a hotel or similar can indicate which facilities, if any, are available to such.

non-smoking **1.** A compartment or area in a train or other vehicle where smoking is not permitted.
2. An area in a hotel, restaurant or other establishment where smoking is not permitted.

non-stop A trip that is continuous from end to end. All non-stop journeys are through services, although a through service does not have to be non-stop.

non-transferable When a ticket, voucher, reservation or other travel service can be used only by the person for whom it was originally provided.

noon Midday or 1200 hours.

normal fare A fare carrying no special restrictions of validity or use.

Norman **1.** A native or inhabitant of Normandy.

N

2. A member of the peoples of mixed Scandinavian and Frankish origin established in the 10th century. The Normans invaded Britain in 1066.
3. The style of Romanesque architecture introduced to Britain by the Normans.

North America The region comprising Bermuda, Canada, Mexico, the United States and the West Indies. Generally regarded as a continent in its own right. The island of Greenland is considered as being in North America.

North Atlantic Drift The northern extension of the Gulf Stream that warms the coasts of Iceland, Norway and Spitzbergen.

North Pacific Current The Pacific equivalent of the North Atlantic Drift. It brings the warm waters of the Kuroshio to the north-west coast of North America.

North Pole The northernmost point of the earth.

northern hemisphere That part of the earth north of the equator.

northern lights *See aurora borealis.*

nose The projecting front of an aircraft or other vehicle.

nose wheel The front landing wheel of an aircraft.

nouvelle cuisine Literally "new cooking". A style of cooking that pays particular attention to the presentation of the food. The style is becoming less fashionable.

NT National Trust. *See Appendix 7a.*

NTO National Tourist Office. *See tourist office.*

NUC *See neutral unit of construction.*

null and void Invalid, not binding.

nullify To invalidate.

Nunavut The new name for the eastern (Inuit) part of Canada's Northwest Territories, split in two in 1999. Nunavut is an Inuit word meaning "Our Land". It covers an area of around 1 million square miles (2,560,00 square kilometres), approximately 20% of Canada's landmass.

nursery slope A gentle ski run used to teach the art of skiing or snowboarding.

NVQ *See national vocational qualification.*

N

O
O

OAG *See official airline guide.*

OAP (UK). *See old age pensioner.*

oasis A fertile spot in a desert, often around a pool of water.

observation car A carriage on a train built to allow a good view. Also known in the US as a bubble car or dome car.

occidental Of or relating to the Western nations.

occupancy The number of people using a particular facility.

occupancy rate Similar to load factor but relating to bed nights (that is, the number of hotel beds occupied multiplied by a given number of nights).

ocean A large sea. There are only five (some say six) oceans on the earth and alphabetically they are: Arctic; Atlantic (sometimes split into North and South); Indian; Pacific and Southern.

oceanarium A large seawater aquarium.

ocean-going Of a ship. One designed to cross large stretches of water.

Oceania A general geographical description of the area containing the islands of the central and south Pacific ocean, including Melanesia, Micronesia and Polynesia. Sometimes extended to include Australia, New Zealand and the Malay Archipelago.

oceanic Of, relating to or near to an ocean.

octopush A form of underwater hockey played in a swimming pool.

OECD The Organisation for Economic Co-operation and Development whose members currently comprise: Australia, Austria, Belgium, Canada, Czech Republic, Denmark, Finland, France, Germany, Greece, Hungary, Iceland, Ireland, Italy, Japan, Republic of Korea, Luxembourg, Mexico, The Netherlands, New Zealand, Norway, Poland, Portugal, Spain, Sweden, Switzerland, Turkey, United Kingdom and the USA.

off season Another name for low season.

official airline guide An American directory to international flights.

off-line carrier A carrier other than the one whose reservations system is being used to make a booking.

off-line point A city not served by a particular carrier.

offload To remove and/or refuse to carry a booked passenger. This may be because of overbooking, although there are other reasons.

off-peak Used or in use at times of lesser demand.

off-piste Away from the prepared ski-runs.

off-season *See off-peak.*

offshore At sea some distance from the shore.

OK Confirmed. The official abbreviation on most travel documents.

old age pensioner (UK). An elderly person. This expression tends to be considered derogatory these days and terms such as senior citizen are often preferred. Persons of pensionable age can usually obtain discounts on most forms of travel.

Old World Europe, Asia and Africa.

omnibus *See bus.*

on board When a person has boarded a ship or other vessel.

one-class A means of transport, usually a ship, where all passengers have access to all facilities and public areas. Although they are all the same class, there will often be significant differences between the quality of accommodation provided in the various cabins.

one-way rental A car rental that terminates at a station other than that at which it started. In many cases an

additional "one-way rental" charge will be payable by the hirer.

one-way trip A journey from origin to destination with no booked return.

on-line carrier The carrier whose system is being used to make a booking.

onshore 1. To be on land. Often used when referring to a person or item that might otherwise be on board a ship (e.g. the Captain's onshore at present).
2. Of a wind. Blowing from the sea to the land.

open sea An expanse of sea away from the land.

open skies The philosophy or policy of allowing unrestricted access to airspace by any carrier. In other words, total deregulation.

open-date A ticket or document that has been paid for, but with which no reservation is associated.

open-jaw A return journey that has either different originating and terminating points or where the turnaround points are different. For example, London/Montreal/Manchester or London/Montreal - Vancouver/ London.

option (UK). A provisional booking, usually for a holiday, held without payment while a customer decides. Many tour operators no longer offer options, claiming that proper selling skills on the part of travel agents would do away with the need for them.

optional extra Anything bought by a customer that is additional to

o

the basic holiday or other arrangement.

Ordnance Survey maps (UK). A series of very detailed maps produced by the Ordnance Survey, an official survey organisation.

organiser Under the EC Package Travel regulations, this is anyone who organises, other than "occasionally", a package holiday. This does not have to be a commercial organisation; a person arranging a package on a purely voluntary basis is still bound by the regulations. For example, a local publican arranging a weekend trip to the Munich Oktoberfest will probably be deemed an organiser. The only loophole is the "occasionally" caveat, but since this is not defined, it would be unwise to rely on it as a defence in law.

oriental Of or relating to Eastern civilisation.

origin 1. The starting point for a journey.
2. Where a person initially comes from.

Orthodox Christian (main) The civilisation that started in Turkey around AD 680 and survives today.

Orthodox Christian (Russian) The civilisation that started in the upper Dnieper basin around AD 950 and survives today.

ORV Austrian Travel Agent Association (Osterreich Reiseburo Verband). *See Appendix 7c.*

Ottoman The civilisation that started in Turkey around AD 1320 and lasted until AD 1919.

out of date A document whose validity has expired.

outboard A motor attachable to the outside of the stern of a boat.

outbound That part of a journey which is towards an ultimate destination.

outcrop A stratum of rock emerging from the surface of the soil.

outfall The mouth of a river, stream, drain, etc., where it empties.

outing A short trip or excursion, especially from one's home.

outlying Remote. Far from a centre.

outrigger 1. A beam or spar projecting out from the side of a ship or boat to add stability.
2. A boat fitted with outriggers.

outside cabin A cabin on a ship with a window or porthole. It is important to remember that a cabin on the outside of a ship but which has no porthole or window is not considered to be "outside".

overbooking The practice of selling more accommodation than is actually available. Known as overselling in the US.

over-capacity More seats or beds or other accommodation than is needed to meet the needs of customers.

overpass A road or railway that passes over another by means of a bridge.

overriding commission Sometimes simply referred to as "override". Officially the extra commission paid by principals to their general sales agents to enable them to pay full commission to other agents. These days the term is often used to describe any commission paid in excess of the "standard" amount.

overseas Foreign or abroad.

overselling (US). *See overbooking.*

Oyashio The Pacific's equivalent of the East Greenland Current, flowing south through the Bering Strait.

O

P
p

p.m. Post meridiem. The suffix used with the 12 hour clock to denote times between 12 noon and 12 midnight.

Pacific *See oceans.*

Pacific Rim Those countries and regions surrounding the Pacific Ocean, especially the eastern Asian nations.

package holiday This now has a strict definition in EU legislation, as follows: "The pre-arranged combination of not fewer than two of the following when sold or offered for sale at an inclusive price and when the service covers a period of more than 24 hours or includes overnight accommodation: (a) transport; (b) accommodation; (c) other tourist services not ancillary to transport or accommodation and accounting for a significant proportion of the package". In simple language, any arrangement that includes something more than just travel is likely to be a package.

Package Travel, Package Holidays And Package Tours Regulations 1992 The regulations, made under the EEC Council Directive 90/314 and colloquially known in the trade as the "EC Directive", were introduced in an attempt to harmonise consumer protection throughout the EC. The legislation is backed up by UK law and contravention of its provisions can be a criminal offence.

Padania A name claimed for the area of Italy from Umbria and Tuscany northwards. A local political party, the Northern League, would like to see the area become an independent country within the EU.

paddle steamer A vessel propelled by paddles, either on its side or at its stern.

page To call for someone in a hotel or similar environment. Originally this was done by means of a person who walked around calling or showing the person's name; these days it is usually done by means of a public address system.

pagoda A Hindu or Buddhist temple or sacred building, usually a tower with many tiers, most common in Far Eastern countries.

PAI Personal accident insurance. An optional insurance that covers injury or death caused to the driver and passengers travelling in the rental vehicle. However, such cover is normally included in a normal travel insurance policy so there is usually little point in buying it.

painter A short length of rope used to tie up a boat.

palatial Of accommodation, like a palace. Very luxurious.

pampas Large treeless plains in South America.

Pampero A strong, cold wind in South America, blowing from the Andes to the Atlantic.

pandemic An epidemic so bad as to be almost out of control.

panhandle (US). A narrow strip of land projecting from one state into another.

panorama An unbroken view of the surrounding area.

Papal States Historically the states of central Italy belonging to the Pope.

paper 1. A familiar term for a ticket or other document, more commonly used when carriers each had their own individually printed tickets.
2. A theatrical term meaning to give away free tickets.

par of exchange The official term to denote the recognised value of one currency in terms of another.

parador A Spanish hotel owned by the government. Often created from old castles or other ancient buildings, they offer a high standard of accommodation, frequently in areas where normal commercial provision might not be feasible.

paragliding An aerial sport in which participants jump from a height with a parachute-like canopy strapped to their backs.

parallel A line of latitude.

paramotoring An aerial sport in which the user flies wearing a paraglider canopy and propelled by a pusher propeller.

parasailing An aerial sport in which participants, wearing parachutes, are towed though the air by a motor boat.

parascending A generic term for the main parachuting sports. *See parasailing, paragliding.*

paratyphoid A disease resembling typhoid, caused by different but related agents.

parish 1. A district having its own church and clergy.
2. A district constructed for the purposes of local government.

parkway 1. (US). An open, landscaped highway.
2. (UK). A railway station, often on the outskirts of a town, that has extensive parking facilities.

Pars A GDS used by TWA and Northwest Airlines.

part charter An arrangement whereby a tour operator contracts for some of the seats on an aircraft, rather than booking the whole aircraft.

partner fare A special fare issued to an accompanying partner at a reduced rate.

party A name sometimes used as an alternative to group.

pass 1. A narrow way through a mountain, etc.
2. A permit, usually free, giving access to an amenity.

P

passage A name sometimes used as an alternative to journey.

passenger A person, other than the driver or crew, travelling in or on some form of vehicle.

passenger coupon The coupon or coupons of a ticket or voucher that are retained by the passenger. Passenger coupons will usually give outline details of the conditions of carriage and may also act as a baggage check.

passenger mile One passenger carried for one mile. When the number of passengers carried is multiplied by the number of miles travelled, a total passenger/mile figure is obtained for that carrier.

passenger name record (PNR) Airline jargon for a booking stored in a reservations computer.

passenger sales agent An IATA term for a travel agent appointed to sell passenger (as opposed to freight or cargo) tickets and services.

passenger space ratio A shipping term for the GRT divided by the passenger capacity of a vessel. The lower the number the higher the density and the less space there is likely to be for each passenger. A PSR of 20 is on the high side and a PSR of 40 is low. Only the most luxurious ships would have PSRs in excess of 50.

passenger transport authority A public organisation set up to control public passenger transport services.

Passover The Jewish spring festival that celebrates the liberation of the Israelites from the Egyptians.

passport An identity document that allows its bearer to travel to countries other than his or her own.

passport control The point in a port or at a border where travellers have to show their passports.

PATA Pacific and Asian Travel Agents Association. *See Appendix 7d.*

path 1. A small track or trail. 2. A determined route along which something moves. (E.g. flight path)

patio 1. A paved area adjacent to a house 2. An inner courtyard in a Spanish or Latin American house.

patois The dialect of the locals in an area, that might differ significantly from the official language of the country.

patriality Having the right to live in the UK through the British birth of a parent or grandparent.

pavé French. A paved street, road or path.

pavement 1. (UK). That section of the highway reserved for the use of pedestrians. 2. (US). The roadway or its surface.

pax A common abbreviation meaning passengers.

payload The proportion of the total weight of a vehicle that can produce revenue. Payload can be of passengers, cargo or both.

peak season Another name for high season.

Ped Xing (US). A pedestrian crossing.

pedalo A small, pedal-operated pleasure boat.

pedicab A pedal-operated rickshaw.

pedometer An instrument, carried or worn by a walker, that measures the distance travelled.

pedway (US). A route built for pedestrians in an urban area.

penalty fare A fare charged, often with a surcharge, to a passenger on board public transport without a valid ticket or authority to travel in the class and/or on the route travelled.

peninsula An area of land surrounded by water or projecting into the sea and connected to the mainland by a relatively small area.

pension A European term for a small hotel. Some grading systems require certain minimum facilities from establishments before they can be categorised as hotels and in cases where these standards are not met, a pension designation may be given.

penthouse An apartment on the roof of a building. Often used by hotels to denote their highest (and usually best) accommodation.

peoples Persons making up a community, tribe, race, nation, etc.

per diem *See diem.*

perestroika A Russian expression meaning the practice of restructuring or reforming a political system. Its application in the former Soviet Union has lead to the emergence of many new or revived states and countries.

perishability Anything that is perishable will deteriorate rapidly if it is not used and although many assume that this only applies to goods such as fresh fruit, it is also an important concept in travel. An unsold space on a particular flight perishes as soon as the doors are closed. Even though the seat itself is still there, that space on that flight can never be sold again.

permafrost Subsoil that is permanently frozen, as found in extreme northern and southern latitudes. Permafrost can create difficulties for builders since any constructions placed on it may cause it to melt through conduction of heat. This can lead to instability in the building.

permanent way (UK). The completed track of a railway.

Perpendicular A form of Gothic architecture, popular in England in the 15th and 16th centuries, characterised by the vertical tracery in the larger windows.

personal accident insurance (PAI) A term meaning payment of a specified amount, paid to the insured in the event of certain specified injuries caused through accident. Typically a policy will make a payment in the case of death, injury such as loss of a limb, or permanent total disablement.

P

personal liability insurance This is cover against the insured's legal liability in respect of a tort he or she has perpetrated against a third party. This cover is only payable to the third party if the insured is found to have committed the tort. In other words, theoretically the third party must institute legal action and obtain judgement in his or her favour.

personal money insurance This covers the loss of personal money when being carried or securely stored. Since money loss is common, all insurance companies place stringent conditions on this cover.

personal possessions insurance This covers the replacement (or repair if possible) of personal possessions that have been damaged or stolen. Cover is also often given under this section to allow for the purchase of "emergency" items (such as clothing) necessary should the items be lost on the outward journey.

PEX A type of excursion fare usually available to passengers booking and travelling on the same day.

phaeton **1.** An open four-wheeled horse-drawn carriage. **2.** (US). A vintage touring car.

Phoenician The Semitic peoples of ancient Phoenicia in southern Syria and the Lebanon.

phonetic alphabet There is an official phonetic alphabet that is used world-wide throughout the travel industry. It is in English, since this is the official language of international air travel and traffic control and is as follows:
Alpha, Bravo, Charlie, Delta, Echo, Foxtrot, Golf, Hotel, India, Juliet, Kilo, Lima, Mike, November, Oscar, Papa, Quebec, Romeo, Sierra, Tango, Uniform, Victor, Whisky, X-ray, Yankee, Zulu.

physical feature Any feature that is an actual part of the landscape (as opposed to a building or construction), such as a mountain or lake. Most physical features have been formed naturally, but for the purposes of this definition they need not be. In the travel industry, the important physical features are those which influence holiday choice. Thus, the Alps are important to skiers and mountain climbers, the Norfolk Broads (an artificially formed feature) to boating and fishing enthusiasts, etc.

physical geography Geography dealing with physical features.

piazza A public open square, especially in Italy.

picnic A meal eaten out of doors.

picnic site A place where travellers may stop to have a picnic.

pictogram An informative sign or symbol created by means of a stylised image. The sign of a deleted cigarette to indicate that smoking is prohibited is a good example. Pictograms are a good way of overcoming the difficulties that can otherwise exist in airports and other places where there are large numbers of foreign travellers.

pictograph **1.** *See pictogram.* **2.** Ancient hieroglyphic writing in picture form.

pidgin A simplified language, often containing words from several languages, used to communicate between people having no common language.

pidgin English A pidgin whose main language is English..

piece concept The airline baggage system where the amount allowed as free allowance is based on the size and number of items, rather than their weight.

pied-à-terre A house, flat, etc. kept for occasional use.

piedmont A gentle slope leading from the foot of the mountains to a region of flat land.

pier 1. A bridge-like structure, raised on piles and leading out to sea, etc. 2. A projection from an airport terminal building leading towards an aircraft stand.

pilgrim One who visits a sacred place for religious reasons.

pilgrimage A journey taken by a pilgrim or group of pilgrims.

pillar valve The valve attached to one end of a diving cylinder.

pilot 1. A person who flies an aircraft. 2. A person licensed to navigate ships into and out of ports and harbours. Joins a ship to advise the captain on its handling during these procedures.

pinnace A ship's small boat, usually motor-driven.

Pioneer Club A body of specialist UK travel agents who have undertaken a USTTA (subsequently Visit USA) training programme.

PIR *See property irregularity report.*

pissoir French. A public urinal.

piste A skiing term referring to a track of firm, compacted snow laid out as a run.

piste basher *See piste groomer.*

piste groomer A large tractor with very wide caterpillar tracks designed

to flatten ski runs. Also known as "piste basher" or "snow cat".

piston engine When applied to an aircraft it refers to an internal combustion engine similar to the type used in most cars. Aircraft using piston engines will either be quite small, or old, or both.

PIT. Polska Izba Turystycna. *See Appendix 7c.*

pitch 1. The distance between the front edge of an aircraft seat and the front edge of the seat behind. 2. The fore and aft motion of a ship.

pizza pie (US). *See snowplough (2).*

place name The name given to a town, village, etc.

plague 1. (When preceded by "The") a contagious bacterial disease, usually transmitted by rat fleas. 2. Any deadly disease spreading rapidly over a wide area.

plain A general term used to describe a level tract of land, especially one with few trees.

plan management An IATA term meaning that department of IATA responsible to the agency administrator for the administration, management and development of the Billing and Settlement Plan in the different areas where it is applicable. It includes the local representative of the plan management in the area of a Plan and such local representatives may also act as the agency sales manager.

plane 1. A familiar term for an aircraft. Abbreviation from aeroplane. 2. When a boat travels at speed and

P

rises in the water so that the front part of the hull is clear of the surface.

plat du jour A French catering term meaning "dish of the day". In other words, the chef's daily recommendation in a restaurant.

plate **1.** A small embossed metal plate used in a ticket validating machine. Different plates give details of the carrier and the issuing agent.
2. A large part of the earth's crust. *See plate tectonics.*

plate tectonics The physical situation associated with the movement of the earth's plates upon its fluid interior that lead to phenomena such as volcanoes and earthquakes.

plateau A large, flat, elevated area of land.

platform **1.** A railway expression meaning the raised area of a station where passengers embark and disembark. Not all countries have platforms at their railway stations and this will slow passenger loading considerably since it will be done by means of steps.
2. A raised area in an auditorium or similar from which a speaker may address an audience.

playa Spanish. A beach.

plaza A market place or open square in a town in Spanish speaking countries.

Plimsoll line (or mark) Actually a series of lines, painted on the outside of a ship's hull to indicate the various safe levels to which the vessel may be loaded. There are several lines denoting the levels for varying situations such as fresh and salt water,

summer and winter, etc. (Samuel Plimsoll 1824-1898).

ply Of a vehicle, to travel regularly between two or more points.

ply for hire To offer the services of a vehicle, typically a taxi, to members of the public on an ad hoc basis.

PNR *See passenger name record.*

point of sale display A marketing term used to describe material used to promote a product or service at the place where it is provided. An example in travel could be a show-card promoting a particular destination.

point-to-point air fare A fare that is valid only between a specified pair of points which allows no stopover en route and may not be combined with other fares.

polar Of, at or relating to the poles.

polder An area of land reclaimed from the sea. These are especially common in low countries such as Holland.

pole star A star in Ursa Minor that remains stationary relative to the earth and appears in the direction of true north.

poles The most northerly and southerly points of the Earth's surface and the points about which it rotates. True north and true south are measured from the poles. Magnetic north and south are the points towards which compasses point and are not quite the same are true north and south. Furthermore, the magnetic poles move slowly around the true poles and a constantly varying adjustment must be made to a

P

magnetic compass reading if a true bearing is needed.

poliomyelitis An infectious viral disease that can cause paralysis.

political geography Geography that deals with the political aspects of an area.

pollution The spoiling of the environment by the impact of harmful things such as effluents and noise.

polyglot 1. Of or relating to many languages.
2. A multi-lingual person.

Polynesia The collective name for the islands of the central and south Pacific ocean including: American Samoa, Cook Islands, Easter Island, French Polynesia, Hawaii, Kiribati (east), New Zealand, Niue, Pitcairn Islands, Tokelau, Tonga, Tuvalu, Wallis and Futuna and Western Samoa.

Polynesian civilisation The civilisation of Samoa and Tonga that lasted from around 500 BC to AD 1775.

pond A very small, enclosed body of water.

pontoon 1. A floating support for a temporary bridge.
2. A flat-bottomed boat.

pool agreement An arrangement where two or more carriers agree to serve a route and accept each other's tickets. The revenue earned is "pooled" and divided between the carriers in proportion to the number of services each provides.

poop The aftermost and highest deck of a ship.

pooped When a following wave overtakes a boat and breaks over its stern, possibly swamping it.

population The inhabitants of a place referred to collectively.

port 1. An originating, en route or destination point for a vessel, usually a ship.
2. The left hand side of a ship or aircraft, facing forward. Portside is always denoted by a red navigation light.

port of call A scheduled stop on the itinerary of a cruise or line service.

port surcharge A fee charged to rental companies delivering or collecting hire vehicles at a port or airport.

port taxes Charges levied on passengers arriving and/or departing from a port. Similar in principal to airport taxes.

porter 1. A person employed to carry luggage and generally give assistance at an airport or railway station, etc.
2. (US). A sleeping car attendant.

porthole The circular window in a ship or boat.

POS *See point of sale.*

posada A small Spanish roadhouse or restaurant.

posh Now taken to mean anyone or anything that is high class or exclusive. It is generally believed that the term originated from the days when ships were not air-conditioned and passengers travelling from the UK to India and the Far East would prefer to travel on the side of the ship

P

furthest from the sun. For this journey that meant travelling out on the port side and returning on the starboard side and of course, the shipping lines would charge a premium for such cabins. Those passengers who could afford the extra would travel Port Out, Starboard Home, or POSH. Although this definition is popular, there is little evidence to support it and other suggestions for its origin include the claim that it is derived from an earlier French slang word, posh, a dandy. Alternatively that it is an abbreviated form of polish or polished.

positioning The movement of an aircraft, ship or other vehicle from where it is to where it can begin to earn revenue. Positioning is costly and some carriers, particularly cruise lines, seek to defray these costs by offering positioning voyages for which they can sell accommodation at particularly attractive rates.

positive buoyancy The state of being lighter than water and therefore floating.

post-date To date a document later than its actual date of issue. Usually done to delay payment to the carrier and thus officially frowned upon.

pothole A deep hole or system of caves.

pourboire Literally, from the French "for a drink". A tip or gratuity.

pousada A Portuguese government-owned hotel, built in the local style.

powder snow 1. Snow that has just fallen.
2. Snow falling in dry climatic

conditions, especially in the Rocky Mountains.

powerboat A powerful motor vessel, often used for racing.

powwow A conference or meeting for discussion. (Originally between North American Indians).

pp In travel, per person. However there are at least four other meanings so the abbreviation should be used with care.

prairie A large area of treeless grassland, mostly found in North America.

pre-boarding An arrangement by which passengers with special needs may be allowed onto an aircraft before the bulk of the passengers.

pre-book To reserve in advance.

precinct 1. An enclosed or clearly defined area, such as a pedestrian precinct in a town (from which vehicles are excluded).
2. (US). A police district.

precipice A steep cliff.

precipitation Rain or snowfall.

pre-existing condition An insurance term relating to a condition, such as an illness, that existed before the insurance was contracted. Many companies will not cover claims arising from such conditions.

préfect The chief administrative officer of a department, especially in France.

préfecture A district under the control of a préfect.

preferred supplier A principal with which a travel agency has a special agreement. This is usually that it will give extra sales support in return for additional commission or other benefit.

premier First in class or importance.

premium The amount payable in consideration for a contract of insurance.

premium traffic The name given to those, such as business travellers, paying the higher fares on a service.

prepaid ticket advice A notification to a distant point that a passenger has paid for a ticket. Usually used if a passenger wishes to collect the document from a point other than that of payment (at the airport of departure, for example).

pre-payment Payment made in advance for a service.

president 1. The elected head of a republic.
2. (US). The head of a company or corporation.

pressurised Modern aircraft fly at heights where the air is too thin to be breathed comfortably. To ensure the comfort and well-being of passengers, such aircraft are filled with air at a much higher pressure than that of the outside atmosphere.

Prestel (UK). British Telecom's viewdata service. *See viewdata.*

prestige Of a higher class or standard than normal.

price grid The way in which prices are often displayed in travel literature, such as brochures. Commonly the details of the holiday are listed down and the departure dates across. The intersection points on the grid show the price for that holiday at that time.

price-fixing An agreement between suppliers to maintain prices at an agreed (usually high) level. Now illegal in many countries, including the US and UK.

price-ring *See price fixing.*

prime meridian The meridian of longitude at 0° that passes through Greenwich.

principal The name given to an individual or organisation in the Travel Industry, responsible for organising or providing some sort of facility. The facility might be transport and airlines, shipping lines, railways, car rental companies and bus and coach operators are obvious examples. Providers of accommodation, such as hotels, motel and holiday centres are also principals. Other principals provide services which may be less obvious, such as travel insurance companies.

principality A country, territory or state governed by a Prince (such as Monaco).

priority boarding An arrangement for a person to board an aircraft or other vehicle before the other passengers. Usually arranged for elderly or infirm passengers.

private 1. Accommodation in a private dwelling
2. When a passenger on an inclusive holiday elects not to take accommodation for its full duration and will make "private" arrangements.

P

private facilities The provision of washing and toilet facilities in a hotel room.

privy Usually US. A toilet or lavatory, possibly outdoors.

pro rata In proportion. A pro rata payment would be made in proportion to the rest of the payment. (E.g. if a rate were £70 for one week with extra days pro rata, each extra day would be charged at one seventh of the weekly rate, that is, £10.)

pro tem An abbreviation for pro tempore, meaning "for the time being", temporarily.

projection Since the Earth is a globe it is not possible to show it accurately on a flat map. The ways in which the globe can be represented in a single plane, more or less accurately, are known as projections.

promenade (UK). A public walkway along the seafront.

promenade deck An upper deck on a ship that is designed for passengers to walk around.

promontory A piece of high land jutting into the sea.

promotional fare A specially reduced fare designed to attract customers who might otherwise choose some other carrier or method of transport.

propeller A large screw-shaped device that provides thrust for an aircraft or ship. The action of the screw forces water or air to the rear thus creating the thrust.

property irregularity report (PIR) A form used by airlines to record details of a problem with a passenger's property - usually baggage that has gone missing.

propjet An aircraft with propellers driven by a jet turbine engine.

protectorate A state that is controlled and protected by another.

province The principal administrative division of a country, etc. *See appendix 4 for a list of Canadian Provinces.*

provisional booking A booking that has not yet been confirmed by the agent or passenger and where space is being held pending a decision. *See also option.*

provisioned charter Rental of a boat or yacht or similar vessel that includes fuel and provisions but does not include crew.

prow The pointed or projecting part of the front of a ship.

PSA Passenger Shipping Association Ltd. *See Appendix 7a.*

PSARA Passenger Shipping Association Retail Agents Scheme. *See Appendix 7a.*

PSV (UK). *See public service vehicle.*

PTA 1. *See prepaid ticket advice.* 2. *See passenger transport authority.*

pub (UK). *See public house (1).*

public holiday A day when most commercial premises and government departments are closed. *See also bank holiday.*

public house 1. In Great Britain a building designed for the sale and consumption of alcoholic drinks.

Almost invariably abbreviated to "pub".
2. In some countries, a brothel.

public service vehicle A vehicle, such as a bus, operated to serve the needs of the public.

public transport Vehicles travelling on fixed routes and offering carriage to the public, usually on payment of a fare.

publican 1. (UK). The keeper of a pub **2.** Australian. The keeper of a hotel.

published fare The fare shown in a carrier's tariff.

Pullman Originally an American railroad company that ran vehicles of a higher than usual standard, which included sleeping accommodation. In the UK it referred to luxury day carriages, providing meals at all seats. Few now remain except on special services, such as the UK portion of the Venice-Simplon Orient Express. (George Pullman 1831-1897).

pullman berth A name sometimes given to an upper berth that can be folded away when not in use.

punt A narrow, flat-bottomed boat used mainly on rivers and generally propelled by means of a long pole.

purser The person who looks after the welfare and accommodation of the passengers on board a ship or aircraft.

put about Of a ship or boat, to turn around.

P

Q
q

quad An abbreviation for quadricycle. *See also cycle.*

quad chair A chair lift with seats for four passengers.

quad room A room for four people.

quadricycle A small four-wheeled vehicle, usually powered by a small motorcycle engine. The expression "quad-bike", often used to describe such vehicles, is incorrect, since the abbreviation "bike" means a two-wheeled cycle. Thus a "quad-bike" would be an impossible creation, a four-wheeled, two-wheeler.

quag Or quagmire. A marsh or bog.

quarantine A period of time during which animals or people, who may possibly have been exposed to a disease, are isolated from others to avoid the chance of transmitting infection. Animals imported into the British Isles must currently undergo a six month quarantine period, although it is likely that this requirement will soon be relaxed.

quarter-deck Part of the upper deck of a ship, situated towards the stern, usually reserved for officers.

quay A wharf or pier.

quayside The land near a quay.

queen room A hotel room with a queen-sized bed

Queen's highway (UK). A public road. The designation "King's" or "Queen's" will change according to sex of the Sovereign.

queue 1. (UK). A line of people waiting for something.
2. The making available of an item on an agent's computer terminal. For example, if an agent has made a request for a reservation that cannot immediately be confirmed (possibly because the service is full), the request is queued. When space becomes available, the agent's computer is automatically accessed by the principal and the details advised.

quick release A style of belt buckle that allows for quick removal. It is particularly favoured by divers as it facilitates the swift removal and jettison of weight belts and cylinders.

quicksand Loose wet sand into which an object or person is likely to sink.

quin room A room for five people.

quote A price calculated for a service and advised to a potential customer so that he or she may decide whether to accept the offer.

R
r

rabies A contagious and usually fatal virus disease of dogs and other mammals. Can be transmitted to humans through saliva. Endemic in most of the world although not in the British Isles where quarantine has largely kept it out.

RAC Royal Automobile Club. *See Appendix 7a.*

race Each of the major divisions of humankind, distinguished by variations in language, religion, physical characteristics, etc.

rack railway *See cog railway.*

rack rates The rates advertised by hotels and other principals before any discounts. So called because these are the prices on the leaflets "in the rack".

racking policy A marketing philosophy adopted by some travel agencies. Essentially it means which brochures an agency will display and where it will display them.

radar **Ra**dio **d**etection **a**nd **r**anging. A system for detecting the range and presence of objects such as vehicles. Now an integral part of all transport systems.

raft A flat, floating construction of timber and other buoyant materials.

rail map A map showing the railway routes of a country or area.

rail travel Travelling on a railway.

railcar A railway vehicle consisting of a single powered carriage.

railcard (UK). Various types of card that allow their holders discounts off rail travel fares.

railhead The beginning or end of a railway.

railroad (US). A railway.

Railtrack The organisation responsible for running most of the track and many of the stations on the railways of Britain.

railway A means of transport in which the vehicles run on metal rails. Railways have the advantage of needing far less separation between each vehicle than do other means of transport and they are thus much more economical in their use of land space.

rain forest Luxuriant and dense jungles growing in tropical areas.

rain shadow A region sheltered from rainfall, usually by mountains.

Raj The period of British rule in India.

rajah An Indian ruler or dignitary.

R

rake-off Commission or share on a deal, often an underhand one.

Ramadan The ninth month of the Muslim year, during which fasting is observed from dawn to dusk.

ramjet A type of jet engine in which the air is drawn in and compressed by the forward motion of the vehicle, rather than by a fan.

ramp *See apron.*

rapid transit A system or vehicle designed for high speed transport of passengers in urban areas.

rapids A section of a river where the water runs very fast, often over rocks.

RATA Russian Association of Travel Agents. *See Appendix 7c.*

rate The appropriate charge for an item or service, often expressed as an amount for a specific time. (E.g. a rate of £20 per day).

ravine A deep narrow gorge.

Réaumur An obsolete temperature scale in which water freezes at 0° and boils at 80°.

rebate A discount or an amount refunded.

re-book To reinstate a booking or to book a passenger again.

reception The area in a hotel or office building where travellers check in and where they may request hotel and other services.

receptionist A person working in reception.

réchauffé Food that has been warmed up.

recompression The act of re-pressurising a diver, usually in a recompression chamber after the onset of decompression sickness.

recompression chamber Pressurised steel chamber used for the compression, decompression and recompression of the occupants at air pressures which equate to various depths of water.

reconfirmation The rule that states that passengers who break an air journey for more than 72 hours may need to advise the airline of their intention of using their next reservation. There are many variations to this rule.

record locator The identification for a file or record in a computer.

recreational vehicle (RV) Originally an American term for a camper type vehicle, now usually used to denote any motorhome.

red and green system A customs clearance system that allows incoming passengers to choose the green channel (if they have no goods to declare) or the red channel (if they have goods to declare). Spot checks are made on passengers transiting the green channel to try to prevent smuggling.

red carpet Preferential treatment afforded to an important visitor or traveller. Traditionally a red carpet was laid for the person to walk upon.

Red Crescent The equivalent to the Red Cross in Muslim countries.

Red Cross An international aid organisation.

red ensign The flag of the British merchant navy.

red eye A colloquial expression for an overnight flight especially coast-to-coast in the US.

red light district An area of a town or city where brothels and other aspects of the sex industry are located.

red run A European grading given to ski runs that are quite difficult but not sufficiently difficult to be categorised as black. US resorts do not use this grading.

reef A ridge, often of coral, at or just under the surface of the sea.

re-embark To get back on board a vessel.

re-entry visa A visa that allows a traveller back into a country.

refuelling stop It is not always possible for aircraft to refuel at a point of turnaround and thus a stop is required en route to take fuel on board. Passengers cannot join or leave a flight at a refuelling stop.

regime A method or system of government. The term tends to be used in a derogatory way about governments that are not well thought of.

region An area of land having more or less definable boundaries.

register The official record, maintained by hotels, of the names and other details of guests.

registered baggage Baggage that has been put into the care of a carrier who will undertake to handle and convey it until arrival at the passenger's destination.

regulator Also called demand valve. A valve that reduces the high pressure contained in an aqualung cylinder to a usable pressure so that the diver is able to breathe.

reissue 1. To issue a document again, usually to make some change or changes to it.
2. A document so reissued.

relief map A map showing hills, valleys, etc., by means of colour rather than by simple contour lines.

relief road (UK). A road taking traffic around a congested area.

remark A note or endorsement on a document to convey a special instruction.

Renaissance The period during the 14th to 16th centuries during which there was a revival of art and literature using classical models. The name is often given to art, architecture, etc. of this period.

rental day In car rental terms, a day is 24 hours. Any rental which exceeds the 24 hour period may incur an additional day's rental charge.

rep *See representative.*

repatriation The bringing home of a traveller from abroad, usually for reasons of sickness or emergency.

representative Technically anyone who represents a company or organisation. In travel parlance, the expression is usually taken to mean a tour operator's employee, retained in a resort to attend to the needs of its customers.

republic A state in which power is

R

held by the people or their elected representatives, not by a monarch,

request **1.** Where a facility has been asked for but not confirmed.
2. Usually used on air tickets. When a flight is full and the customer is on a waiting list for space. Because of the possible confusion between meanings, some travel clerks use the abbreviation WL for a waiting list, but this is not an official airline abbreviation.

request stop (UK). A stop at which a vehicle, usually a bus, will only stop on the instruction of a passenger or potential passenger.

re-route To change the routeing on a ticket or itinerary.

reservation A ticket shows that a passenger has paid for travel but does not guarantee that space is, or will be, available on any service. A reservation guarantees space but the passenger will not be carried unless a valid ticket is also held. Many tickets have reservation and travel details shown on the one document, but on services where most passengers travel without reservations (rail is a good example), a separate reservation document is usually necessary.

reservation system Any system that is set up to control the sale of facilities such as holidays. Most reservation systems are now computerised.

reserve To make a booking.

reserved Space that has been booked or set aside for a customer.

resort A city, town, village or other development stayed in by holidaymakers for a specific reason.

Since individual preferences vary, almost anywhere can be considered a resort. However, major centres such as London, although attracting large numbers of visitors, are not usually called resorts. In the USA the term is now often used to describe a large scale hotel and leisure complex, or even a large hotel with extensive grounds and facilities.

resort condominium A block of separate apartments in a North American resort complex.

rest house A place for travellers to rest in, possibly overnight. Typically found in the Indian subcontinent.

restaurant An eating establishment offering a range of food often with table service.

restaurateur A person who owns or runs a restaurant (note that the word is spelt without an "n" before the second "t").

restroom (US). A lavatory.

retail travel agent Usually the first point of contact for someone wishing to make travel arrangements. A the name "retail" implies, almost a shop where travel can be bought. In the UK, the term usually refers to a shop or office, although in some countries a "travel agent" can also be a person.

re-time To set a new schedule for a service, typically on a railway.

return ticket Mainly UK. A round trip ticket.

revaccination A repeat vaccination to boost or reinforce the original.

revalidation The process of amending

R

a detail of a ticket or reservation. The expression usually refers to airline tickets, on which agents may change flights or dates of travel only.

revalidation sticker A sticker which is attached to a ticket to show that certain details have been amended.

reverse thrust The system by which the exhaust of a jet engine can be directed forward into the direction of travel. This can be used to reverse an aircraft on the ground or to create a powerful braking effect after landing.

ria A long narrow inlet formed by the submergence of a river valley, especially in north-west Spain.

Richter scale A logarithmic scale that records the severity of earthquakes. Its values range from 0 to 9 and to date the most severe earthquake ever recorded measured 8.6.

rickshaw A light two-wheeled vehicle usually drawn by a person or people on foot.

ridge A long narrow hilltop or similar.

ridgeway A road or track along a ridge.

rift valley A steep-sided valley caused by subsidence of the earth between two faults. The river Jordan lies at the bottom of the deepest rift valley on dry land.

rigging The arrangement of sails, ropes, etc., on a sailing ship.

right of abode (UK). A person's right to take up residence in a country.

right of way 1. A right established to travel across another's land.
2. A path having such a right.

3. The order of precedence of a ship or other vehicle.

ring road (UK). A bypass.

rip A stretch of rough or fast running water in the sea or a river, caused by the meeting of currents.

river A substantial stream of water, flowing to an ocean or sea (or sometimes to a lake). The ten greatest rivers, or combinations of rivers, in order of length, are:
• Nile-White Nile-Albert Nile-Victoria Nile-Victoria Nyanza-Kagera-Luvironza
• Amazon
• Mississippi-Missouri-Jefferson-Beaverhead-Red Rock
• Yenisey-Angara-Selenga
• Yangtze Kiang
• Ob'-Irtysh
• Hwang Ho (Yellow River)
• Zaire (Congo)
• Lena-Kirenga
• Amur-Argun'
The longest river in Europe is the Danube.

Riviera Popular tourist region in south-east France and north-west Italy bordering the Mediterranean Sea. The coastal strip stretches from Cannes to La Spezia. The French Riviera is also known as the Côte d'Azur, the Italian Riviera is divided into the Riviera di Ponente in the west and the Riviera di Levante in the east. Main coastal resorts include Cannes, Nice, Monte-Carlo, Genoa and La Spezia.

riviera Any coastal region with a sub-tropical climate, especially in southern France and north-west Italy.

road A generic term for any path or

R

way with a specially prepared surface and intended for the use of pedestrians, animals or vehicles wishing to move easily around an area.

road map A map showing the roads of a country or area.

road train A large road locomotive pulling a number of trailers. Commonly used in Australia.

road warrior Marketing jargon for a business traveller, especially one who demands such things as special facilities in hotels and portable computer technology

roadhouse An inn or similar establishment on or near a road.

roadside The strip of land next to a road.

roadway That part of a bridge used for traffic.

roaring forties Areas of high wind at approximately 40° to 50° north and south of the equator.

ROE An abbreviation for rate of exchange. This abbreviation is commonly used on air tickets when the purchasing currency differs from the currency on which the fare is based.

ROH *See run of house rate.*

roll The side to side movement of a ship.

roll on, roll off The system used on most car ferries that allows vehicles to be driven on and driven off, as opposed to being loaded by crane.

rolling stock 1. The locomotives, carriages, goods wagons and other vehicles used on a railway.
2. (US). The road vehicles of a company.

Roman numerals The system of numbering, often used for additional pages such as indices, that uses letters and letter combinations: I (=1), V (=5), X (=10), L (=50), C (=100), D (=500), M (=1000). No zero (0) is used in the Roman numbering system. *See also Arabic numerals.*

Romanesque A style of architecture prevalent in Europe between 900 and 1200 AD with massive vaulting and rounded arches.

Romany *See Gypsy.*

rondavel A round hut or similar simple building, especially in South Africa.

room night One room occupied for one night. A measurement of accommodation use.

room only *See European Plan.*

room service The provision of drinks, meals, etc., in a hotel room.

roomette 1. (US). A single compartment in a railway sleeping car.
2. (US). A small room available for letting.

rooming list A list giving details of clients booked, usually when a group is involved.

ro-ro *See roll on, roll off.*

rotating wing aircraft An aircraft whose wings rotate in flight to provide lift. This is usually a helicopter or similar.

rough passage A crossing over rough seas.

round the world (RTW) 1. A journey round the world.
2. An air fare using this construction.

round trip 1. A journey to one or more places and then back to the originating point.
2. An airline term meaning a return trip comprising two fare components only, the fares for which are the same, but for which the routes are different. *See also circle trip.*

rounding Fares for most transport operators are calculated to a nearest whole unit. In the case of UK rail, for example, this is usually 5 pence. Any calculation (for a reduction, for example) must be rounded to the specified unit before the fare is used.

routeing The way or course taken between the start and finish of a journey. Every fare will be available by a specific route or routes and the restriction as to what route is available for any ticket will be shown somewhere on the document.

rover ticket A ticket allowing unlimited travel in a particular area for a specified time. Usually restricted to the services of one carrier.

RQ An abbreviation for request. *See request.*

RT *See round trip.*

RTW *See round the world.*

rubberneck A derogatory term for a tourist or sightseer.

rudder That part of a ship or aircraft that controls its direction.

rule of the road The decision that countries have made to decide whether to drive on the left or right. Most countries (around three-quarters) drive on the right.

running gear The suspension and wheels of a vehicle.

running lights Sometimes called navigation lights. The lights that a vessel must display when travelling at night.

run-of-the-house rate A flat price at which a hotel has agreed to offer rooms to a group.

runway A long, straight, flat and wide pathway from which aircraft take off and onto which they land.

rural Of or relating to the countryside.

Rust Belt The areas of the north and north-east United States characterised by older, heavy industry, particularly the steel and auto industries, and cold weather.

RV *See recreational vehicle.*

ryokan A Japanese term for a traditional wayside inn.

R

S
s

Sabbath The day of rest and religious observance kept by Jews on a Saturday. Agents should be aware of the possible implications on travel arrangements.

sabbatical Leave granted at intervals to a university teacher for study or travel, originally every seven years. The term is now often used to denote any extended leave period granted to an employee.

Sabre A GDS sponsored by American Airlines.

safari A trip into a wildlife area, such as a game reserve, for photography or occasionally hunting. Safaris are particularly popular in East Africa. The expression "safari" derives from the Swahili word for travel.

safari park *See wildlife park.*

safety announcement Verbal instructions for the use of the safety and evacuation equipment on board a ship or aircraft given by the crew soon after the start of a journey.

safety deposit A facility offered by hotels for the safekeeping of their guests' valuables.

SAGTA School & Group Travel Association. *See Appendix 7a.*

sahib A polite form of address used in India. From the Urdu "friend, lord".

sail The large piece of material, traditionally canvas, fixed to a ship's mast to catch the wind.

sailboard A small boat with a mast and sail used in windsurfing.

sailboat (US). A sailing boat.

sailing boat (UK). A boat propelled by sails.

sailing list An obsolete term that meant a shipping line's timetable. Where they exist, shipping lines now call them timetables.

sailing ticket A control document used on some shipping and ferry services that experience very heavy peak demand.

sailplane An engineless heavier-than-air aircraft used for sustained unpowered flight. Originally sailplanes differed from gliders in that gliders needed a permanent tow and sailplanes could fly using upward wind currents: Nowadays the distinction is rarely made.

sales agency agreement An agreement for the sale of a principal's services. Most principals will have a specific form or structure for such agreements.

salinity The concentration of salt in a liquid, typically the sea. The higher the salinity the more buoyant the water.

sally port An opening in a fortification from which the defenders could "sally forth" or come out in attack.

saloon 1. A public room on a ship. 2. (US). A bar. 3. (UK). An enclosed motor car with no partition between driver and passengers. 4. (UK). A railway carriage serving as a lounge, etc.

saloon keeper (US). A bartender.

salt A sailor (often "old salt" to imply knowledge and experience).

salt flat The dried up bed of a salt lake that leaves a plain covered in salt.

salt lake A lake of salt water.

salubrious Of a climate or place, healthy.

salvage The rescue of a ship or other vessel or its property following an accident or similar.

salvage tug A tug designed to rescue disabled vessels.

samovar A Russian urn used for making tea. At one time a standard provision on Russian long-distance trains.

sampan A small boat often used in the Far East.

sample room A room that displays merchandise.

sand yacht *See land yacht.*

sandbank A deposit of sand forming a shallow place in the sea or a river.

sandbar *See bar (2).*

Sargasso Sea An area of the North Atlantic in which there are large amounts of sargasso seaweed, forming island-like clumps.

satellite printer location The place in which a satellite ticket printer is located. The official IATA definition is: "An accredited agent's place of business in one country, controlled by a host location in the same country - which is located on the premises of a customer of the agent, such customer not being an agent or tour operator, - which is not accessible to the general public, - whose sole purpose is the issuance, by means of a satellite ticket printer, of traffic documents to the customer or its employees, and - which is entered on the agency list as a satellite ticket printer location."

satellite state A small country dependent on or controlled by another.

satellite ticket printer A ticket printer located away from an agency that can be used to print out traffic documents in a distant location. Satellite ticket printers can only be controlled by the agency.

satellite town A small town dependent on a nearby larger town or city.

SATH 1. Society for the Advancement of Travel for the Handicapped. *See Appendix 7a.* 2. The Society for the Advancement of Travel for the Handicapped. *See Appendix 7b.*

S

satnav Satellite navigation. A navigation system using information from satellites, increasingly common on ships and aircraft.

saturation diving Diving for prolonged periods whereby all body tissues are saturated with disolved nitrogen to the maximum extent for the depth in question.

savannah Or savanna. Tropical grasslands bordering on the equatorial rain forests in both the northern and southern hemispheres.

Saxon Of or relating to the Germanic peoples that conquered parts of England in the 5th and 6th centuries.

scale of map The ratio of size to actual territory on a map or chart. For example, on a scale of one centimetre to the kilometre.

Scandinavia The geographical region comprising: Denmark, Norway and Sweden. Often extended to include Finland and Iceland.

scenery The general appearance of the features of a landscape, etc.

scenic Picturesque or attractive as regards its view.

schedule An alternative name for a timetable.

scheduled carrier A carrier that operates a scheduled service.

scheduled service A service which operates at advertised set times between points, regardless of passenger demand.

scheduled territories An obsolescent term for those countries in the sterling area. That is, those countries whose currency was closely tied to that of the UK and between which the normal exchange control restrictions did not apply.

schooner 1. A fore and aft rigged sailing ship with two or more masts.
2. (US). A tall beer glass.
3. (UK). A large measure glass, particularly for sherry.

schuss A straight downhill ski-run.

Scirocco Alternatively sirocco. A hot dry wind that blows from the Sahara to the southern part of France.

scree A mountain slope covered with small, loose stones or rocks.

screw A ship's propeller.

scrub An area of low bushes or stunted forest growth.

scuba Self-contained underwater breathing apparatus. An aqualung.

scupper 1. An opening in the side of a ship that allows any accumulation of water to escape.
2. To sink a vessel deliberately.

scuttle 1. A hole in a ship's deck fitted with a cover.
2. To sink a ship deliberately, usually by letting in water through the sea cocks.

sea A large body of water, usually salt. The ten largest seas, in order of size, are:
• South China Sea
• Caribbean Sea
• Mediterranean Sea
• Bering Sea
• Gulf of Mexico
• Sea of Ockhotsk
• East China Sea

S

- Hudson Bay
- Sea of Japan
- Andaman Sea

sea anchor A device dragged from a ship to control its drift.

sea breeze A breeze blowing off the sea onto the land.

sea cock A valve situated below the waterline in a ship to let water in or out.

sea legs This expression refers to the ability to walk properly on the decks of a ship, even when it is pitching and rolling. It usually takes a day or two for a passenger to acquire his or her sea legs.

sea sickness A feeling of nausea caused by the rolling and pitching of a vessel at sea. The condition is caused by upset to the balance organs in the ear.

sea travel Travelling by ship, hovercraft, hydrofoil or other seaborne vessel.

sea view A hotel room with a view of the sea. Since such rooms are preferred by many guests, a supplement is usually payable.

sea wall A wall or embankment constructed to prevent encroachment by the sea.

seafront That part of a coastal town or resort that faces onto the shore.

seaplane An aircraft that can operate from water.

seashore That part of the land close to the sea.

season **1.** Any one of the four divisions of the year characterised by clearly identifiable climatic characteristics. The differences between the seasons become more pronounced as one moves towards the poles.
2. In travel, a particular time of the year during which demand or activity is at a certain and identifiable level.

season ticket A ticket available for a series of journeys, admissions, etc., in a given period.

seasonality The variation for demand for products and services that is due to different seasons.

seat belt A retaining device fitted to many vehicles that holds passengers in their seats in the event of accident or violent movement. The use of seat belts in cars and coaches is obligatory in many countries while their use in aircraft is universal.

seat only (UK). A seat on an air charter service for which no associated hotel accommodation is provided. In the UK it is theoretically illegal to sell seats on charter flights unless they are part of a package so the seat only sale is actually a package tour but with accommodation so cheap and negligible that passengers do not use it. Since this is simply a way of bypassing regulations (and diverting traffic from scheduled carriers) many countries will not accept travellers arriving on these sorts of arrangements.

seat rotation A system used on coach tours where passengers change seats at regular intervals so as to ensure that everyone has an opportunity to occupy the better seats.

S

seating plan A diagram showing the layout of seats on a vehicle or in a hall, etc.

seaward Towards the sea.

seaway An ocean or estuarial traffic lane.

second 1. A sixtieth of a minute of time.
2. A sixtieth of a minute of arc.

second class 1. Originally applied to railways that conveyed passengers in first, second or third class accommodation. Most railways now only have two classes, first and second or in the case of the railways of Britain, first and standard.
2. Sometimes applied to hotels. Difficult to define exactly since there is such a wide range of grading systems. Obviously inferior to first class or de luxe and probably best avoided in less well developed parts of the world.

second floor 1. (UK). The floor two levels above the ground floor.
2. (US). The floor immediately above the ground floor.

second sitting The later of two meal times on a ship.

sector A complete portion of an itinerary or journey, which can comprise several legs or segments.

security tax A charge levied to cover the cost of screening of passengers and their luggage to try to detect acts of terrorism.

sedan 1. Originally an enclosed chair carried by two porters to provide transport.
2. (US). A saloon car.

segment That portion of a passenger's journey from boarding to disembarking. Since a vehicle may stop several times en route, a segment could comprise several legs. *See also leg.*

seiche A fluctuation in the water level of a lake or other enclosed body of water caused by changes in barometric pressure, rather than by tidal influences.

seif A long narrow sand dune.

self-catering Any type of accommodation that allows or expects guests to arrange their own meals.

self-drive In car rental, a vehicle operated by the renter.

self-righting Of a small boat, one that returns automatically to the upright position after a capsize.

selling point A feature or aspect of a holiday or other arrangement that makes it of particular benefit to a prospective customer.

semaphore 1. An early signalling method involving the use of hand-held flags, each position representing a letter.
2. A signal, usually on a railway, that makes use of a moving arm, rather than coloured lights.

semi-basement A storey in a building that is partly below ground level.

semi-tropical *See sub-tropical.*

senior citizen An elderly or retired person.

SEO Society of Event Organisers. *See Appendix 7a.*

S

sepulchre A tomb cut into rock, or built of stone or rock.

serein Fine rain that occasionally falls from cloudless skies in the tropics.

serial number The number or code on a document that indicates its position in the batch.

service area An area beside a road, usually for the supply of fuel, refreshments, etc.

service bus Australian. A motor coach.

service charge An additional amount added to a bill to cover the cost of service. Such charges are supposed to replace the traditional tip, but many establishments try to obtain both. In theory, if the service has been poor, a customer would have the right to deduct the service charge.

service industry An industry, such as travel, that provides services rather than goods.

service road A road running parallel to a main road giving access to shops, etc.

service station An establishment selling fuel and providing services to motorists.

serviced accommodation Any accommodation provided by an organisation, such as a hotel, that provides a range of additional services.

set down To offload passengers.

set meal A meal with no choice of dishes.

seven seas The oceans of the world. *See ocean.*

sex tourism Tourism that attracts visitors to destinations where they may seek sexual encounters. Although this is frowned on by many, the practice is widespread in such countries as Thailand and Cuba.

sextant An instrument that measures angular distance, used in navigation.

SFTA Swiss Federation of Travel Agents. *See Appendix 7c.*

shakedown cruise Usually US. The first cruise operated after a ship has been built or re-fitted. It is intended to identify any flaws or deficiencies before the vessel enters full service.

Shangri La An imaginary paradise on earth supposedly located somewhere in Tibet.

shanty A small, crudely built dwelling.

shantytown A residential area made up of shanties, often found on the outskirts of large conurbations, and occupied by immigrant workers.

shark billy Short stick with pointed end used for fending off sharks.

shebeen An unlicensed house that sells alcohol, especially in Ireland and Scotland.

sheikhdom A country or state ruled by a sheikh.

shingle Small stones or pebbles.

ship 1. A large waterborne vessel, often of many thousands of tons in weight and hundreds of feet in length. Ships should never be referred to as boats, although this description may correctly be given to the lifesaving vessels mounted on a ship's decks. 2. (US). An aircraft.

S

ship density *See passenger space ratio.*

ship of the desert A camel.

shipboard A term that means anything that is used or occurs on board a ship.

ship-canal A canal large enough to take seagoing vessels.

shire (UK). A county, especially one whose name ends in …shire.

shooting brake (UK). An estate car.

shore The land along the edge of a body of water.

shore excursions Short duration trips to various attractions arranged at ports of call for passengers on cruise ships.

short break A short duration trip usually taken in addition to a main holiday. Many short breaks are to cities or similar destinations that boast a wide range of attractions.

short haul An inexact term that is applied generally to journeys within one continent.

short takeoff and landing Any aircraft that can operate from a shorter runway than is needed for conventional types.

shoulder season The period between high season and low season.

shuttle service A service that operates at regular intervals rather than to a timetable of varying departures.

sick flag *See yellow flag.*

sickbay That part of a ship used as a hospital.

sidereal time Time measured by the apparent motion of the stars. A sidereal day is about 20 minutes 23 seconds longer than a solar day.

side-road A road joining or leaving a main road.

sidewalk (US). The area on a highway reserved for pedestrians.

siding **1.** An area of track on a railway used for the marshalling and storage of rolling stock.
2. (US). External cladding material for a building.

sierra A mountain range.

siesta A rest taken in the middle of the afternoon. Once common in hot countries, it is becoming less so with the advent of air conditioning and the demands for full-time working.

sightseeing trip A visit to one or more tourist attractions.

signal box (UK). A building from which the signals and points of a railway are controlled.

signal tower (US). *See signal box.*

Silicon Valley Electronics and computer research and manufacturing area in the Santa Clara Valley, California, stretching from Palo Alto in the north to San Jose in the south.

silver service Restaurant service where the food is brought to the table on large dishes from which it is served in portions to meet the needs of each diner.

single When applied to a hotel room, means a room for one person only.

s

single chair A chair lift designed to carry only one person.

single entry visa A visa valid for one visit only.

single occupancy rate A special rate charged to a lone guest occupying a multiple bedded room. It would usually be more than the price for a single room, but less than the full rate for the multiple bedded room

single supplement An extra amount payable by those wishing to occupy accommodation on their own. It is important to realise that this supplement is for the sole occupancy, not for any additional facilities. Indeed, many single rooms are inferior to their double counterparts.

single-decker (UK). A bus or coach with only one deck.

Sinic The ancient Chinese civilisation that lasted from around 1600 BC until 220 AD.

site of special scientific interest (SSSI) (UK). An area designated as being of special scientific importance and thus often having restricted access.

six pack chair A chair lift designed to carry six people.

sked (US). *See schedule.*

Skeleton Coast The desert coast of Namibia between Walvis Bay and the Angolan border. A national park and part of the Namib Desert, the name comes from the number of ships wrecked on its treacherous rocks or lost in the fogs created by the cold Benguela current.

skerry Scottish. A reef or rocky island.

ski évolutif A method of learning to ski where beginners start with special short skis, graduating to longer ones as they improve.

ski lift Any one of a number of types of device to carry skiers up a slope.

ski poles The two metal rods held by a skier to assist propulsion, turning, etc.

ski sticks *See ski poles.*

skiable vertical The vertical distance that a skier can ski down without having to take a lift up.

ski-bob A single track vehicle, similar in layout to a bicycle, but with skis instead of wheels.

Skidoo A brand name for a make of snowmobile, often used as a generic name for all such vehicles.

ski-jump A man-made slope with a sharp drop from which skiers jump.

ski-plane An aircraft with skis rather than wheels.

skipper A familiar expression for the captain of a ship or aircraft.

skirt The flexible surround that contains the air of a hovercraft or similar vehicle.

ski-run A slope prepared for skiing.

skis **1.** A pair of long narrow pieces or wood, fibreglass or plastic, fitted to the underside of a pair of special boots, that allow rapid travel over snow.
2. The act of using a pair of skis.

skyjack *See hijack.*

S

slack water The time when the tide is turning, especially at low tide.

Slave Coast Coastal strip of west Africa, the coasts of present-day Togo, Benin and western Nigeria. The name comes from the trade in slaves between the 16th and 19th centuries.

sleeper **1.** A railway sleeping car. On UK railways a single or two-berth sleeping compartment. UK sleepers have proper beds and bed linen and sexes are segregated. They cost a little more than a couchette but are cheaper than a Wagon Lit.
2. The wooden or concrete transverse supports that hold the metals of a railway track in proper alignment. Known as ties in the USA.

sleeping car *See sleeper (1).*

sleigh A sledge, especially one for riding on, often drawn by horses or reindeer.

SLI *See supplementary liability insurance.*

slip (US). An artificial slope in a marina or dock where boats can be brought into or out of the water.

slip road (UK). A road that enters or leaves a motorway or similar.

slip-carriage *See slip-coach.*

slip-coach A coach or carriage of a train that is detached while the train is in motion and brought to a stand at a station. This avoids the necessity for braking and accelerating the entire train. Slip coaches are no longer used on UK railways.

slipstream A current of air or water driven back by a moving vehicle.

sloop A small single masted vessel with foresail and jib.

slot An allocated time of departure or arrival at an airport. Slots are at a premium in busy airports like Heathrow.

smallpox A once deadly, contagious viral disease that has now been eliminated in the wild although strains are still kept in a few laboratories.

SMB *See surface marker buoy.*

smog Fog mixed with smoke.

smokestack *See funnel.*

smuggle To attempt to bring in goods to a country secretly and illegally.

SNAV Société Nationale des Agences de Voyage. *See Appendix 7c.*

snorkel Also schnorkel. A "J" shaped tube that enables a diver to breathe ordinary air at the surface without having to raise his or her head and face out of the water.

snorkelling The act of swimming face down in the water using a snorkel to breathe.

snow cat *See piste groomer.*

snow-blindness A sight condition caused by looking too long at snow reflecting bright sunshine, without using sunglasses.

snowboard A wide, single ski.

snow-cap A mountain top covered with snow.

snowdrift A bank of snow heaped up by the wind.

snowfield Officially a permanent wide expanse of snow. However the term is colloquially used to describe non-permanent expanses in such expressions as "virgin powder snowfields" that commonly melt in the summer.

snowline Officially the level above which snow never entirely melts. However, the term is often used to describe the line where the snow begins and ends on a mountain, even when this is a movable point. Weather forecasters, for example, may speak of the snowline moving down as the temperature drops and moving up as it rises.

snowmobile A vehicle, usually fitted with tracks, for travelling over snowfields.

snowplough 1. A device for clearing or moving snow.
2. The name given to the commonest way of teaching people to ski. It is derived from the inverted "V" shape made by the skis in the "snowplough" position.

snowshoe A device that fits over ordinary boots to allow the wearer to walk on snow without sinking. Useful for those who are unable to ski although snowshoeing is now becoming popular in its own right.

sojourn A temporary stay.

solar day The length of a day as measured by the apparent movement of the sun. The normal measurement of time on earth.

solstice Either of the two times in a year when the sun is at its greatest distance from the equator. The summer solstice is on June 21, the winter solstice on December 22.

Somali current This warm current runs off the north-east coast of Africa flowing north in June, July and August and south during other times of the year.

sommelier A wine waiter.

son et lumière From the French "sound and light". An entertainment making use of illuminations and recorded music, etc., to give a dramatised history. Often used at historic man-made attractions, such as the Pyramids.

SOS An international distress signal. Contrary to popular belief it is not an acronym for "save our souls". The letter group was chosen because of its simple and memorable combination of dots and dashes in Morse code (· · · — — — · · ·).

souk A market place in Muslim countries.

sound 1. A narrow passage of water connecting two other bodies of water.
2. To test the depth and quality of the bottom of a body of water.

South America The region that includes all the countries in the land mass south of Panama, the Falkland Islands and the Galapagos Islands. Usually regarded as a continent in its own right.

South Equatorial Current Originating close to the equator and flowing westward, this current is diverted northwards by the Brazilian coast and feeds the source of the Gulf Stream.

south pole The southernmost point of the earth.

South Sea, South Seas The southern Pacific Ocean.

S

Southern Cone The region of South America comprising Brazil, Paraguay, Argentina and Uruguay.

Southern Cross A distinctive constellation shaped like a cross and visible only from the southern hemisphere.

southern hemisphere That part of the earth south of the equator.

southern lights *See aurora australis.*

Southern Ocean *See oceans.*

souvenir A memento bought as a reminder of a journey or visit. Souvenirs are a major earner of foreign exchange in most resorts.

sovereign A supreme ruler, especially a monarch.

spa A natural source of water that may be used for drinking and/or bathing. The effects of spa water are said to be beneficial and many spa towns have exploited this facility to attract visitors for many years. Originally named after the town of Spa in Belgium.

SPAA Scottish Passenger Agents Association. *See Appendix 7a.*

space available basis *See standby.*

Space Coast Area of coastline east of Orlando, Florida, stretching from New Smyrna Beach in the north to Palm Bay in the south. Encompasses many sites relating to the US space programme, as well as numerous beach resorts and wildlife reserves.

spaghetti junction (UK). A motorway junction having several levels. So-called because of its supposed resemblance to strands of spaghetti.

spar 1. A pole used for the mast or a major spar of a ship.
2. The main structural member of an aircraft's wing.

Spartan The civilisation of ancient Laconia that lasted from around 900 BC until AD 396.

spear gun A device for propelling a spear at speed through the water.

special-interest attraction Any tourist attraction that is designed to appeal to a specific hobby or interest.

special-interest holidays A general term given to any holiday arrangement for those wanting something which meets their particular interests or hobbies. For example, bird watching, golfing, diving, etc.

special-needs accommodation Accommodation designed for guests with disabilities.

speedboat A small, fast boat.

SPF *See sun protection factor.*

SPH Skiers per hour. *See uplift capacity.*

spinnaker A large triangular sail.

spit A point of land projecting into a body of water.

split season Travelling out and back in different seasons.

split ticketing The issuing of separate tickets for a multi-sector journey to undercut the through fare. For example, a London/Hong Kong/London fare, plus a Hong Kong/Tokyo/Hong Kong fare might prove cheaper than the direct fare London/Tokyo/London. Technically

S

this commonly used form of construction is illegal but rarely are perpetrators prosecuted or even inconvenienced.

sporting attraction An attraction that capitalises on its ability to offer visitors the chance to participate in or enjoy a sport or recreation.

spot height A specific height marked on a map, for example, the summit of a mountain.

spouse A husband or wife. At one time carriers' special fares for accompanying partners were restricted to spouses. These days such fares are usually available to any partner.

spouse fare See partner fare.

spring tide The tide just after new and full moon, when there is the greatest difference between high and low water.

squall A sudden and violent gust or storm of wind.

square-rigged A form of rigging where the principal sails are arranged at right angles to the length of the ship and extended by horizontal yards attached to the masts.

SS When placed in front of a ship's name means steamship.

SSSI See site of special scientific interest.

SST See supersonic transport.

stabiliser A historical term for an ABTA initiative to regulate the travel industry. Although it was a restrictive practice it was allowed to continue by the courts as it was held to be in the public

interest. Following the legal provisions implicit in the EC Legislation on Package Travel it became unnecessary and is now obsolete.

stabilisers Devices on a ship to help prevent roll. They create considerable drag when in use and so will only be deployed when really necessary.

STAG Society of Travel Agents in Government Inc. See Appendix 7b.

stage decompression A specific depth at which the diver must remain before completing the journey to the surface - to enable accumulated nitrogen to escape from the body without danger of contracting decompression sickness.

stagecoach Historically a large, closed horse-drawn coach running to a timetable between various points. Sometimes still used to describe similar motor coach services.

stalactite A deposit of crystallised minerals hanging from the roof of a cave or cavern caused by mineral-laden water seeping through the cavern roof. Most resemble a stone icicle.

stalagmite A deposit of crystallised minerals rising from the floor of a cave or cavern caused by drops of mineral-laden water falling from a stalactite.

stall The condition that occurs when the airflow over an aircraft's wings is insufficient to maintain lift. The aircraft will simply fall in the air when it stalls and will crash unless corrective action is taken.

stamp To endorse a ticket or other

S

items by means of a rubber or metal stamp.

standby fare A general term for a discounted fare offered to passengers who are prepared to wait until the last minute to obtain accommodation on a vehicle.

starboard The right hand side of a vessel looking forward. Denoted by a green light.

state 1. An organised political community under one government. 2. An organised political community forming part of a federal republic. *See Appendix 3 for a list of US states and appendix 5 for a list of Australian states.*

stateless Of a person. One who has no nationality or citizenship.

stateroom 1. A state apartment in a palace or hotel. 2. A private room on a ship. Originally the term was reserved for the best cabins, but some shipping lines refer to all their sleeping accommodation as staterooms. 3. (US). A private compartment on a train.

station A stop or terminus for trains or buses.

station wagon (US). An estate car.

status box The space on an air ticket that indicates whether a reservation has been confirmed or not.

statute mile A distance of 1,760 yards or approximately 1.6 kilometres. The usual measure of distance in countries using imperial measurements.

STB Scottish Tourist Board. *See Appendix 7a.*

steam engine An engine that produces its power by burning fuel in a boiler to produce steam. This in turn drives a piston or turbine. Steam engines are now used mainly in large static installations such as power plants. However, in transport they can still be found in larger liners and on a few railways.

steamer *See steamship.*

steam-hauled A railway expression indicating that a train is hauled by a steam-powered locomotive. Usually only found on preserved lines or tourist trains.

steamship A ship powered by steam engines. Usually denoted by the abbreviation SS in front of its name.

steerage Historically the cheapest accommodation on a ship, situated far aft.

stem An alternative name for a ship's bow.

steppe A level, grassy plain with extreme temperature variations.

sterling area *See scheduled territories.*

stern The rear part of a ship.

steward A male passenger attendant on a ship, aircraft or train.

stewardess (UK). A female steward.

stock 1. In travel, the unissued tickets and other documents held pending use. 2. *See rolling stock.*

STOL *See short take off and landing.*

stopoff *See stopover.*

stopover A deliberate interruption to a journey, agreed in advance, between the origin and destination points of a journey. Not all fares will allow stopovers and there is an official IATA definition of stopover to help decide whether one is allowed at a given fare.

storey A floor of a building.

stowaway A person who has hidden aboard a vehicle in the hope of obtaining free transport.

STP *See satellite ticket printer.*

STP location *See satellite printer location.*

strait A narrow passage of water joining two seas or other larger areas of water.

stratus A type of cloud characterised by its generally low, flat base and grey colour.

stream A small river or similar flowing body of water.

street A public road in a town or village.

street furniture The various signs and other artefacts provided in a road or street to assist users.

streetcar (US). A tramcar.

studio A one-bedroomed apartment.

sub-aqua Relating to any underwater activity, especially diving.

subcontinent A large land mass, smaller than a continent.

subject to load Often abbreviated to subload. When a carrier agrees to convey a passenger if space is available. Most discounted tickets are subject to load and the greater the discount the lower the priority of the holder of the subload ticket. *See also standby.*

subload *See subject to load.*

submarine 1. Beneath the sea. 2. A vessel capable of operating beneath water. Submarine excursions are now common in resorts where there are underwater attractions, such as coral reefs.

subrogation Once an insurance company has indemnified a claimant, by repayment or replacement or other agreed settlement, the claimant relinquishes his or her rights to claim against any other party. In essence, the right to do so has passed to the insurance company which itself could claim against a negligent party if it wished.

subsonic Less than the speed of sound (approximately 1225kph or 760 mph at sea level).

sub-temperate The cooler parts of a temperate climatic zone.

subterranean Under ground.

subtropical A climate zone slightly cooler than tropical.

suburban Often abbreviated to suburb. The area around a city.

subway 1. (UK). An underground passage, often beneath a road. 2. (US). An underground railway.

suite Accommodation with at least two rooms, including one bedroom and usually a kitchen.

S

sultan A Muslim sovereign.

sultanate A state ruled by a sultan.

sultry Of the weather, hot or oppressive.

Sumerian The civilisation of ancient Sumeria that lasted from before 3,500 BC to 1700 BC.

summit The highest point of a feature, especially a hill or mountain.

sumptuous Particularly lavish or costly.

sun deck The deck of a ship designed for sunbathing.

sun protection factor The indicator of the effectiveness of sun creams and lotions.

Sunbelt The areas of south and south-west United States made popular by holidaymakers and those in retirement. The term applies mainly to Florida, Arizona and southern California. Rapid development has taken place due to the good weather, incentives to industry and the availability of cheap labour from Mexico.

sunbelt An area receiving more than the average amount of sunshine.

sunblock Cream or lotion formulated to protect the skin against the sun's rays. *See SPF.*

sunlust The desire to travel to a sunny destination.

sunscreen *See sunblock.*

Sunshine Coast Resort coast north of Brisbane, Australia, stretching from Bribie Island to Tin Can Bay, less developed than the Gold Coast to the south.

sunstroke Acute exhaustion or collapse caused by over-exposure to the sun.

suntrap (UK). A place sheltered from the wind, etc., and designed to catch the sun.

sunup (US). Sunrise.

superelevation The amount by which the outer edge of a road or railway is above the inner edge.

superhighway **1.** (US). A particularly fast main road with multiple carriageways in each direction. **2.** In full the information superhighway. The means by which information can be transferred rapidly between computers by means of the Internet and similar networks.

superior Of accommodation. A better class or category than that normally provided, usually attracting a supplement.

supersonic Faster than the speed of sound (approximately 1225 kph or 760 mph at sea level).

supersonic transport (SST) Any vehicle capable of travelling at more than the speed of sound. The only SST in commercial passenger service at present is Concorde.

superstructure Any structure built onto another structure. Thus the superstructure of a ship will include all the cabins and entertainment facilities built onto the hull.

supplement A fee for an extra, or better, grade of service.

supplementary liability insurance A car rental term. The cover afforded by third party insurance may be limited, especially in the USA. In order to obtain adequate cover ($1,000,000 is recommended), SLI can be purchased.

supplier Another term for a principal.

surcharge An extra charge on a customer's bill. Surcharges may arise for various reasons but are less common than was the case a few years ago, when many tour operators were applying surcharges to avoid losses caused by currency fluctuations.

surface demand Air supplied to a diver underwater by tubes from a surface source.

surface lift *See drag lift.*

surface marker buoy A small buoy floating on the surface and towed by a diver using a long line to indicate his or her whereabouts underwater.

surface travel A generic term that can denote any form of travel that is not by air, but usually refers to travel over the ground.

surfboard A long narrow buoyant board on which riders are carried over the surf.

surrender Of a ticket or other document, to give it up on demand.

surrey (US). A light four-wheeled horse-drawn carriage often used for sightseeing. The name comes from Surrey, the English county where they were first made.

sustainable tourism Tourism that has a minimal effect on the natural and cultural environment of the area visited.

SVQ Scottish Vocational Qualifications. The Scottish equivalent of NVQ.

swallow An area where a river appears to sink into the ground, only to reappear later.

swamp An area of waterlogged land.

sweepback The angle at which an aircraft's wings are set back from the right-angle.

swell The heaving of seas that do not break into waves, often after a storm.

S

T
t

T Junction A road junction where one road joins another at right angles without crossing it.

t.b.a. *See to be advised.*

t.b.n. To be notified. *See to be advised.*

TAANZ Travel Agents Association of New Zealand. *See Appendix 7c.*

table d'hôte A menu in a restaurant that is available at a fixed price and which contains relatively few choices.

tableland An extensive elevated region.

tables As related to diving. A compilation of figures in graph form denoting various depths, and times allowed at those depths, with the desired decompression stops.

tachograph A device fitted to vehicles such as coaches that measures the speed, duration of stops and number of hours a driver works.

tack The direction in which a sailing vessel moves as determined by its own direction and that of the wind.

taffrail The rail around a ship's stern.

taiga A stretch of coniferous forest, especially in Siberia.

tail wind A wind blowing in the same direction as a vehicle is travelling.

tailor made A holiday or other arrangement designed especially for a particular client.

tailplane The smaller horizontal projections from the fuselage of an aircraft, situated towards the rear. These serve to stabilise the machine and provide most of the control.

take a chance A marketing device used by some cruising companies. By taking a chance on the exact cabin and cruise, prospective passengers can pay a substantially reduced fare. Their accommodation will then be allocated around a month before sailing.

take off The moment when an aircraft leaves the ground and starts to fly.

taking air Or taking big air. A skiing expression that means leaving the snow and jumping into the air, intentionally or inadvertently, while skiing or snowboarding.

tall ship A sailing ship with a tall mast or masts.

Tannoy A brand name for a type of public address system, but often used in the UK to denote any such system.

tapas Small savoury dishes, often served at a Spanish bar.

taproom A room in which alcoholic drinks, usually beer, are served.

tariff A rate or charge. The expression is often used to refer to a listing of rates, as in "Air Tariff", a listing of air fares.

tarmac A type of road surface (an abbreviation of **tarmac**adam). Often used casually to denote a paved area of an airfield, or even a runway.

tavern An old fashioned name for an inn.

taverna A Greek name for an eating place or sometimes a small hotel.

taxi 1. A car or similar vehicle licensed to ply for hire. The name is derived from taximeter, and not the other way round.
2. The movement of an aircraft on the ground.

taxi way Paved tracks on which aircraft move between the parking and loading area and the runway.

taximeter The device that calculates the distance travelled and the fare payable for a cab journey.

T-bar A type of drag lift found mainly in Austria, Switzerland and Germany. The lift carries two skiers side by side but is awkward to use due to the difficulty of keeping the two passengers balanced.

TC Timeshare Council. *See Appendix 7a.*

tech stop *See technical stop.*

technical stop A planned stop on an air journey that is not scheduled for passenger pick up or drop off. Usually this will be for refuelling or crew change. Passengers may not need to leave the aircraft, but this will depend on local restrictions.

téléférique Another name for a cable car, commonly used in France and Switzerland.

Telemark skiing The original method of downhill skiing, invented in the Telemark area of Norway in the 1860's.

temperate A climate zone characterised by its lack of extremes of temperature and its unpredictable weather. The United Kingdom is in a temperate zone.

temperature-humidity index A value that gives the measure of discomfort experienced due to the combined effects of the temperature and humidity of the atmosphere.

tempest A violent, windy storm.

tender 1. A launch or similar vehicle that takes passengers from a ship to the dock when the ship is forced to anchor away from land.
2. The putting in of a bid for business. Common now among business travel agents who are often expected to re-tender for a company's travel account at regular intervals.

tent A portable or temporary dwelling made of canvas or other cloth. Often the cheapest form of accommodation, although many modern tents are quite luxurious.

terminal 1. A building at an airport, bus station or similar that is used to process arriving and departing passengers.
2. The VDU and associated equipment in a travel agency that is connected to a GDS or other system.

T

terminus (UK). The station at the end of a railway line or bus route.

terra firma A rather pretentious expression meaning solid earth (as opposed to air or sea). For example, "When we're back on terra firma" means when we've landed.

terra incognita An unknown or unexplored area.

terrace 1. A raised, flat area outside a house or similar.
2. A flattened area of hillside used for growing crops, etc.

terrain The physical features of an area. *See also topography.*

terrestrial Of or relating to the earth.

territorial waters The waters under the jurisdiction of a country or state, especially that part of the sea a stated distance from the country's shore.

territory Any piece of land belonging to, or under the jurisdiction of, a state or country.

The West European, as opposed to Oriental.

theft protection A car rental insurance giving cover should the rented vehicle be stolen.

theme cruise A cruise designed to appeal to a certain section of the public. For example, an archaeological cruise.

theme park An entertainment centre, usually spread over a large area with a number of separate entertainment facilities, based on a particular special interest.

themed attraction Any tourist attraction that has chosen a particular special subject or topic on which to base its activities, displays, etc.

thermocline Boundary between waters of differing temperature.

third age The period in life of active retirement. Often the time when many people travel extensively.

third class The third-best category of accommodation. Usually best avoided in less developed countries.

third party insurance The cover against claims made by another person, in respect of injury, damage, death or other loss.

Third World That part of the world that is less advanced or developed, such as many parts of Africa.

thoroughfare A road or path open at both ends for the passage of traffic.

through fare A fare for travel between two points. Usually through fares will allow en route stopovers, unlike point to point fares. The publication of a through fare for a journey does not mean that a through service exists.

through service A service that does not require a passenger to change. Through services are not necessarily non-stop services.

throughway 1. A thoroughfare.
2. (US). (often thruway) a motorway.

throwaway Any item included in an inclusive tour that is not intended to be used. The accommodation in a seat only arrangement is a good example.

thrust An aviation term indicating the force generated by an aircraft engine.

thunder The sound of lightning caused by the rapid heating of air by the electrical discharge. The sound of thunder is generated at the same time as the lightning and the interval between the two is caused by the different speeds at which light and sound travel. Light travels at approximately 186,300 miles per second and sound at about 760 miles per hour. Each 5 second delay between seeing the lightning and hearing the thunder is equal to about a mile, which gives a rapid way of estimating how distant a storm is.

thunderbolt A flash of lightning with an almost simultaneous crash of thunder, caused by the nearness of the storm. Often imagined to be different from, or more destructive than, a more distant event.

thundercloud A tall cumulus cloud, producing thunder and lightning.

thunderstorm A storm producing rain, thunder and lightning.

TIAA Travel Industry Association of America. *See Appendix 7b.*

TIC *See tourist information centre.*

ticket **1.** A document that proves entitlement to travel on a specific journey, subject to conditions of carriage. It is not the same as a reservation. In itself it does not guarantee passage at any particular time.
2. A document allowing entry to an event or place, etc.

ticket agent An obsolescent term for a travel agent, especially one that dealt with theatre bookings.

ticket collector A person responsible for checking tickets or travel documents, usually on a train or at the barrier of a station.

ticket office A place where tickets are made available.

ticket on departure If a passenger is unable or unwilling to collect a ticket at the purchasing point, a ticket can be made available for collection at the departure point. *See also PTA.*

ticket printer A printer that prints the details on automated tickets.

ticket tout A person who obtains tickets, usually for a concert or sporting event or similar, and then sells them at a substantial profit when no more tickets can be obtained from official sources.

ticketed point mileage The published mileage between the origin and destination points on an airline ticket. The MPM is the maximum distance that can be travelled in excess of the TPM without surcharge.

ticket-holder A person who has legitimately obtained and carries a ticket for a journey or facility.

ticketless travel *See electronic ticketing.*

tidal wave A dangerous and destructive wave, usually produced by an earthquake.

tide The regular rise and fall of the surface of seas and oceans that occurs about every 12 hours 25 minutes.

tidetable A table indicating the times of high and low tides.

tideway The channel in which a tide

T

runs, especially the tidal part of a river.

tied house (UK). A pub owned by a brewery and thus usually obliged to sell primarily the brewery's own products. *See free house, guest beer.*

tiller The horizontal handle fitted to a boat's rudder by which it is turned.

Timbuktu Actually a real destination in north-west Africa (Mali) but often used simply to denote a distant or inaccessible place.

time and mileage A car rental tariff that is based on the time for which the vehicle has been rented and the distance driven. Usually taken by business travellers; holiday renters usually take an unlimited mileage tariff.

time series charter A charter based on the use of a vehicle, usually an aircraft, for an agreed length of time.

time zone The world is divided into 24 time zones, changing approximately every 15° of longitude. It is important for people in the travel industry to know how to convert times between various zones, since this has an effect on apparent journey times as well as the times during which business can be transacted between countries.

timeshare The concept where people "buy" a period of time in accommodation. This time is then reserved for their use year on year. Other customers will buy other time slots in the same accommodation.

timetable A list of departure and arrival times of a mode of transport. The complexity of a timetable is directly related to the number of connection possibilities afforded by the transport system, with rail timetables usually being the most complex.

tip *See gratuity.*

to be advised Used when a particular item of information is not available at the time. Commonly used by agents when they are awaiting a detail about the customer (the full name, for example). Principals may also use the expression if they are unable to give full details about a booking, such as a timing or accommodation details.

TOC *See train operating company.*

TOD *See ticket on departure.*

toilet A lavatory or WC.

token A staff or similar object carried by the driver or guard of a train to control access to a section of single track taking two-way traffic.

toll **1.** A fee charged for the use of a road, bridge or similar. **2.** (US). The charge for a long-distance telephone call.

toll booth The place where a road toll is collected.

toll free (US). A "free" telephone call, generally one where the called number pays.

tonnage **1.** A general term meaning ships, as in "new tonnage on that route". **2.** A measurement of a ship's capacity with 4 different meanings. Gross registered tonnage or g.r.t.; net registered tonnage or n.r.t.; displacement tonnage, which is the weight of water displaced by a vessel (and thus its actual weight); dead-weight tonnage is the carrying capacity by weight. Most passenger shipping companies quote g.r.t. in their brochure since this is the most useful measurement when determining a ship's likely comfort. Displacement tonnage is usually quoted for warships (and sometimes for US merchantmen) Dead-weight tonnage is usually quoted for tankers.

topography That variety or mix of natural or artificial features that make up a landscape.

topside The side of a ship above the waterline.

tornado A violent storm, covering a relatively small area and characterised by whirlwinds (revolving, funnel shaped clouds).

torrent A rushing stream of water.

torrid Extremely hot and dry weather.

totalitarian Of or relating to a centralised and dictatorial form of government.

touch of the sun A colloquial expression for a feeling of sickness caused by exposure to too much sun. Less severe than sunstroke.

touchdown The moment of landing of an aircraft.

tour A trip that visits a number of places. Tours are often operated by coach and frequently have a guide. Tours with guides are usually known as "escorted tours".

tour conductor Someone who escorts a tour, usually acting as a manager and guide.

tour escort *See tour conductor.*

tour leader *See tour conductor.*

tour manager A person who manages and supervises a pre-established tour itinerary, ensuring that it is carried out according to schedule and to standard.

tour operator An organisation that puts together an inclusive holiday for sale to the public. Tour operators are not regarded as principals in the UK travel industry, although there are occasions when they could be considered as such. Tour operators are more commonly regarded in much the same way as a wholesaler would be in the case of manufactured products. *See also organiser.*

tour organiser *See tour operator.*

tourism The all-embracing term for the movement of people to destinations away from their place of residence for pleasure, and the multifarious peripheral activities associated with this.

tourism apartheid Where discrimination exists against local people in favour of free-spending foreign tourists.

tourist A person who engages in tourism.

tourist attraction Anything, natural or artificial, that attracts visitors. An example of a natural attraction might be the Florida Everglades, and an artificial attraction in the same state could be Walt Disney World. *See Appendix 6 for a select list of tourist attractions.*

tourist card A document required by certain countries before they will

T

allow a person admission. The requirements for obtaining a tourist card are similar to, but usually less onerous than, those required for obtaining a visa.

tourist class *See economy class.*

tourist enclave An area of separate tourist accommodation, often provided for safety or security reasons.

tourist generating country A country from which large numbers of tourists originate, as opposed to a tourist receiving country. Some countries (the United Kingdom is a good example) are both originating and receiving.

tourist guide A person who possesses an area-specific tourist guide qualification recognised by the appropriate public authority in the country concerned. The tourist guide's role is to guide visitors from home or abroad, in languages of their choice, interpreting the natural and cultural heritage of the area of qualification.

tourist information centre (UK). An office (usually run by a tourist board or local authority) which gives information about a destination.

tourist offices These exist to promote tourism to a country or region and are usually funded by the governments of the countries they promote. In many countries (including the UK) incoming tourists contribute a major portion of foreign exchange earnings. It is the desire to increase these "invisible exports" that prompts governments to set up and maintain tourist offices.

tourist receiving country A country that large numbers of tourists visit, as opposed to a tourist generating country. Some countries (the United Kingdom is a good example) are both originating and receiving.

tourist region An area visited by tourists that has a specific name or identity. This will often differ from the name for the region used geographically. For example, the stretch of coast between Valencia and Alicante is officially in the Comunidad de Valenciana, but all holidaymakers know it as the Costa Blanca.

tourist trap A scathing expression for a destination or attraction that is becoming popular and is supposedly overrun with tourists. Usually used by those who have just begun to aspire to somewhere slightly newer or better.

tow path From towing path. A path alongside a canal or navigable river, originally used by draught horses to haul barges.

town A large urban area with a name and boundaries, not large enough to be classed as a city.

TP *See theft protection.*

TPI *See third party insurance.*

TPM *See ticketed point mileage.*

track 1. A rough path through countryside.
2. A railway line.
3. The course of an aircraft in flight.

track-laying Of a vehicle, one that lays its own tracks as it progresses. A tank is probably the best known example, but track-laying vehicles are often used for haulage where the ground is poor or slippery.

tract A region or area of indefinite size.

trade body Most trades and professions have their own representative organisations that usually come into existence soon after the business area starts to grow and large numbers of new entrants come into it. Trade bodies set common standards and practices so that members of the trade or profession can work together more effectively. Furthermore, they provide a common voice to represent the needs of the industry to try to obtain the best trading conditions from government.

trade discount A discount given by one business to another business, that may or may not be in the same industry. A travel agent's discount is an example.

trade fair An exhibition set up to meet the interests of people and organisations involved with a particular industry and to provide commercial opportunities.

trade mission A tour arranged for business or government representatives to visit a destination with a view to obtaining more business.

trade show *See trade fair.*

trade winds The steady winds that blow across the oceans from about 30° north to about 30° south. In the northern hemisphere they blow from north-east to south-west; in the southern, from south-east to north-west. Very important in the age of commercial sailing, they are now of interest only to the occasional sailor or balloonist.

traffic In travel, any movement of people and or vehicles between two points, by road, rail, air or sea.

traffic calming The deliberate slowing of road traffic by the construction of obstacles, such as humps or chicanes, in the roadway.

traffic conference area An IATA classification of the world's major airline routes into three areas.
TCA 1 is North and South America
TCA 2 is Europe and Africa
TCA 3 is Asia and Australasia

traffic document The official IATA term for a passenger ticket or similar document. Traffic documents may be issued manually, mechanically or electronically and include any of the following:
Carriers' own traffic documents - passenger ticket and baggage check forms; automated ticket/boarding passes; miscellaneous charges orders; multiple purpose documents; agents refund vouchers and on-line tickets supplied by members to accredited agents for issue to their customers and Standard traffic documents - billing and settlement plan passenger ticket and baggage check forms; standard off-premise automated ticket/boarding passes; standard miscellaneous charges orders; neutral multiple purpose documents; BSP agent refund vouchers and other accountable forms supplied to accredited agents for issue under the billing and settlement plan.

traffic evaporation When new roads are built to ease congestion, their very existence attracts extra traffic, thus creating as much congestion as they were intended to save. It has been found that the closure of road has the opposite effect with drivers switching permanently to alternative methods of travel. This phenomenon has been dubbed traffic evaporation.

traffic rights Usually applicable to air travel, but can apply to any form of transport. In a journey between two points, A and B, a carrier may travel via one or more intermediate points, say C and D. The carrier will have the right to carry passengers between A and B, but not necessarily between A and C or C and D. *See also freedoms of the air.*

trail 1. A path created for use. Leisure uses include walking, horse-riding, cycling, etc.
2. (US). A ski run or marked route for snowmobiles.

trailer 1. An unpowered vehicle drawn by a powered vehicle.
2. (US). A caravan.

train A collection of vehicles linked together. Generally only used for rail travel where trains of a kilometre in length are not unknown.

train ferry A ferry designed to carry railway vehicles across water.

train operating company One of the companies operating rail services in the UK.

tram (UK). Abbreviation for tramcar.

tramcar A vehicle that uses a tramway.

tramp steamer A cargo vessel that travels from point to point on an ad hoc basis, as determined by the demands for cargo.

tramway 1. (UK). A light railway, often running along the roads and penetrating into the very heart of towns.
2. (US). An alternative name for a cable car.

transaction fees *See management fees.*

transatlantic Across the Atlantic.

transcontinental Across a continent.

transfer The transport provided for passengers between their point of arrival and their accommodation.

transferable Capable of being transferred. In travel, a ticket or document that can be passed on to another, which is not usual.

transit Used for determining one's position at sea, a transit is a line joining two fixed objects such as "lining up" a church spire in the foreground with another feature in the distance.

transit lounge A room at an airport for transit passengers.

transit passenger A passenger who has disembarked at an intermediate point, usually to change services, and who will be continuing on a connecting service. In many countries, transit passengers do not need to undertake immigration and customs clearance provided they stay in a designated transit area.

transit visa A visa issued to someone who is simply travelling through a country and not remaining for any significant period.

transocean Across an ocean.

T

transom Vertical strong point, forming the rear of a boat, onto which an outboard motor may be attached.

transpacific Across the Pacific.

transport The actual movement of passengers or goods. Along with accommodation and entertainment, one of the three main elements of travel and tourism. Transport or transportation is usually categorised as surface, sea or air.

transportainment A new portmanteau word to describe "themed transport". That is, vehicles designed to carry visitors around an attraction that are built in character with the attraction itself. The term first appeared in connection with the new Silver Springs attraction in Maryland, USA.

transportation order An IATA term meaning an agent's own order form authorised by an IATA member for use by the agent, against which the member issues its ticket.

trans-ship To transfer from one form of transport to another.

travel agent *See business travel agent, retail travel agent, leisure travel agent.*

travel bureau Another name for a travel agent, less commonly used nowadays.

travel clerk *See travel consultant.*

travel consultant The name usually given to those working in a travel agency and dealing directly with customers.

travel counsellor *See travel consultant.*

travel industry Tourism is not travel; travel is part of the overall business of tourism and the travel industry exists to serve people's travel requirements.

travel insurance Although travel is not considered hazardous, there are certain risks which travellers may incur which they would not be exposed to were they at home. For this reason, all prudent travellers effect insurance and indeed, many travel companies will not deal with persons who refuse to take out insurance. It is usually a criminal offence under the terms of the EC Package Travel legislation for travel agents not to advise their customers about insurance.

travel sickness Nausea caused by motion while travelling.

traveller In reality, an all-embracing term for someone who goes from one place to another. However, some consider the term more appropriate to those (such as "new tourists") who travel independently and reserve the term tourist for those who use pre-arranged facilities.

travellers cheques A form of money that is more secure than cash. The principle of the travellers cheque is that it is purchased for a specific value and then signed by the purchaser. When it is accepted by a vendor of goods or services, the purchaser signs it again and the signature match proves validity.

travolator A level or inclined moving walkway, without the steps used on an escalator.

trek A special interest holiday that will involve walking or another active method of travel, usually to less developed areas

tributary A river or stream flowing into a larger river or lake.

trike An abbreviation for tricycle. *See also cycle.*

trilingual The ability to speak three languages.

trimaran A three-hulled catamaran.

trip Another name for a journey, originally one taken for pleasure. These days a distinction is often made by qualifying the word by preceding it with a descriptor. E.g. business trip or pleasure trip.

triplane An aeroplane with three pairs of wings. The configuration is no longer used.

triple A room suitable for three people.

triple chair A chair lift designed to carry three people.

tripper A person on a trip, usually for pleasure.

triptyque A term of French origin that describes a customs permit allowing passage of a motor vehicle.

trishaw A three-wheeled rickshaw.

trolley 1. A bus propelled by electricity, drawing its current from an overhead wire.
2. (US). A tramcar.

tropical storm A severe storm, but not as fierce as a hurricane or cyclone.

tropics Those areas of the world situated between the tropics of Cancer at 23° 30" north and Capricorn at 23° 30" south.

true north North according to the earth's axis, not as indicated by a magnetic compass. *See poles.*

true south South according to the earth's axis, not as indicated by a magnetic compass. *See poles.*

TS The Tourism Society. *See Appendix 7a.*

tsunami A tidal wave, usually caused by an earthquake.

TTA Travel Trust Association Ltd. *See Appendix 7a.*

tube The name given to the underground railway network in London and some other parts of the UK.

tubing A popular modern version of tobogganing that involves sliding down a slope, or specially prepared run in a "tubing park", on an inflated lorry inner tube.

tug 1. A small, powerful boat used to tow ships into and out of their moorings.
2. A small, heavy tractor used to move aircraft around an airport.

tugboat *See tug (1).*

tuk-tuk A small three-wheeled scooter taxi, common in India and Thailand.

tundra A large, treeless arctic region, usually having a marshy surface with underlying permafrost.

turboprop 1. A jet engine designed to drive a propeller rather then rely solely on jet thrust.
2. An aircraft equipped with turbo-prop engines.

turbulence The violent movement of air. This can cause an aircraft to shake, sometimes violently, which is why airlines recommend that passengers keep their seat belts fastened at all times during a flight.

turnaround The time allowed or taken to prepare a vehicle, following its arrival, for its next journey.

turnpike (US) A toll road.

turnstile A special form of gateway that will admit only one person at a time. Turnstiles allow control of access and exit and can be designed to provide additional functions such as cash collection and usage counts.

Turquoise Coast Coastal resort region of southern Turkey. The main town is Antalya, other resorts include Alanya and Side.

TURSAB Association of Turkish Travel Agencies. *See Appendix 7c.*

tuxedo (US). *See dinner jacket.*

twelve hour clock Although the travel industry thoughout most of the world now uses the 24 hour clock, there are still some countries, most importantly the USA, where the 12 hour clock is still used. In this system times before 1200 are referred to as a.m. and times after, when the hour is reset to zero, are referred to as p.m. Thus 1300 hours is known as 1.00 p.m.

twenty-four hour clock With the main exception of the USA, the travel industry uses the twenty-four hour clock. In this system, times between midnight and noon are counted from 0000 to 1200 (no dots or hyphens should be used) and times thereafter from 1201 to 2359.

twenty-four hour delegate rate *See daily delegate rate.*

twin A hotel room with two beds

Twin Cities The two cities of Minneapolis and St Paul situated either side of the Missouri river, USA.

twin double Another name for a double double room.

twin screw A description of a vessel having two propellers, one on each side of its keel.

twin-set An aqualung with two diving cylinders.

twister (US). A familiar expression for a tornado.

typhoid An infectious bacterial fever endemic in many countries, usually spread by contaminated food or water.

typhoon A violent tropical storm. The Pacific region's equivalent to an Atlantic hurricane.

T

U
u

UAE United Arab Emirates.

UATP *See universal air travel plan.*

uberrimæ fidei An insurance term meaning "of utmost good faith". In insurance contracts, the uberrimæ fidei principle imparts an obligation on persons buying insurance to reveal every material fact within their knowledge concerning the desired policy. A claim can be refused should it come to light that an insured person had not acted in good faith and had failed to reveal a fact known when the insurance was effected. A good example would be the failure to reveal a pre-existing medical condition.

UK *See United Kingdom.*

Ulster The geographical region comprising the six counties of Northern Ireland and the counties of Cavan, Donegal and Monaghan.

ultima thule A far-away, unknown region.

UM An airline code used to indicate Unaccompanied Minor.

umiak An Eskimo open boat, traditionally made from skins stretched over a wooden frame.

UMTS *See universal mobile telecommunications system.*

UN *See United Nations.*

unaccompanied minor An underage traveller taking a trip on his or her own. Special facilities are provided for these passengers.

uncharted An area that has not been explored or mapped.

unchecked baggage *See hand baggage.*

under canvas A colloquial term for accommodation in tents.

under way In motion. Typically used to refer to a ship moving under its own power.

undercarriage The wheels and associated mechanisms of an aircraft.

undercart A familiar term for undercarriage.

underdeveloped A country or region that has not yet reached its potential level of economic development.

underground 1. Below ground. **2.** (UK). An underground railway.

underground railway A railway that has a significant part of its route below ground. Commonly used in large towns and cities.

underpass A road or railway that

passes under another by means of a short tunnel.

undertow When the current below the surface of a stretch of water flows in an opposite direction from that on the surface. This is especially dangerous to swimmers from a beach when the undertow is away from the land.

UNESCO *See United Nations Educational, Scientific and Cultural Organisation.*

UNICEF United Nations Children's Fund.

unicycle A cycle with only one wheel.

Union flag The United Kingdom's national flag. Often referred to, incorrectly, as the Union Jack, which name it only takes when flying from a jackstaff.

Union Jack *See Union flag.*

Union of Soviet Socialist Republics The state that was the Soviet Union. Now divided into several independent states.

unique selling point (Or proposition). A selling point that is unequalled by other providers. It is usually better for suppliers of travel services to try to create a USP rather than to compete on price.

United Kingdom A geographical entity comprising England, Scotland, Wales and Northern Ireland.

United Nations An international gathering of countries established to promote world-wide peace and security. Although nearly every state in the world is a member (only Kiribati, Nauru, Switzerland, Taiwan, Tonga, Tuvalu and the Vatican City are not), many UN interventions have had limited success.

United Nations Educational, Scientific and Cultural Organisation A specialised agency of the UN. Its purpose is to contribute to peace and security by promoting collaboration amongst nations by education, science and culture. UNESCO also promotes heritage sites world-wide.

United States of America Comprising the 50 states plus Puerto Rico, the US Virgin Islands, Guam and certain other Pacific Islands. Not the same as America, or the Americas, which is the name for the entire continent of North and South America.

universal air travel plan (UATP) The credit card scheme operated by IATA.

universal mobile telecommunications system A proposed new high-capacity system that will allow the genuinely universal use of portable telephones.

unlade To unload a ship.

unladen A vehicle without passengers or cargo.

U

unlimited mileage A car rental tariff where the hirer has paid a set amount to cover a duration of hire and where no extra amount is payable whatever the distance travelled.

unmapped *See uncharted.*

UNO United Nations Organisation. *See*

United Nations.

unpressurised When applied to aircraft refers to an aircraft without a pressurised cabin. Usually only found on smaller aircraft that fly at relatively low altitudes or in less developed countries where older aircraft are still in service.

unpretentious Simple or unaffected. Often used to describe accommodation of a modest standard.

UNPROFOR United Nations Protection Force.

unpublished fare A fare that is not advertised in tariffs, etc. Often an air fare made available through a consolidator.

UNRWA United Nations Relief and Works Agency.

unscheduled Not in the advertised schedule. Often used to describe a stop on a journey that has become necessary through abnormal operational circumstances.

unsurfaced Of a road, etc. Not having a proper surface suitable for vehicles.

up-anchor *See weigh anchor.*

UPAV Union Professionelle des Agences de Voyages. *See Appendix 7c.*

up-country Toward the interior of a country.

upgrade A term (usually, but not exclusively used by airlines) which means the switching of a passenger to accommodation in a higher class than that originally paid for. *See also complimentary upgrade.*

uplift capacity The number of skiers a lift, or the total numbers of lifts in a resort, can carry up a slope in one hour.

upmarket Of a holiday or other travel arrangement, towards or relating to the more expensive.

upper works That part of a ship that is above water when it is fully laden.

upscale (US). *See upmarket.*

uptown (US). The residential or more sophisticated part of a town or city.

urban 1. Living or situated in a city. **2.** Of, or relating to, a town or city.

urban tourism Tourism concentrated in urban areas.

US 1. The USA. **2.** (UK). Unserviceable.

USA *See United States of America.*

useful load The load that can be carried by a vehicle in addition to its own weight.

user friendly Any system or procedure that is supposed to be easy to use. Many systems that claim to be user friendly are the very reverse.

USP *See Unique Selling Point.*

USSR *See Union of Soviet Socialist Republics.*

USTI United States Tourism Industries. *See Appendix 7b.*

USTS United States Travel Service. *See Appendix 7b.*

USTTA United States Travel and Tourism Administration. *See Appendix 7b.*

UT Universal Time. The new official term for the time standard presently called Greenwich Mean Time. *See also Greenwich Mean Time.*

UTC Universal Time Coordinate. *See Universal Time.*

Utopia An imaginary perfect place or situation.

V

vacancy Availability of space or accommodation.

vacate To leave accommodation.

vacation (US). A holiday.

vaccination The process of introducing a vaccine into a person's body.

vaccine A protective substance made from the organisms that cause a particular disease. It will stimulate the production of antibodies in humans and thus afford them protection from that disease.

validation The official term for making a ticket good for travel, usually by stamping or imprinting. A validation stamp will contain, at least, the name of the issuing office and the date of issue of the document

validator A machine for endorsing an agency's name and other details on documents.

validity An indication as to whether a document is good for use. The most common use of the term refers to the dates between which the document can be used - its period of validity.

valley A long and often narrow depression in the land, usually between two ranges of hills or mountains. Many valleys have a river running along the bottom.

Valley of the Sun The valley in which Phoenix, Arizona is situated, together with most of its major suburbs including Mesa and Scottsdale. One of the fastest-growing parts of the Sunbelt.

Valsalva manoeuvre Technical term for equalising the pressure inside the ear-drum with that on the outside. Achieved by holding the nose firmly closed and then trying to breathe out through it, until the ears are felt to gently "pop." The technique is typically used by divers but all will find it useful when travelling by air, especially during descent.

van 1. An enclosed vehicle designed for the conveyance of goods.
2. (UK). The railway carriage provided for the use of the guard and the conveyance of luggage.

vaporetto A small motor boat, especially one used on the canals of Venice.

vapour trail *See contrail.*

VDU *See Visual Display Unit.*

vehicle Any machine designed for the transport of passengers or goods.

veld Also *veldt.* A South African term for open country or grassland.

Venice of... Suzhou in China has long been known as the "Venice of the East" due to its many canals. For the same reason Manchester, UK is nicknamed the "Venice of the North" and Fort Lauderdale, Florida, is nicknamed "Venice of America".

venue Any place where people have agreed to meet or to set something up.

verandah (Also veranda). A raised platform, sometimes roofed, along the side of a house.

verify To check the accuracy of something.

vertical drop The difference in height between the top of the top lift in a resort and the bottom of the lowest lift. This is one of the most important indicators as to how much skiing is likely to be available in an area.

vertical integration The terminology used to describe the ownership, by one organisation, of both the means of production and the means of distribution of a commodity. In travel, for example, the same organisation could own an airline, a tour operator and a travel agency.

vertical take off and landing Of an aircraft that can take off vertically, for example, a helicopter

very important person The endorsement VIP is made on a booking to indicate the superior status of the traveller. Such status is usually reserved for public figures. *See also CIP.*

vessel In travel, a waterborne vehicle.

vestibule 1. A hall or ante-chamber. 2. (US). An enclosed entrance to a railway carriage.

VFR *See visiting friends and relatives.*

via An expression derived from the Latin for road that now simply means "by way of".

viaduct A bridge, often constructed of a number of short spans, that conveys a road or railway across a valley.

vicinity The local area.

victoria A low, light four-wheeled horse-drawn carriage with a collapsible top.

view That which can be seen from a particular point. Usually expected to be attractive.

viewdata A computerised information and booking service, generally using dial-up lines. Now being replaced by more sophisticated systems such as CRS.

Viking One of the Scandinavian seafaring traders and/or pirates who were active in north-east Europe during the 8th to 11th centuries.

villa Self catering accommodation, usually in a private, detached house or bungalow. The name originally applied to prestigious houses (or villas) privately owned, and rented to selected guests. Now however, a villa could be in a specially built complex containing many similar properties

village A group of houses and other buildings, larger than a hamlet and smaller than a town.

VIP *See very important person.*

visa An authority, usually stamped into a passport, permitting travel to or via a country. Certain countries have restrictions on travel by their own

V

residents and in such cases an exit visa may be needed which will permit travel out of the country. Many countries charge substantial amounts for visa issue, realising that it is an easy way to raise revenue.

Visigoth A member of the branch of the Goths who settled in France and Spain during the 5th century, ruling Spain until the early 8th century.

visit 1. To go to a place for a short period.
2. (US). A chat.

visiting friends and relatives A term used to describe travellers whose main purpose for their journey is to visit friends or relatives who live abroad.

visitor One who is undertaking a visit.

visitor attraction *See attraction.*

visitor's book A register in which visitors to an attraction or similar record their names.

vista A long narrow view, especially between trees.

visual display unit A monitor or similar used to display computer data.

void An endorsement in the itinerary box of a ticket (usually air) that shows that the particular sector is not valid for use.

volcano A mountain formed through the expulsion of lava from the earth's interior. Volcanoes can be active, that is, still likely to erupt, dormant (inactive) and therefore unlikely to erupt, or extinct and very unlikely to erupt.

voltage The pressure of an electrical supply. In most of Europe the mains supply is delivered at between 220 and 250 volts. In most of the Americas it is delivered at 110 volts. Travellers must take care when using appliances in other countries since poor operation or damage can arise if suitable adjustment or adaptation is not made.

voluntary changes Changes to an itinerary that are made at a passenger's own request.

voucher A name for a document that may be exchanged for services such as meals or accommodation, in the same way that a ticket may be exchanged for travel. In many cases either name can be used, as for example in the case of meals where some companies refer to a meal voucher and others to a meal ticket

voyage A journey, especially one by sea.

voyager A person on a voyage.

VTOL *See Vertical Take Off and Landing.*

V

W pattern In order to maximise the use of an aircraft, airlines try to avoid ferry mileage and one way of doing this is the W pattern of operation. For example, an aircraft may take passengers from Gatwick to Palma, pick up passengers there and take them to Cardiff, pick up more passengers there and take them to Palma then pick up a further load and take them back to Gatwick. This type of intensive utilisation is more common with short haul charter operations than it is with long haul or scheduled services.

w.e.f. (UK). With Effect From.

w.p. *See working pressure.*

wadi A rocky watercourse, usually in Arabia, that is dry for most of the year.

Wagon-Lit A European sleeping car. Much more comfortable than a couchette but usually very expensive. Wagon Lits are not operated on UK railways, but UK rail sleepers are at least as good as most Wagon Lits.

waiter 1. (UK). A man employed to serve customers in a restaurant or similar establishment with food, drinks or other requirements.
2. (US). A person of either sex providing waiting services as described above.

waiting list (Or wait-list). When a facility is fully booked, most principals will maintain a waiting list of potential customers wanting to join. Once the waiting list reaches such a length that it is unlikely that all those on it will be accommodated, the principal will refuse to add further names and the waiting list is said to be "closed".

waiting room A room provided, especially at a railway or bus station, for passengers to stay while awaiting the arrival of their service.

wait-list *See waiting-list.*

waitress (UK). A woman employed for the same job as a waiter.

waive To refrain from insisting on, or using, a right.

waiver An act or instance of waiving. For example, if a damage waiver is paid to a car rental company, the company will not insist on its right to collect a charge if the car suffers damage.

wake The waves caused by the motion of a ship through water.

walking tour A holiday on foot, usually of several days.

walkway A passage or path, often a

W

raised passageway connecting parts of a building or similar.

wanderlust The desire to travel or explore.

warrant A document, often issued by the military or a government department, that can be exchanged for tickets or other travel documents.

Warsaw Convention An international agreement, reached in 1928, which limits the liability of airlines for loss or damage to passengers carried internationally. It has been considerably modified over the years, but most of its terms and conditions still apply.

wash-out A breach in a road or railway track caused by flooding.

washroom (US). A room with washing and lavatory facilities.

WATA World Association Of Travel Agents. *See Appendix 7d.*

watch A period of duty for a seaman, usually 4 hours. *See also dog watch.*

water bus A boat carrying passengers on a regular service on a river, lake, canal, etc. Usually the journeys will be relatively short.

water closet A lavatory with a means for flushing with water. Usually abbreviated to WC.

water park A recreational area where the facilities are mainly based on activities involving water.

water taxi A small boat, usually motor-driven, taking passengers on a casual basis. Commonly used in cities such as Venice.

watercourse A stream or artificial channel.

waterfall A stream or river flowing over a precipice. Waterfalls are often spectacular and are therefore significant tourist attractions. The ten largest waterfalls, in order of height, are:
- Angel
- Tugela
- Utigård
- Mongefossen
- Yosemite
- Østre Mardøla Fosse
- Tyssestrengane
- Kukkenaam
- Sutherland
- Kile

The Angel Falls are approximately 20 times the height of Niagara Falls.

waterfront The area adjacent to water, often a dock or harbour.

watering hole 1. A place at which animals regularly drink. Often a focal point for visitors to game reserves, etc. **2.** Colloquial. A bar or pub.

waterline The point on a ship's hull up to which the water reaches.

waterman A boatman plying for hire.

water-ski A sport whose participants are towed across a stretch of water, usually by a speedboat, with special skis attached to their feet.

waterspout An up-welling of water caused by a tornado.

watertight doors Heavy doors that, when closed, divide a ship into a series of separate compartments. This minimises the risk of sinking following damage to the hull that allows the entry of water.

waterway Any route used for travel by water, but usually applied to rivers and canals.

watt A measurement of power. In an electrical appliance it will be shown on the data plate. Dividing the power rating of the appliance by the voltage at which it is being operated will give an indication of the current that will be drawn.

wave The undulations in the sea, caused by wind. The distance between the crests of waves will vary according to the weather conditions and the body of water.

wave machine A devise for producing waves in a swimming pool.

way station (US). A minor railway station.

waybill A list of passengers or goods on a vehicle.

wayside The edge of a road or other land route.

WC A universal term for a lavatory or toilet. *See water closet.*

weather The day to day variations of temperature, rainfall, humidity, etc. Unlike climate, which indicates the overall situation of a region, weather can be variable and unpredictable. The UK is an example of a region with a mild and temperate climate but with very unpredictable weather.

week Officially a period of seven days reckoned from Saturday night. In travel it usually means a period of seven days from the start of a provided facility.

weekday A day other than at the weekend.

weekend The days at the end of the normal working week when many businesses are shut. In most of Europe and the USA it falls on Saturday and Sunday, but Moslem and Jewish countries observe different closing days.

weigh anchor To raise the anchor of a ship prior to sailing.

weir A small dam built across a river to raise its level or regulate its flow.

well-appointed Of accommodation, etc. Having all the expected fixtures and fitments, etc.

well-travelled A person who has travelled a great deal.

West Indies The islands enclosing the Caribbean Sea including the groups: Bahama Islands, Greater Antilles, Lesser Antilles.

Westerlies The winds that blow from mainly west to east, between latitudes 30° and 70°. In the northern hemisphere their prevailing direction is from the south-west; in the southern hemisphere it is from the north-west.

Western civilisation Started around AD 675 and still flourishes.

western hemisphere The half of the earth that contains the Americas.

wet lease To hire a vehicle, usually a ship, boat or aircraft, with all its crew and supplies.

wet suit Protective rubber suit worn by divers that allows water to enter the suit before being largely retained in place. The layer of water thus formed provides an extra layer of insulation.

wetland A marsh, bog or similar area.

wharf A structure projecting into water to which vessels can be moored.

wherry **1.** A light rowing boat. **2.** (UK). A large, light barge.

whirlpool A powerful circular eddy in water.

whirlwind A tornado.

whirlybird A familiar term for a helicopter.

whistle stop **1.** (US). A small, unimportant railway station. **2.** A very fast tour or journey with few and brief stops.

white ensign The flag of the British Royal Navy and the Royal Yacht Squadron.

white night A night in extremely high latitudes when it never gets properly dark.

white out A condition, often caused by blizzard conditions, where it is impossible to see anything except white snow in the air and on the ground.

white tie A name given to the very formal mode of evening dress for men that involves the wearing of a tail coat and white bow tie.

white-water rafting An extreme sport involving taking a raft or similar vessel through a stretch of very rough water, often rapids on a river.

wholesaler In commerce, an organisation that buys in bulk from a manufacturer to sell to retailers. In travel, this is usually a tour operator.

wide-bodied aircraft An aircraft with two or more aisles that carries larger numbers of passengers than conventional types. The Boeing 747 is probably the best known example.

Wild Coast Scenic coastal area between East London and Port Shepstone in South Africa.

Wild West The western USA during its historical period of lawlessness.

wilderness A wild or undeveloped region.

wildlife attraction Any attraction, such as a wildlife park, where animals, birds or other fauna are on view to visitors.

wildlife park Sometimes known as a safari park. A place where exotic animals are kept in a semi-wild state in conditions that allow them to be viewed by visitors.

wind chill Fierce, cold winds can often make the temperature seem colder by many degrees. The amount by which they do this is known as the wind chill factor.

wind force The force of the wind as measured by the Beaufort scale. *See Beaufort scale.*

wind shear A sudden downward rush of air, often experienced in storm conditions. Wind shear has caused several aircraft accidents.

windbound When a sailing vessel is unable to operate because of contrary winds.

windjammer A merchant sailing vessel.

windward On the side from which the wind is blowing.

W

Windward Islands The group of Caribbean islands including Grenada, Martinique, St Lucia, St. Vincent and the Grenadines.

wine bar A bar or small restaurant serving drink and food.

wine waiter In larger restaurants the wine and other beverages may be served by a special waiter who is involved only with this duty.

wings The large projections from the fuselage of an aircraft that create the lift that support it during flight.

wingspan The measurement across the wings or an aircraft.

winter sports Sports performed on snow and ice, such as skating, sledging, skiing, etc.

wipe out 1. A familiar term given by winter sports enthusiasts to a crash or fall from a snowboard or skis. **2.** A similar accident from a surfboard.

withdrawal of services insurance A "loss of enjoyment" insurance cover paid when a pre-arranged service or facility was not provided, regardless of any financial loss.

workday (US). A day on which work is usually done.

working pressure The maximum pressure to which a diving cylinder should be normally charged for everyday use.

World Heritage Site Those sites designated by UNESCO as being of special historical, cultural or natural importance.

World Travel Market The most important travel exhibition in the world, held at Earl's Court, London, in November each year. Attendance is restricted to persons connected with the Travel Industry.

Worldspan A GDS owned by Delta and other airlines.

Worldwide Fund for Nature One of the world's largest private nature conservation organisations. Its aim is to conserve the natural environment by preserving species and ecosystem diversity.

WP Word processor

write out To issue a document manually.

WTB Wales Tourist Board. *See Appendix 7a.*

WTM *See World Travel Market.*

WTO World Tourism Organisation. *See Appendix 7d.*

WWF *See Worldwide Fund for Nature.*

W

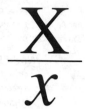

xebec A small, three-masted Mediterranean sailing vessel.

xenophobe One who distrusts foreigners.

xenophobia Fear or distrust of foreigners.

x-rays Short wave radiation that can pass through many solid materials. X-rays are sometimes used for baggage screening at airports and other sensitive places. Since they can affect photographic film, travellers should ask for their baggage to be hand-searched if they are in any doubt as to the photographic safety of the screening equipment.

X

Y
y

yacht **1.** A small sailing vessel used for pleasure.
2. A large motor vessel used by very wealthy or titled individuals, including royalty.

yard **1.** A measure of length equal to 0.9144 metres.
2. A nautical expression meaning a spar slung across a mast to hold a sail.
3. (UK). An enclosed piece of ground at the back of a house.
4. (US). The garden of a house.

yaw Of a ship or aircraft. To fail to hold a straight course; veering from side to side.

yawl A two-masted sailing vessel.

yellow fever A tropical disease caused by a virus and difficult to cure. Travellers should ensure that they are vaccinated before visiting endemic zones.

yellow flag A flag displayed by a vessel in quarantine.

yellow line (UK). A line painted at the edge of a road to indicate that parking restrictions exist.

YHA Youth Hostels Association. *See Appendix 7a.*

yield The income resulting from the control and allocation of space, as provided at various price levels.

Yield Improvement Plan IATA's most recent attempt to regularise air ticket sales so that travellers pay the "official" price, rather than the heavily discounted fares sold by bucket shops. It has had little success, since most governments seem firmly wedded to the idea of "free market forces". In fact, although under the UK Civil Aviation Act of 1971, it is illegal for airlines to sell ticket at prices lower than those agreed with the CAA, no airline has ever been prosecuted for this common offence

yield management The control of the way in which space is used on aircraft and other means of transport. Typically a carrier will adjust the ratio of accommodation available at various rates so as to maximise the load factor and revenue of a service.

YIP *See Yield Improvement Plan.*

youth A young person, generally aged between the early teens and early twenties.

youth fare A fare offered to people up to the age of approximately 25 years.

Y

youth hostel An inexpensive form of accommodation originally restricted to young people. Most youth hostels will now accept travellers of any age.

Youth Training Scheme (UK). A government sponsored training scheme intended to ensure that all young people have access to vocational training.

YTS *See Youth Training Scheme.*

Y

Z
z

zenith The highest point, often used to describe a period of prosperity, etc.

zephyr A soft, gentle breeze.

Zeppelin A pioneering German manufacturer of airships, whose name is still sometimes used as a generic term for this type of aircraft. The first regular airline service was operated by Zeppelins.

zero emission vehicle A vehicle that produces no emissions at the point of operation. Presently the only successful ZEV's are electrically or cable operated although experiments are ongoing. One current line of investigation is the use of compressed air as a fuel.

ZEV *See zero emission vehicle.*

zócalo A Mexican term for the main square and focal point of a town.

zone An area or region having particular properties that make it special or identifiable.

zoo An abbreviation for zoological garden or park and now a place where visitors can see animals in captivity and other attractions. Many zoos are now finding a new role in the conservation and preservation of endangered species.

zorbing An extreme sport invented in New Zealand in 1996 that involves being lashed into a large plastic ball that is then rolled down a steep hill. Participants are, apparently, usually uninjured by the experience.

Z

APPENDIX 1

Nationalities & Languages

Please note:

1. The inclusion or omission of a country, state, territory or language has no political or other significance.

2. Where no name is shown, this is simply because research has failed to find a commonly accepted term.

3. Apart from the principal languages listed, many countries have a large number of other local languages and dialects, often several hundred.

4. For more information on states and territories generally, and languages in particular, consult the relevant pages of your Columbus Press *World Travel Guide*.

Name of Country
The name generally used to describe citizens of that country
Main languages spoken

A

Abu Dhabi.
See United Arab Emirates

Afghanistan
Afghan
Dari, Pashtó

Ajman
See United Arab Emirates

Albania
Albanian
Albanian, Greek

Algeria
Algerian
Arabic, French

American Samoa
Samoan
Samoan, English

Andorra
Andorran
Catalan, French, Spanish

Angola
Angolan
Portuguese

Anguilla
Anguillan
English

Antigua and Barbuda
Antiguan
English

Argentina
Argentine or Argentinian
Spanish

Armenia
Armenian
Armenian, Russian

Aruba
Aruban
Dutch, Papiamento, English, Spanish

Australia
Australian
English

Austria
Austrian
German

Azerbajan
Azerbajani
Azerbajani, Russian

B

Bahamas
Bahamanian
English

Bahrain
Bahraini
Arabic, English

Bangladesh
Bangladeshi
Bengali

Barbados
Barbadian
English

Barbuda
Barbudan
English

Belarus
Russian

Belgium
Belgian
Flemish, French

Belize
Belizian
English, Spanish

Benin
Beninese
French

Bermuda
Bermudan or Bermudian
English

Bhutan
Bhutanese
Dzongkha

Bolivia
Bolivian
Spanish

Bonaire
Dutch, Papiamento

Bosnia-Herzegovina
Bosnian
Serbo-Croat and Croato-Serb

Botswana
Tswana
English, Setswana

Brazil
Brazilian
Portuguese

British Virgin Islands
English

Brunei Darussalom
Bruneian
Malay, English

Bulgaria
Bulgarian
Bulgarian

Burkina Faso
Burkinese
French, Moré, Dioula, Peulh

Burma
See Myanmar

Burundi
Burundian
Kirundi, French

C

Cambodia
Cambodian
Khmer, Chinese, Vietnamese

Cameroon
Cameroonian
French, English

Canada
Canadian
English, French, Inuktitut

Cape Verde Republic
Cape Verdean
Portuguese, Creole, English

Cayman Islands
Cayman Islander
English

Central African Republic
French, Sangho

Chad
Chadian
Arabic, French, Sara

Chile
Chilean
Spanish

China, People's Republic
Chinese
Mandarin, Cantonese

Colombia
Colombian
Spanish

Comoro Islands
Comoran
French, Arabic

Congo
Congolese
French, Lingala, Kilcongo

Congo, Dem Rep
Congolese
French, Lingala, Kilcongo

Cook Islands
Cook Islander
Cook Islands Maori, English

Costa Rica
Costa Rican
Spanish

Côte d'Ivoire
French

Croatia
Croatian
Croatian (Croato-Serb)

Cuba
Cuban
Spanish

Curaçao
Dutch, Papiamento

Cyprus
Cypriot
Greek, Turkish, English

Czech Republic
Czech
Czech

D

Denmark
Dane
Danish, English

Djibouti
Djiboutian
Arabic, French, Afar, Somali

Dominica
Dominican
English, Creole

Dominican Republic
Dominican
Spanish

Dubai
See United Arab Emirates

E

Ecuador
Ecuadorian
Spanish

Egypt
Egyptian
Arabic, English, French

El Salvador
Salvadorean
Spanish

England
Englishman, Englishwoman
English

Equatorial Guinea
Equatorial Guinean
Spanish, Fang, Bubi

Eritrea
Eritrean
Arabic, Tigrinya, Italian

Estonia
Estonian
Estonian, Russian, English

Ethiopia
Ethiopean
Amharic, English

F

Falkland Islands
Falkland Islander
English

Fiji
Fijian
Fijian, Hindi

Finland
Finn
Finish, English

France
Frenchman, Frenchwomen
French

French Guiana (Guyane)
French, Creole

Fujairah
See United Arab Emirates

G

Gabon
Gabonese
French, Fang

Gambia, The
English

Georgia
Georgian
Georgian, Russian

Germany
German
German

Ghana
Ghanaian
English

Gibraltar
Gibraltarian
English, Spanish

Great Britain
Briton
English

Greece
Greek
Greek

Greenland
Greenlander
Greenlandic, Inuit, Danish

Grenada
Grenadian
English

Guadeloupe
Guadeloupian
French, Creole

Guam
Guamanian
English, Chamorro

Guatemala
Guatemalan
Spanish

Guernsey
English, Norman-French dialect

Guinea Republic
French, Susu, Malinké, Fula

Guinea-Bissau
Portuguese, Guinean Creole

Guyana
Guyanese
English

H

Haiti
Haitian
French, Creole

Honduras
Honduran
Spanish, English

Hungary
Hungarian
Hungarian

I

Iceland
Icelander
Icelandic, Danish, English

India
Indian
English plus 14 other official languages

Indonesia
Indonesian
Bahasa Indonesian (Malay)

Iran
Iranian
Persian (Farsi), Arabic

Iraq
Iraqi
Arabic, Kurdish

Ireland
Irishman, Irishwoman
English, Gaelic

Isle of Man
Manxman, Manxwoman
English, Manx Gaelic

Israel
Israeli
Hebrew, Arabic, English

Italy
Italian
Italian

J

Jamaica
Jamaican
English

Japan
Japanese
Japanese

Jersey
Jerseyman
English, Norman-French dialect

Jordan
Jordanian
Arabic, English

K

Kazakhstan
Kazakh

Kenya
Kenyan
Kiswahili, English

Kiribati
Kiribati, English

Korea, Democratic People's Republic
Korean
Korean

Korea, Republic
Korean
Korean

Kuwait
Kuwaiti
Arabic, English

Kyrgyzstan
Kyrgyz
Kyrgyz, Russian

L

Lao, Democratic People's Republic
Laotian
Lao, French, Vietnamese

Latvia
Latvian
Latvian, Russian

Lebanon
Lebanese
Arabic, French, English

Lesotho
Mosotho, pl. Basotho
Sesotho, English

Liberia
Liberian
English, Bassa, Kpelle, Kru

Libya
Libyan
Arabic

Liechtenstein
Liechtensteiner
German, Alemmanish

Lithuania
Lithuanian
Lithuanian, Russian

Luxembourg
Luxemburger
French, German, Letzeburgesch

M

Macau
Portuguese, Cantonese

Macedonia
Macedonian
Macedonian

Madagascar
Malagasy or Madagascan
Malagasy, French

Malawi
Malawian
English, Chichewa

Malaysia
Malaysian
Bahasa Malay

Maldives
Maldivian
Dhiveli

Mali
Malian
French

Malta
Maltese
Maltese, English

Martinique
French, Creole

Mauritania
Mauritanian
Arabic, French

Mauritius
Mauritian
English, Creole, Hindi, Bojpuri

Mexico
Mexican
Spanish, English

Moldova
Moldavian
Moldavian (Romanian), Russian

Monaco
Monégasque or Monacan
French, Monégasque

Mongolia
Mongolian
Mongolian Khalkha

Monserrat
English

Morocco
Moroccan
Arabic, Berber, French

Mozambique
Mozambican
Portuguese

Myanmar (formally Burma)
Burmese
Burmese

N

Namibia
Namibian
English

Nauru
Nauruan
Nauruan, English

Nepal
Nepalese
Nepali, Maithir, Bhojpuri

Netherlands
Dutchman or Dutchwoman or
Netherlander
Dutch

New Caledonia
French, Polynesian, Melanesian

New Zealand
New Zealander
English, Maori

Nicaragua
Nicaraguan
Spanish

Niger, Republic of
Nigerian
French, Hausa

Nigeria
Nigerian
English

Niue
Niuean, English

Northern Ireland
Ulsterman, Irishman or Irishwoman
English

Norway
Norwegian
*Norwegian (Bokmål and Nynorsk),
Lappish*

O

Oman
Omani
Arabic, English

P

Pakistan
Pakistani
Urdu, English

Panama
Panamanian
Spanish, English

Papua New Guinea
Papua New Guinean or Papuan
English, Pidgin English, Hiri Motu

Paraguay
Paraguayan
Spanish, Guaraní

Peru
Peruvian
Spanish, Quechua

Phillippines
Filipino, Filipina
Filipino (Tagalog), English

Poland
Pole
Polish

Portugal
Portuguese
Portuguese

Puerto Rico
Puerto Rican
Spanish, English

Q

Qatar
Qatari
Arabic

R

Ras al Khaimah
See United Arab Emirates

Réunion
French, Creole

Romania
Romanian
Romanian

Russian Federation
Russian
Russian

Rwanda
Rwandan
Kinyardwanda, French, Kiswahili

S

Saba
Dutch, English

Samoa
Samoan
Samoan, English

San Marino
Italian

São Tomé e Príncipe
Portuguese, Fôrro, Agolares

Saudi Arabia
Saudi Arabian or Saudi
Arabic

Scotland
Scot, Scotsman, Scotswoman
English, Scots Gaelic

Senegal
Senegalese
French, Wolof

Seychelles
Seychellois
Creole, English, French

Sharjah
See United Arab Emirates

Sierra Leone
Sierra Leonean
French, Krio

Singapore
Singaporean
Mandarin, English, Malay, Tamil

Slovak Republic
Slovakian
Slovak

Slovenia
Slovenian
Slovene

Solomon Islands
Solomon Islander
English, Pidgin English

Somalia
Somali
Somali, Arabic

South Africa
South African
English, Afrikaans

Spain
Spaniard
Spanish, Catalan, Galician, Basque

Sri Lanka
Sri Lankan
Sinhala, Tamil, English

St Eustatius
English, Papiamento

St Kitts and Nevis
English

St Lucia
St. Lucian
English, French patois

St Maarten/St. Martin
Dutch, English, Papiamento, French

St Pierre et Miquelon
French, English

St Vincent and the Grenadines
Vincentian
English

Sudan
Sudanese
Arabic

Suriname
Surinamer or Surinamese
Dutch, Sranan Tongo (Creole)

Swaziland
Swazi
English, Siswati

Sweden
Swede
Swedish, Lapp, English

Switzerland
Swiss
German, French, Italian

Syria
Syrian
Arabic, French, English

T

Tahiti
Tahitian
Tahitian, French

Taiwan
Taiwanese
Mandarin

Tajikistan
Tajik, Russian

Tanzania
Tanzanian
Swahili, English

Thailand
Thai
*Thai, English, Malay, Chinese
(Tachew)*

Togo
Togolese
French, Ewe, Watchi, Kabiyé

Tonga
Tongan
Tongan, English

Trinidad and Tobago
Trinidadian and Tobagan or
Tobagonian
English

Tunisia
Tunisian
Arabic, French

Turkey
Turk
Turkish

Turkmenistan
Turkoman
Turkmen

Turks and Caicos Islands
English

Tuvalu
Tuvaluan
Tuvaluan, English

U

Uganda
Ugandan
English, Luganda, Kiswahili

Ukraine
Ukrainian
Ukrainian

Umm al Qaiwain
See United Arab Emirates

United Arab Emirates
Arabic

United Kingdom
See under separate countries

United States of America
American
English, Spanish

Uruguay
Uruguayan
Spanish

US Virgin Islands
Virgin Islander
English, Spanish, Creole

Uzbekistan
Uzbek
Uzbek

V

Vanutu
Bislama (Pidgin English)

Vatican City
Italian

Venuezuela
Venezuelan
Spanish

Vietnam
Vietnamese
Vientnamese, English, French

W

Wales
Welshman, Welshwoman
English, Welsh

Y

Yemen
Yemeni
Arabic

Yugoslavia
Yugoslav
Serbo-Croat

Z

Zambia
Zambian
English

Zimbabwe
Zimbabwean
English, Shona, Ndebele

APPENDIX 2

Countries

The list below gives selected information on all the world's independent states. Many of these have dependencies, overseas possessions, colonies and the like, and apart from a few common-sense exceptions (such as Réunion and Gibraltar) these have not been included. The matter of defining what is and what is not a state is by no means clear-cut, but no political or other subjective stance has been adopted. For further information on states and territories worldwide, please consult the relevant pages of your *World Travel Guide* and *World Travel Atlas*.

Some **Country** names have been shortened for reasons of space. **Visitor Arrivals (VAs)** for 1989 and 1998 are expressed in 000s and have been supplied by the World Tourism Organisation. A country whose entry for 1989 is marked • did not in that year exist in its present form, or did not exist at all. In a few cases VA figures are not available. The **Rank** figure grades each country by 1998 arrivals. Although every country has an **International Dialing Code (IDC)**, calls to some parts of some countries may still need to be placed through the international operator. The **Currency Codes (CC)** are those specified by the International Standards Organisation, although other abbreviations for certain currencies are also in common use.

* Arrival figures for China include Hong Kong for both 1989 and 1998. The IDC 852 is still used for calls to Hong Kong.

Country	VAs'89	VAs'98	Rank	IDC	CC	Country	VAs'89	VAs'98	Rank	IDC	CC
Afghanistan	8	4	202	93	AFA	Belize	70	140	143	501	BZD
Albania	14	20	188	355	ALL	Benin	75	152	141	229	XOF
Algeria	1,207	648	83	213	DZD	Bermuda	418	372	109	1 441	BMD
Am. Samoa	26	21	187	684	USD	Bhutan	1	5	200	975	BTN
Andorra	n/a	n/a	–	376	ESP	Bolivia	194	387	102	591	BOB
Angola	40	50	175	244	AOR	Bonaire	34	63	168	599	ANG
Anguilla	29	45	177	1 264	XCD	Bosnia-H'vina	•	100	152	387	BAM
Antigua & B.	189	230	130	1 268	XCD	Botswana	448	740	78	267	BWP
Argentina	2,492	4,859	27	54	ARS	Brazil	1,403	3,135	38	55	BRL
Armenia	•	35	180	374	AMD	Brit. Virgin Is.	176	250	127	1809 49	USD
Aruba	344	651	82	297	AWG	Brunei	393	800	76	673	BND
Australia	2,080	4,012	32	61	AUD	Bulgaria	1,521	2,630	41	359	BGL
Austria	18,202	17,282	10	43	OMR	Burkina Faso	80	140	143	226	XOF
Azerbaijan	•	170	138	994	AZM	Burundi	82	12	195	257	BIF
Bahamas	1,575	1,590	58	1 242	BSD	Cambodia	20	220	131	855	KHR
Bahrain	1,342	1,922	51	973	BHD	Cameroon	87	135	145	237	KMF
Bangladesh	128	163	139	880	BDT	Canada	15,111	18,659	9	1	CAD
Barbados	461	477	93	1 246	BBD	Cape Verde	19	52	173	238	CVE
Belarus	•	260	124	375	BYB	Cayman Is.	210	382	103	1 345	KYD
Belgium	4,991	6,152	22	32	BEF	Cent. Af. Rep.	5	20	188	236	XOF

Country	VAs'89	VAs'98	Rank	IDC	CC	Country	VAs'89	VAs'98	Rank	IDC	CC
Chad	12	8	198	235	XOF	Haiti	122	150	142	509	HTG
Chile	797	1,595	57	56	CLP	Honduras	176	303	119	504	HNL
China*	15,346	33,600	5	86	CNY	Hungary	14,490	14,660	14	36	HUF
Colombia	733	1,600	55	57	COP	Iceland	131	205	133	354	ISK
Comoros	13	27	184	269	KMF	India	1,736	2,398	44	91	INR
Congo	33	44	179	242	CDF	Indonesia	1,626	4,900	26	62	IDR
Congo, DR	51	32	183	243	ZRZ	Iran	89	900	68	98	IRR
Cook Is.	33	45	177	682	NZD	Iraq	1,025	340	112	964	IQD
Costa Rica	376	825	73	506	CRC	Ireland	3,484	6,073	23	353	IEP
Côte d'Ivoire	192	302	120	225	XOF	Israel	1,177	1,950	50	972	ILS
Croatia	•	4,200	30	385	HRK	Italy	25,935	34,829	4	39	ITL
Cuba	315	1,200	63	53	CUP	Jamaica	829	1,230	62	1 876	JMD
Curacao	204	195	134	5 999	ANG	Japan	2,835	4,100	31	81	JPY
Cyprus	1,378	2,235	47	357	CYP	Jordan	639	1,260	61	962	JOD
Czech Rep	7,079	16,325	12	420	CZK	Kazakstan	•	n/a	–	7	TEN
Denmark	1,688	2,480	43	45	DKK	Kenya	735	1,062	65	254	KES
Djibouti	41	20	188	253	DJF	Kiribati	3	4	202	686	AUD
Dominica	37	60	171	1 809	XCD	Korea DPR	97	130	148	850	KPW
Dominican Rep.	1,219	2,362	45	1 809	DOP	Korea Rep.	2,728	4,251	29	82	KRW
Ecuador	335	544	88	593	ECS	Kuwait	89	35	180	965	KWD
Egypt	2,351	3,766	33	20	EGP	Kyrgyzstan	•	13	194	996	KGS
El Salvador	131	530	89	503	SVC	Laos	25	260	124	856	LAK
Eritrea	•	414	100	291	ERN	Latvia	•	242	128	371	LVL
Estonia	•	759	77	372	EEK	Lebanon	n/a	659	81	961	LBP
Ethiopia	77	121	149	251	ETB	Lesotho	169	115	150	266	LSL
Eq'ial Guinea	n/a	n/a	–	240	GQE	Liberia	n/a	n/a	–	231	LRD
Fiji	251	366	110	679	FJD	Libya	95	95	156	218	LYD
Finland	1,581	1,810	53	358	FIM	Liechenstein	77	61	170	41 75	CHF
Fr. Polynesia	140	190	137	689	XPF	Lithuania	•	1,062	65	370	LTL
France	49,549	70,000	1	33	FRF	Luxembourg	875	802	75	352	BEF
Gabon	112	192	136	241	XOF	Macau	2,304	3,590	35	853	MOP
Gambia	85	87	158	220	GMD	Macedonia	•	153	140	389	MKD
Georgia	•	330	114	995	GEL	Madagascar	39	133	146	261	MGF
Germany	16,115	16,504	11	49	DEM	Malawi	117	215	132	265	MWK
Ghana	125	335	113	233	GHC	Malaysia	4,846	6,856	20	60	MYR
Gibraltar	162	73	164	350	GIP	Maldives	158	403	101	960	MVR
Greece	8,082	11,077	16	30	GRD	Mali	32	85	160	223	XOF
Grenada	66	112	151	1 809	XCD	Malta	828	1,175	64	356	MTL
Guadeloupe	284	697	79	590	FRF	Marshall Is.	4	6	199	692	USD
Guam	669	1,406	60	671	USD	Martinique	312	510	90	596	FRF
Guatemala	437	500	92	502	GTQ	Mauritania	n/a	n/a	–	222	MRO
Guinea	49	99	153	224	GNF	Mauritius	263	570	87	230	MUR
Guinea-Bissau	n/a	n/a	–	245	GWP	Mexico	14,962	19,300	7	52	MXN
Guyana	67	60	171	592	GYD	Moldova	•	20	188	373	MDL

APPENDIX 2

Country	VAs'89	VAs'98	Rank	IDC	CC	Country	VAs'89	VAs'98	Rank	IDC	CC
Monaco	245	267	123	377	FRF	Solomon Is.	10	16	193	677	SBD
Mongolia	237	86	159	976	MNT	Somalia	40	10	196	252	SOS
Montserrat	17	5	200	1 664	XCD	South Africa	930	5,981	24	27	ZAR
Morocco	3,468	3,241	37	212	MAD	Spain	32,477	47,743	2	34	ESP
Mozambique	n/a	n/a	–	258	MZM	Sri Lanka	185	382	103	94	LKR
Myanmar	14	194	135	95	MMK	St Eustatius	16	24	186	599	ANG
N. Mariana Is.	326	660	80	670	USD	St Kitts & Nevis	72	85	160	1 869	XCD
Namibia	•	510	90	264	NAD	St Lucia	133	253	126	1 758	XCD
Nauru	n/a	n/a	–	674	AUD	St Maarten	489	435	97	5995	ANG
Nepal	240	435	97	977	NPR	St Vincent & Gren.	50	75	163	1 809	XCD
Netherlands	5,206	6,170	21	31	NLG	Sudan	23	34	182	249	SDP
New Caledonia	82	99	153	687	XPF	Suriname	38	62	169	597	SRG
New Zealand	901	1,450	59	64	NZD	Swaziland	248	325	115	268	SZL
Nicaragua	77	382	103	505	NIO	Sweden	2,113	2,508	42	46	SEK
Niger	24	18	192	227	XOF	Switzerland	12,600	11,025	17	41	CHF
Nigeria	161	640	84	234	NGN	Syria	411	891	70	963	SYP
Niue	1	2	204	683	NZD	Taiwan	2,004	2,253	46	886	TWD
Norway	1,867	2,697	40	47	NOK	Tajikistan	n/a	n/a	–	7	TJR
Oman	136	612	86	968	OMR	Tanzania	138	447	95	255	TZS
Pakistan	495	381	107	92	PKR	Thailand	4,810	7,720	19	66	THB
Palau	•	64	167	680	USD	Togo	115	96	155	228	XOF
Panama	192	439	96	507	PAB	Tonga	21	27	184	676	TOP
Papua N. Guinea	49	69	166	675	PGK	Trinidad & Tob.	190	325	115	1 868	TTD
Paraguay	279	360	111	595	PYG	Tunisia	3,222	4,700	28	216	TND
Peru	334	815	74	51	PEN	Turkey	3,921	9,200	18	90	TRL
Philippines	1,190	2,167	48	63	PHP	Turkmenistan	•	304	118	993	TMM
Poland	3,293	18,820	8	48	PLZ	Turks & Caicos	48	93	157	1 649	USD
Portugal	7,116	11,800	15	351	PTE	Tuvalu	1	1	207	688	AUD
Puerto Rico	2,444	3,255	36	1 787	USD	UAE	629	1,811	52	971	AED
Qatar	110	451	94	974	QAR	Uganda	41	238	129	256	UGX
Reunion	182	377	108	262	FRF	UK	17,338	25,475	6	44	GBP
Romania	1,857	3,075	39	40	ROL	Ukraine	•	850	71	380	UAH
Russian Fed	•	15,810	13	7	RUB	Uruguay	1,240	2,163	49	598	UYU
Rwanda	19	2	204	250	RWF	US Virgin Is.	450	415	99	1 340	USD
Saba	24	10	196	599	ANG	USA	36,365	47,127	3	1	USD
Samoa	54	71	165	685	WST	Uzbekistan	•	270	122	7	UZS
San Marino	437	632	85	378	ITL	Vanuatu	23	51	174	678	VUV
São Tomé	4	2	204	239	STD	Vatican City	n/a	n/a	–	39	ITL
Saudi Arabia	1,677	3,700	34	966	SAR	Venezuela	412	834	72	58	VEB
Senegal	259	309	117	221	XOF	Vietnam	215	1,630	54	84	VND
Seychelles	86	131	147	248	SCR	Yemen	65	81	162	967	YER
Sierra Leone	86	50	175	232	SLL	Yugoslavia	•	279	121	381	YUM
Singapore	4,397	5,600	25	65	SGD	Zambia	113	382	103	260	ZMK
Slovakia	957	900	68	421	SKK	Zimbabwe	474	1,600	55	263	ZWD
Slovenia	•	971	67	386	SIT						

APPENDIX 3
USA States

ISO* Name
Admission to the Union, State capital
State nickname

AK Alaska
3rd Jan 1959, Juneau
The Last Frontier

AL Alabama
14th Dec 1819, Montgomery
Heart of Dixie

AR Arkansas
15th June 1836, Little Rock
Land of Opportunity

AZ Arizona
14th Feb 1912, Phoenix
Grand Canyon State

CA California
9th Sept 1850, Sacramento
Golden State

CO Colorado
1st Aug 1876, Denver
Centennial State

CT Connecticut
9th Jan 1788[†], Hartford
Constitution State / Nutmeg State

DC District of Columbia
*(Federal District, coextensive with
the city of Washington)*

DE Delaware
7th Dec 1787[†], Dover
First State / Diamond State

FL Florida
3rd Mar 1845, Tallahassee
Sunshine State

GA Georgia
2nd Jan 1788[†], Atlanta
Empire State of the South / Peach State

HI Hawaii
21st Aug 1959, Honolulu
Aloha State

IA Iowa
28th Dec 1846, Des Moines
Hawkeye State

ID Idaho
3rd July 1890, Boise
Gem State

IL Illinois
3rd Dec 1818, Springfield
Prairie State

IN Indiana
11th Dec 1816, Indianapolis
Hoosier State

KS Kansas
29th Jan 1861, Topeka
Sunflower State

KY Kentucky
1st June 1792, Frankfort
Bluegrass State

LA Louisiana
30th Apr 1812, Baton Rouge
Pelican State

APPENDIX 3

MA Massachusetts
6th Feb 1788[†], Boston
Bay State

MD Maryland
28th Apr 1788[†], Annapolis
Old Line State

ME Maine
15th Mar 1820, Augusta
Pine Tree State

MI Michigan
26th Jan 1837, Lansing
Great Lakes State / Wolverine State

MN Minnesota
11th May 1858, St Paul
Gopher State / North Star State

MO Missouri
10th Aug 1821, Jefferson City
Show Me State

MS Mississippi
10th Dec 1817, Jackson
Magnolia State

MT Montana
8th Nov 1889, Helena
Treasure State

NC North Carolina
21st Nov 1789[†], Raleigh
Old North State / Tar Heel State

ND North Dakota
2nd Nov 1889, Bismarck
Flickertale State

NE Nebraska
1st Mar 1867, Lincoln
Cornhusker State

NH New Hampshire
21st June 1788[†], Concord
Granite State

NJ New Jersey
18th Dec 1787[†], Trenton
Garden State

NM New Mexico
6th Jan 1912, Santa Fe
Land of Enchantment

NV Nevada
31st Oct 1864, Carson City
Silver State

NY New York
26th July 1788[†], Albany
Empire State

OH Ohio
1st Mar 1803, Columbus
Buckeye State

OK Oklahoma
16th Nov 1907, Oklahoma City
Sooner State

OR Oregon
14th Feb 1859, Salem
Beaver State

PA Pennsylvania
12th Dec 1787[†], Harrisburg
Keystone State

RI Rhode Island
29th May 1790[†], Providence
Ocean State / Little Rhody

SC South Carolina
23rd May 1788[†], Columbia
Palmetto State

SD South Dakota
2nd Nov 1889, Pierre
Mount Rushmore State

TN Tennessee
1st June 1796, Nashville
Volunteer State

TX Texas
29th Dec 1845, Austin
Lone Star State

UT Utah
4th Jan 1896, Salt Lake City
Beehive State

VA Virginia
25th June 1788[†], Richmond
Old Dominion

VT Vermont
4th Mar 1791, Montpelier
Green Mountain State

WA Washington
11th Nov 1889, Olympia
Evergreen State

WI Wisconsin
29th May 1848, Madison
Badger State

WV West Virginia
20th June 1863, Charleston
Mountain State

WY Wyoming
10th July 1890, Cheyenne
Cowboy State / Equality State

* International Standards Organization abbreviation.

† Original thirteen states: date of ratification of the Constitution.

APPENDIX 4

Canadian Provinces & Territories

ISO*Name
Entry to the Dominion, Province/
territory capital
Language**

AL Alberta
1st Sept 1905, Edmonton
English

BC British Columbia
20th July 1871, Victoria
English

MN Manitoba
15th July 1870, Winnipeg
English

NB New Brunswick
1st July 1867, Fredericton
English [†]

NF Newfoundland and Labrador
31st March 1949, St John's
English

NS Nova Scotia
1st July 1867, Halifax
English

NT Northwest Territories
1870, Yellowknife
English

NU Nunavut (territory)
1st April 1999, Iqaluit
Inuktitut [††]

OT Ontario
1st July 1867, Toronto
English

PE Prince Edward Island
1st July 1873, Charlottetown
English

QU Québec
1st July 1867, Québec
French

SA Saskatchewan
1st Sept 1905, Regina
English

YT Yukon Territory
13th June 1898, Whitehorse
English

*   International Standards
      Organization abbreviation.

**   Although Canada is officially
      bilingual (English & French), this
      line indicates the most commonly-
      spoken language in each region.

†   Approx. 35% of the population are
     French-speaking.

††   The language of the Inuit.

APPENDIX 5

Australian States & Provinces

ISO*Name
Date of Granting of responsible
gov't, State/territory capital
Nickname

AC Australian Capital Territory
1911**, Canberra
Nation's Capital

CL Coral Sea Territory
*(External Territory bordering the
Queensland coast and Gt. Barrier
Reef)*

NS New South Wales
1788†, Sydney
Premier State

NT Northern Territory
1911††, Darwin
Outback Australia

QL Queensland
1859, Brisbane
Sunshine State

SA South Australia
1856, Adelaide
Festival State

TS Tasmania
1856, Hobart
Holiday Isle

VI Victoria
1855, Melbourne
Garden State

WA Western Australia
1890, Perth
State of Excitement

* International Standards
Organization abbreviation.

** Canberra became the seat of the
Australian government on 9th May
1927.

† Date of first settlement: New South
Wales originally covered the whole
island with the exception of
Western Australia.

†† Transferred to Commonwealth
from South Australia in 1911, self-
government within the
Commonwealth granted 1978.

APPENDIX 6A

Tourist Attractions
Alphabetical listing by attraction name

Abu Simbel
Lake Nasser, southern Egypt
Site of the two temples of Rameses II, relocated when Lake Nasser was formed.

Adam's Peak
Southern Sri Lanka
Holy mountain whose summit bears an indentation resembling a giant footprint.

Alcatraz Island
San Francisco, California, USA
Island in San Francisco Bay, famous for its prison, now a museum.

Alcazar, Seville
Seville, Andalucia, Spain
12th century Moorish royal palace-fortress.

Alfama
Lisbon, Portugal
Old Moorish quarter.

Alhambra
Granada, Andalucia, Spain
Fortress/palace of Moorish kings, surrounded by the Generalife Gardens.

Alton Towers
Staffordshire, England
Theme park with rides and gardens.

Amber Palace
Jaipur, Rajasthan, India
Fortress, traditionally reached on elephant-back.

Angel Falls
Canaima National Park, eastern Venezuela
Highest waterfall in the world, on the Churum River.

Anne Frank's House
Amsterdam, Netherlands
Home of the World War II diarist.

Anuradhapura
Anuradhapura, central/northern Sri Lanka
Archaeological site of ancient capital city dating back to the 5th century BC.

Arc de Triomphe
Paris, France
Triumphal Arch celebrating the victories of Napoleon and inscribed with the French national anthem.

Auschwitz
Near Krakow, Poland
World War II concentration camp.

Ayers Rock
Central Australia
see Uluru

Badshahi Mosque
Lahore, Pakistan
One of the largest mosques in the world.

Banaue rice terraces
Luzon, Philippines
Ancient terraces cut into the mountain sides for rice cultivation.

Batu Caves
North of Kuala Lumpur, Malaysia
Natural caves housing the Hindu shrine of Lord Subranamiam, reached by 272 steps.

Bay of Islands
Northland, North Island, New Zealand
Sub-tropical area of beaches and islands.

Bellver Castle
Majorca, Balearic Islands
14th century circular Gothic castle overlooking Palma.

Ben Nevis
Near Fort William, Scotland
The highest mountain in the United Kingdom.

Blackpool Pleasure Beach
Blackpool, England
Pleasure park with rides and amusements.

Blarney Castle
County Cork, Ireland
15th century castle containing the 'Blarney Stone' which, when kissed, is supposed to impart the gift of eloquence.

Blue Grotto
Southwest Malta
Caves known for their beautiful colours.

Bodnath Stupa
Kathmandu, Nepal
Buddhist memorial shrine, of particular significance to Tibetans.

Bolshoi Theatre
Moscow, Russia
Opulent opera and ballet theatre.

Boracay Island
The Visayas island group, Philippines
Considered to have one of the best beaches in the world.

Brandenburg Gate
Berlin, Germany
Famous archway, marking the former border between West and East Berlin.

Bridge over the River Kwai
Kanchanaburi, west of Bangkok, Thailand
Railway bridge replacing the famous bridge constructed by prisoners during World War II.

Broadway
New York, USA
Central commercial and theatre district of New York City.

Bruges
Belgium
Medieval city with canals, bridges and many beautiful buildings including the Town Hall, Belfry and Cathedral of the Holy Saviour.

Buckingham Palace
London, England
London residence of Her Majesty The Queen and scene of the 'Changing of the Guard' ceremony.

Caernarfon Castle
Caernarfon, Wales
13th century castle, scene of the Prince of Wales' investiture.

Calgary Stampede
Calgary, Alberta, Canada
Event held annually in July, with rodeo and chuckwaggon races re-creating the atmosphere of the 'Wild West'.

Cambridge, England
Cambridge, England
University city with many fine buildings and churches.

Canterbury Cathedral
Canterbury, England
Cathedral dating back to the 11th century, the seat of the Primate of the Church of England.

Cape of Good Hope
South of Cape Town, Cape Province, South Africa
Meeting point of the Atlantic and Indian Oceans at the southern tip of the Cape Peninsula.

Capitol, Washington DC
Washington DC, USA
Seat of the U.S. Congress since 1800, built on Capitol Hill.

Carthage
Near Tunis, Tunisia
Site of a great ancient city founded by the legendary Queen Dido.

Caves of Drach
Porto Cristo, Majorca, Balearic Islands
Illuminated caves with footpaths and lakes including Lake Martell.

Champs-Élysées
Paris, France
Elegant tree-lined street, famous for its pavement cafés.

Chartres Cathedral
Southwest of Paris, France
Gothic cathedral dating from the late 12th century, famous for its stained-glass windows.

Chichen Itza
Yucatan Peninsula, Mexico
Mayan archaeological site, including the El Castillo pyramid.

Church of the Nativity
Bethlehem, Israel
Church marking the traditional birthplace of Jesus Christ.

CN Tower
Toronto, Ontario, Canada
A communications and observations tower, one of the tallest free-standing structures in the world.

Colosseum
Rome, Italy
Amphitheatre built in the 1st century AD, in which staged fights were held.

Copacabana Beach
Rio de Janeiro, Brazil
Fashionable beach facing the Atlantic Ocean.

Corrida
Pamplona, Navarra, Spain
Bull-running events held annually at the Festival of San Fermin in July.

Dambulla
Dambulla, central Sri Lanka
Rock temple made up of four large caves.

Dead Sea
Border between Israel and Jordan
Lowest point on the earth's surface, the water having a high mineral content with curative properties and giving great buoyancy when bathing.

Death Valley
California, USA
Arid and barren area, much of which is below sea level; extremely hot in summer.

Delphi
Northwest of Athens, Greece
Site of the oracle of the god Apollo, now an archaeological site

including the Temple of Apollo (4th century BC).

Disneyland Paris
East of Paris, France
Theme park with rides, Disney characters and resort complex.

Disneyland, California
Near Los Angeles, California, USA
Theme park with rides and attractions based on Walt Disney characters.

Doge's Palace
Venice, Italy
Italian Gothic ducal palace famous for its Bridge of Sighs.

Dome of the Rock
Jerusalem, Israel
Muslim shrine built over the rock where Muslims believe Mohammed rose to heaven.

Drottningholm Castle
Near Stockholm, Sweden
Palace visited by boat, containing a 17th century theatre.

Dunn's River Falls
Ocho Rios, Jamaica
Series of waterfalls which can be climbed.

Durbar Square
Kathmandu, Nepal
Square surrounded by Buddhist and Hindu temples and the old Royal Palace.

Easter Island
Pacific Ocean, to the west of mainland Chile
Belonging to Chile, famous for its 'Moai' (giant stone statues) and 'Ahus' (burial platforms).

Edinburgh Castle
Edinburgh, Scotland
Castle dating from the 11th

century, sited on high cliffs overlooking the city.

Efteling
Southwest Netherlands
Theme park with rides and attractions based on cartoon characters.

Egyptian Museum
Cairo, Egypt
Best known for its treasures from the tomb of Tutankhamun.

Eiffel Tower
Paris, France
An observation tower built of iron in 1889 for the World Fair, named after its designer.

Empire State Building
New York, USA
Famous skyscraper offering panoramic views of the city.

Ephesus
South of Izmir, Turkey
Archaeological site of a former city, with well-preserved streets and theatre.

Everglades
Florida, USA
Wilderness area of marshland, including Everglades National Park.

Fez medina
Fez (also spelt Fes), Morocco
One of the largest medinas (markets) in the world, in the oldest of Morocco's 'imperial cities'.

Floating Market, Bangkok
Bangkok, Thailand
Colourful market where fruit and vegetables etc. are sold from boats.

Floating restaurants of Aberdeen
Aberdeen, Hong Kong Island, Hong Kong

Popular restaurants moored at the harbour-side.

Fontainebleau Château
Southeast of Paris, France
Palatial home of various French rulers including Napoleon.

Forum
Rome, Italy
Roman meeting place and centre of religion and commerce.

Frogner Park
Oslo, Norway
Park containing unusual sculptures by Gustav Vigeland.

Futuroscope
Near Poitiers, western France
Theme park with various attractions based on the 'moving image'.

Galapagos Islands
On the Equator in the Pacific Ocean, to the west of Ecuador
Islands belonging to Ecuador, famous for their unique animal life and once visited by Charles Darwin.

Garden Route
Cape Province, South Africa
Scenic coastal route between Port Elizabeth and Swellendam, known for its spring flowers.

Giant's Causeway
Antrim, Northern Ireland
Area of unusual polygonal basalt columns, on the Antrim coast.

Giralda Tower
Seville, Andalucia, Spain
Bell-tower dating from the Middle Ages, originally a minaret for a mosque.

Golden Gate Bridge
San Francisco, California, USA
Famous suspension bridge across San Francisco Bay.

Golden Roof
Innsbruck, Austria
Copper roof over a balcony, once part of a 15th century castle.

Graceland
Memphis, Tennessee, USA
Home of the singer Elvis Presley.

Grand'Place
Brussels, Belgium
Cobbled square in the centre of Brussels, surrounded by magnificent buildings including the Town Hall and Maison du Roi.

Grand Canyon
Arizona, USA
Long and deep canyon excavated by the Colorado River, of scenic beauty and geological interest.

Grand Palace, Bangkok
Bangkok, Thailand
18th century palace containing the Wat Phra Kaeo (Temple of the Emerald Buddha).

Great Barrier Reef
Coral Sea, off the coast of Queensland, Australia
A chain of coral reefs stretching approximately 2000 km (1240 miles), containing unique plant and animal life.

Great Mosque, Cordoba
Cordoba, Andalucia, Spain
8th century mosque, now a cathedral, built on the site of a Roman temple.

Great Wall of China
Northern China
Defensive wall over 2000 years old, the longest man-made structure in the world.

Great Zimbabwe
Near Masvingo, Zimbabwe
Archaeological site of former city-state which traded in gold.

Gripsholm Castle
West of Stockholm, Sweden
Castle housing Sweden's National Portrait Gallery.

Gullfoss
Near Geysir, Iceland
A waterfall, literally 'the golden waterfall'.

Hassan Tower
Rabat, Morocco
12th century minaret of a vast, uncompleted mosque.

Hermitage
St Petersburg, Russia
Art gallery within the beautiful Baroque Winter Palace.

Hiroshima Peace Memorial Park
Hiroshima, Honshu, Japan
Park containing a museum and various memorials relating to the devastation caused by the 1945 atomic bomb.

Hollywood
Los Angeles, California, USA
Traditional centre of the U.S. film industry.

Holyroodhouse
Edinburgh, Scotland
Literally the Palace of Holyroodhouse, a royal residence, once the home of Mary Queen of Scots.

Houses of Parliament, London
London, England
Home of the British government (House of Commons and House of Lords), and including the clock tower known as Big Ben.

Iguaçu Falls
(also spelt Iguassu or Iguazu)
Straddling the border between Brazil, Argentina and Paraguay
Wide and spectacular waterfalls on the River Iguaçu, a tributary of the Parana.

Imperial Palace, Beijing
Beijing, China
Within the Forbidden City and dating from the 15th century, once the home of 24 of China's Emperors.

Independence Hall, Philadelphia
Philadelphia, Pennsylvania, USA
Scene of the signing of the U.S. Declaration of Independence in 1776, now a museum.

Jama Masjid
Delhi, India
Great Mosque, the largest in India.

Jeronimos Monastery
Lisbon, Portugal
15th century monastery with ornate architecture.

Jungfrau
Near Interlaken, Switzerland
Mountain in the Bernese Oberland.

Kapellbrucke
Lucerne, Switzerland
14th century wooden Chapel Bridge.

Keukenhof Gardens
Near Haarlem, Netherlands.
Gardens famous for their displays of spring flowers, especially tulips.

Kilimanjaro
Northeast Tanzania
Snow-capped mountain, the highest in Africa.

Knossos
Near Heraklion, Crete, Greece
Archaeological site of a Minoan city,

dating back to 1700 BC, legendary home of the Minotaur.

Kon-Tiki Museum
Oslo, Norway
Exhibits depicting the expeditions of Thor Heyerdahl.

Kremlin
Moscow, Russia
Russian citadel, the most famous being in Moscow and containing the Kremlin Palace, government buildings and cathedrals.

La Scala
Milan, Italy
Literally Teatro della Scala. World-famous opera house.

Lake Balaton
Western Hungary
Lake with sandy beaches and watersports facilities.

Lake Taupo
North Island, New Zealand
Lake with beautiful scenery and watersports.

Lake Tekapo
South Island, New Zealand.
Lake in the foothills of the Southern Alps.

Lake Titicaca
Southeast Peru
Thought to be the highest navigable lake in the world, famous for its floating reed islands.

Las Vegas
Nevada, USA
City renowned for its shows and casinos.

Leaning Tower of Pisa
Pisa, Italy
Bell tower or 'campanile', completed in the 14th century.

Legoland, Denmark
Billund, Denmark
Theme park with rides and brick-built model buildings.

Legoland, Windsor
Windsor, England
Theme park with rides and brick-built model buildings.

Little Mermaid
Copenhagen, Denmark
Statue of one of Hans Christian Andersen's fairy-tale characters, placed near the harbour entrance.

Louvre
Paris, France
National art gallery, part of which was once a palace.

Macchu Picchu
Near Cuzco, Peru
Ancient Inca settlement high up in the Andes mountains.

Madame Tussaud's, London
London, England
Exhibition of life-size wax figures of famous personalities.

Mandalay
Central Myanmar
Buddhist centre with many monasteries and pagodas.

Manneken-Pis
Brussels, Belgium
Irreverent statue of a small boy.

Matmata
South of Gabes, Tunisia
Desert town famous for its underground dwellings and mosque.

Matterhorn
Southwest Switzerland
Mountain in the Valais Alps.

Mdina
Near Rabat, Malta

A well-preserved example of a medieval walled city, the former capital of Malta.

Mecca
Saudi Arabia
Islamic holy city, the birthplace of Mohammed, forbidden to non-Muslims.

Medina
Saudi Arabia
The second-most holy Islamic city (after Mecca), forbidden to non-Muslims.

Meiji Shrine
Tokyo, Japan
Shrine built as a memorial to Emperor Meiji, set in extensive grounds.

Milford Sound
South Island, New Zealand
Scenic sea inlet in Fiordland National Park.

Mirabell Palace
Salzburg, Austria
Palace with formal flower gardens and statues.

Mohammed V Mausoleum
Rabat, Morocco
Burial place of Mohammed V and an outstanding example of traditional Moroccan architecture.

Mont Blanc
French Alps, southeast France
Highest point in the French Alps, straddling the border between France and Italy.

Mont-St-Michel
Normandy, France
Island separated from the mainland at high tide, containing the Abbey of St Michel.

Monte Carlo Casino
Monte Carlo, Monaco
Famous casino with gambling rooms, also housing the Grand Théâtre de Monte Carlo where opera and ballet are performed.

Montserrat Monastery
Northwest of Barcelona, Catalonia, Spain
Benedictine monastery housing the famous Black Madonna, a carved wooden statue.

Moscow State Circus
Moscow, Russia
Home of the world-famous circus.

Mount Cook
South Island, New Zealand
Mountain in the Southern Alps, the highest point in New Zealand.

Mount Everest
Northeast Nepal/border with Tibet
Highest mountain in the world, in the Himalaya range.

Mount Fuji
Southwest of Tokyo, Japan
Japan's highest mountain, a dormant volcano which can be ascended on foot in summer.

Mount Rushmore
South Dakota, USA
Mountainside rock carving depicting the busts of four U.S. presidents.

Munich Beer Festival
See Oktoberfest.

Neuschwanstein Castle
Near Schwangau, Bavaria, Germany
Fairy-tale-like castle of 'mad' King Ludwig II.

Ngorongoro Crater
Northern Tanzania

*Extinct volcanic crater renowned for its
abundance of wildlife.*

Niagara Falls
Ontario, Canada and New York State,
USA
*Waterfalls between Lakes Erie and
Ontario on the U.S./Canadian border,
consisting of the Canadian (or
Horseshoe) and American Falls.*

North Cape
Near Hammerfest, Norway
*Cliff-top viewpoint at the most
northerly point in Europe.*

Notre Dame
Paris, France
*12th century Gothic cathedral on
the Île de la Cité, an island in the
River Seine.*

Oberammergau
Southwest of Munich, Bavaria,
Germany
*Village famous for its Passion Play
held every ten years.*

Oktoberfest
Munich, Germany
*Beer festival held annually
for two weeks in September/October.*

Olympia
Western Peloponnese, Greece
*Site of the original Olympic Games,
with stadium and museums.*

Oxford, England
Oxford, England
*University city with many fine
buildings and churches.*

Pagan
Near Mandalay, Myanmar
*Archaeological area
containing many pagodas
and temples.*

Palace of the Winds
Jaipur, Rajasthan, India
*Palace known for its ornate facade,
glowing bright pink in the sun.*

Palma Cathedral
Palma, Majorca, Balearic Islands
*Gothic style cathedral begun in
the 13th century, with beautiful
rose windows.*

Pamukkale
Near Denizli, Turkey
*Area of calcified waterfalls with
thermal pools, site of ancient
Hierapolis.*

Pantheon
Rome, Italy
*Well-preserved temple, built by
the Emperor Hadrian in the 2nd
century AD.*

Parc Astérix
Northeast of Paris, France
*Theme park based on the cartoon
character Astérix,
with rides and shows.*

Parthenon
Athens, Greece
*5th century BC Temple of Athena
Parthenos on the Acropolis.*

Petra
Southwest Jordan
*Known as the 'rose-red city' because
of the colour of the rocks, out of
which magnificent facades were
carved in Roman times.*

Phang Nga Bay
Near Phuket, Thailand
*Bay with unusual limestone outcrops,
a 'James Bond' film location.*

Phantasialand
Between Cologne and Bonn,
Germany
Theme park with rides and

entertainment based on geographical themes.

Polonnaruwa
Polonnaruwa, central Sri Lanka
Archaeological site of 12th century capital, famous for its Buddha statues carved from the rock.

Pompidou Centre
Paris, France
Modern art gallery and exhibition centre.

Ponte Vecchio
Florence, Italy
14th century bridge across the River Arno, supporting houses and shops.

Port Aventura
Costa Dorada, Spain
Theme park with national themes from around the world.

Prado
Madrid, Spain
National Museum of Painting and Sculpture housing works from the Spanish royal collection.

Pushkin Museum of Fine Arts
Moscow, Russia
Gallery containing international works of art.

Pyramids
Giza and Sakkara (also spelt Saqqara) near Cairo, Egypt.
Ancient royal burial tombs, some almost 5000 years old.

Quaid-i-Azam's Mazar
Karachi, Pakistan
White marble mausoleum of the founder of Pakistan.

Quebrada divers
Acapulco, Mexico
Spectacular sight of divers plummeting from the vertical cliffs.

Raffles Hotel
Singapore
Famous hotel named after the colonial administrator and founder of Singapore, Sir Stamford Raffles.

Ramblas
Barcelona, Catalonia, Spain
Pedestrianised street stretching from the harbour to the Plaza de Catalunya.

Red Fort, Delhi
Delhi, India
17th century imperial palace enclosing a mosque and the Halls of Public and Private Audience.

Red Square
Moscow, Russia
Large square in central Moscow, alongside the Kremlin.

Rialto Bridge
Venice, Italy
16th century bridge over the Grand Canal, containing a double row of shops.

Rijksmuseum
Amsterdam, Netherlands
Art gallery containing famous Dutch and Flemish paintings.

Rock of Gibraltar
Gibraltar
Rocky outcrop famous for its Barbary Apes, overlooking the town of Gibraltar.

Rotorua
North Island, New Zealand
Thermal area with geysers and hot springs.

Royal Barges, Bangkok
Bangkok, Thailand
Exhibition of barges once used by the Thai royal family.

Royal Mile, Edinburgh
Edinburgh, Scotland
Famous street stretching from
Edinburgh Castle to the Palace of
Holyroodhouse.

Royal Pavilion, Brighton
Brighton, England
18th century former royal residence
with oriental-style architecture, now
a museum.

Sacré Coeur
Paris, France
Late 19th century basilica with
distinctive white domes.

Sagrada Familia
Barcelona, Catalonia, Spain
Church of the Holy Family, of
extraordinary design by the architect
Antonio Gaudí.

Sans-Souci Palace
Potsdam, Germany
Ornate palace and gardens, once the
home of Frederick the Great.

Schönbrunn Palace
Vienna, Austria
Sumptuous palace with park
containing the Vienna Zoo.

Sea World, Florida
Near Orlando, Florida, USA
One of the world's largest marine
theme parks.

Sentosa Island
Singapore
Pleasure resort with beaches,
entertainment and museums.

Serengeti Plain
Northern Tanzania
Area including the Serengeti National
Park and scene of the annual
wildebeest migration.

Seville Cathedral
Seville, Andalucia, Spain
Thought to be the largest Gothic
building in the world, built on the
site of a mosque.

Shah Faisal Masjid
Islamabad, Pakistan
Huge mosque capable of
accommodating 100,000 people.

Shakespeare's Birthplace
Stratford-upon-Avon, England
Birthplace of the playwright William
Shakespeare.

Shwe Dagon Pagoda
Yangon, Myanmar
Buddhist shrine thought to be 2500
years old.

Sigiriya
Sigiriya, central Sri Lanka
5th century rock fortress with
palace ruins and well-preserved
wall paintings.

Sistine Chapel
Vatican City, Rome, Italy
Chapel within the Papal Palace,
famous for its ceiling painted
by Michelangelo.

Skokloster
Northwest of Stockholm, Sweden
Baroque palace on Lake Malaren.

Spanish Riding School
Vienna, Austria
Dressage school with the famous white
Lippizaner horses, housed in part of
the Hofburg.

Spanish Steps
Rome, Italy
18th century flight of steps leading up
to the Trinità dei Monti church.

Sphinx
Giza near Cairo, Egypt

*Giant statue with a human head and
an animal's body, dating from
approximately 2500BC.*

St Basil's Cathedral
Moscow, Russia
*16th century cathedral with
unusual domes, commissioned by
Ivan the Terrible.*

St Gallen Cathedral
St Gallen, Switzerland
*Magnificent example of a Baroque
cathedral.*

St George's Castle
Lisbon, Portugal
*Castle with panoramic view
overlooking the city.*

St Isaac's Cathedral
St Petersburg, Russia
*Russian Orthodox Church with
large dome.*

St Mark's Square
Venice, Italy
*Square facing St Mark's Cathedral,
with Campanile (bell tower) and
pavement cafés.*

St Paul's Cathedral, London
London, England
*Cathedral designed by Sir
Christopher Wren in the late 17th
century, famous for its large dome.*

St Peter's Basilica
Vatican City, Rome, Italy
*Domed cathedral built between the
15th and 17th centuries, regarded
as the centre of the Roman Catholic
church world-wide, facing St Peter's
Square.*

St Peter and Paul Fortress
St Petersburg, Russia
*One of the city's oldest buildings,
formerly a prison and now a museum.*

St Sophia, Istanbul
Istanbul, Turkey
*6th century church, later to become a
mosque and now a museum.*

Stanley Market
Hong Kong Island, Hong Kong
Market of street stalls.

Statue of Christ the Redeemer
Rio de Janeiro, Brazil
*Large statue on Corcovado Mountain
overlooking the city of Rio de Janeiro,
commemorating Brazil's
independence.*

Statue of Liberty
New York, USA
*Colossal statue (a gift from France)
commemorating the centenary of the
USA's independence.*

Stonehenge
North of Salisbury, England
*Stone Age ritual monument of
massive stones arranged in a
circular pattern, dating back to
about 3000 BC.*

Sugarloaf Mountain
Rio de Janeiro, Brazil
*Granite mountain overlooking
Guanabara Bay.*

Suleimaniye Mosque
Istanbul, Turkey
*16th century mosque with many
domes.*

Sydney Harbour Bridge
Sydney, New South Wales, Australia
*A single-arch steel bridge spanning
Port Jackson.*

Sydney Opera House
Sydney, New South Wales, Australia
*A building of distinctive design
overlooking Sydney Harbour, used
for concerts, opera, ballet and
theatre productions.*

Table Mountain
Cape Town, South Africa
Flat-topped mountain overlooking the city of Cape Town.

Taj Mahal
Agra, Uttar Pradesh, India
Mausoleum made of white marble, built in the 17th century by Shah Jehan as a monument to his wife.

Teide
Tenerife, Canary Islands
Volcanic mountain, the highest point on Tenerife, also called Pico de Tenerife or Pico del Teide.

Temple of the Tooth
Kandy, central Sri Lanka
Temple containing the sacred relic of the Buddha.

Temple Street Night Market
Kowloon, Hong Kong
Market of street stalls, open at night.

Teotihuacan
Northeast of Mexico City, Mexico
Archaeological site known as the 'City of the Gods', containing the remains of a temple, palace and pyramids dating back 2000 years.

Terracotta Warriors
Xi'an, China
Also known as the 'Terracotta Army'. Over 6000 life-size images of warriors and horses buried in the Tomb of Emperor Qin Shi Huangdi.

Tivoli Gardens
Copenhagen, Denmark
An area of flower gardens, restaurants and an amusement park.

Topkapi Palace
Istanbul, Turkey
Former residence of the Ottoman sultans, overlooking the Bosphorus.

Tower Bridge
London, England
Famous London bridge whose central section can be raised to allow the passage of ships.

Tower of London
London, England
11th century Norman fortress, once used as a prison and royal residence.

Trafalgar Square
London, England
Central square containing Nelson's Column and surrounded by notable buildings such as the National Gallery.

Trevi Fountain
Rome, Italy
Baroque fountain with statues. Throwing a coin into the fountain is believed to ensure the visitor's return.

Trinity College, Dublin
Dublin, Ireland
Part of the University of Dublin, housing the famous 'Book of Kells'.

Uffizi Gallery
Florence, Italy
Art gallery housed in the 16th century Palazzo degli Uffizi.

Uluru
Northern Territory, Australia
Also known as Ayers Rock. Thought to be the world's biggest monolith (single rock mass), with Aboriginal cave paintings. Uluru National Park also includes Kata Tjutu (the Olgas), a group of rock domes.

Uxmal
Yucatan Peninsula, Mexico
Mayan archaeological site with fine stonework.

Vallée de Mai
Praslin, Seychelles
Nature reserve containing the unusual coco-de-mer (sea coconut).

Valley of the Kings & Valley of the Queens
Near Luxor, Egypt
Ancient tombs dating from the 16th century BC on the west bank of the Nile.

Varanasi
Uttar Pradesh, India
Sacred Hindu bathing-place on the River Ganges.

Vasa Museum
Stockholm, Sweden
Museum built to house the 16th century wooden warship recovered from Stockholm harbour.

Vatnajökull
Southeast Iceland
The largest glacier in Europe.

Versailles
Near Paris, France
Magnificent palace and gardens, once the home of Louis XIII and XIV.

Vesuvius
Near Naples, Italy
Active volcano, responsible for the destruction of Herculaneum and Pompeii in the 1st century AD.

Victoria Peak
Hong Kong Island, Hong Kong
Mountain providing a panoramic view of the city and harbour area.

Wadowice
Near Krakow, Poland
Birthplace of Pope John Paul II.

Wailing Wall
Jerusalem, Israel
The original part of the Second Temple, sacred to Jews.

Waitomo caves
North Island, New Zealand
Caves famous for their glow-worms.

Walt Disney World, Florida
Near Orlando, Florida, USA
Theme park with rides and attractions based on Walt Disney characters, also including the EPCOT Center, MGM Studios and Animal Kingdom.

Waterloo
South of Brussels, Belgium
Site of the 1815 Battle of Waterloo, marked by the Lion Mound and various museums.

Westminster Abbey
London, England
Church dating back to the 13th century, used for many royal ceremonies.

White House
Washington DC, USA
Official residence of the President of the USA, dating from the late 18th century.

Windsor Castle
Windsor, west of London, England
Royal residence dating back to the 11th century, overlooking the River Thames.

World Trade Center, New York
New York, USA
One of the tallest buildings in the world, with twin towers.

Xi'an
See Terracotta Warriors

Xochimilco
Mexico City, Mexico
'Floating gardens' where visitors can take boat trips on the Aztec canals.

APPENDIX 6A

York Minster
York, England
Large Gothic cathedral dating back to the 12th century.

Zelazowa Wola
Near Warsaw, Poland
Park containing the birthplace of the composer Chopin.

APPENDIX 6B

Tourist Attractions
Listing by country or region

AUSTRALIA

Great Barrier Reef
Coral Sea, off the coast of Queensland

Ayers Rock/Uluru
Northern Territory

Sydney Harbour Bridge
Sydney, New South Wales

Sydney Opera House
Sydney, New South Wales

AUSTRIA

Golden Roof
Innsbruck

Mirabell Palace
Salzburg

Schönbrunn Palace
Vienna

Spanish Riding School
Vienna

BELGIUM

Bruges
Bruges

Grand'Place
Brussels

Manneken-Pis
Brussels

Waterloo
South of Brussels

BRAZIL

Copacabana Beach
Rio de Janeiro

Statue of Christ the Redeemer
Rio de Janeiro

Sugarloaf Mountain
Rio de Janeiro

Iguaçu Falls (also spelt Iguassu or Iguazu)
Straddling the border between Brazil, Argentina and Paraguay.

CANADA

Calgary Stampede
Calgary, Alberta

Niagara Falls
Ontario

CN Tower
Toronto

CHILE

Easter Island
Pacific Ocean, to the west of mainland Chile.

CHINA

Imperial Palace
Beijing

Great Wall of China
Northern China

Terracotta Warriors
Xi'an

DENMARK

Legoland
Billund

Little Mermaid
Copenhagen

Tivoli Gardens
Copenhagen

ECUADOR

Galapagos Islands
On the Equator in the Pacific Ocean,
to the west of Ecuador

EGYPT

Egyptian Museum
Cairo

Pyramids
Giza and Sakkara (also spelt
Saqqara) near Cairo

Sphinx
Giza near Cairo

Abu Simbel
Lake Nasser, southern Egypt

Valley of the Kings & Valley of the
Queens
West bank of the Nile near Luxor

FRANCE

Disneyland Paris
East of Paris

Mont Blanc
French Alps, southeast France

Versailles
Near Paris

Futuroscope
Near Poitiers, western France

Mont-St-Michel
Normandy

Parc Astérix
Northeast of Paris

Arc de Triomphe
Paris

Champs-Élysées
Paris

Eiffel Tower
Paris

Louvre
Paris

Notre Dame Cathedral
Paris

Pompidou Centre
Paris

Sacré Coeur Basilica
Paris

Fontainebleau Château
Southeast of Paris

Chartres Cathedral
Southwest of Paris

GERMANY

Brandenburg Gate
Berlin

Phantasialand
Between Cologne and Bonn

Oktoberfest
Munich

Neuschwanstein Castle
Near Schwangau, Bavaria

Sans-Souci Palace
Potsdam

Oberammergau
South-west of Munich, Bavaria

GIBRALTAR

Rock of Gibraltar
Gibraltar

GREECE

Parthenon
Athens

Knossos
Near Heraklion, Crete

Delphi
North-west of Athens

Olympia
Western Peloponnese

HONG KONG

Floating restaurants of Aberdeen
Hong Kong Island

Stanley Market
Hong Kong Island

Victoria Peak
Hong Kong Island

Temple Street Night Market
Kowloon

HUNGARY

Lake Balaton
Western Hungary

ICELAND

Gullfoss
Near Geysir

Vatnajökull
Southeast Iceland

INDIA

Taj Mahal
Agra, Uttar Pradesh

Jama Masjid
Delhi

Red Fort
Delhi

Amber Palace
Jaipur, Rajasthan

Palace of the Winds
Jaipur, Rajasthan

Varanasi
Uttar Pradesh

IRELAND

Blarney Castle
County Cork

Trinity College
Dublin

ISRAEL

Church of the Nativity
Bethlehem

Dead Sea
Eastern Israel (border with Jordan)

Dome of the Rock
Jerusalem

Wailing Wall
Jerusalem

ITALY

Ponte Vecchio
Florence

Uffizi Gallery
Florence

La Scala
Milan

Vesuvius
Near Naples

Leaning Tower of Pisa
Pisa

Colosseum
Rome

Forum
Rome

Pantheon
Rome

Spanish Steps
Rome

Trevi Fountain
Rome

St Peter's Basilica
Vatican City, Rome

Sistine Chapel
Vatican City, Rome

Doge's Palace
Venice

Rialto Bridge
Venice

St Mark's Square
Venice

JAMAICA

Dunn's River Falls
Ocho Rios

JAPAN

Hiroshima Peace Memorial Park
Hiroshima, Honshu

Mount Fuji
Southwest of Tokyo

Meiji Shrine
Tokyo

JORDAN

Petra
Southwest Jordan

MALAYSIA

Batu Caves
North of Kuala Lumpur

MALTA

Mdina
Near Rabat

Blue Grotto
Southwest Malta

MEXICO

Quebrada cliff divers
Acapulco

Xochimilco
Mexico City

Teotihuacan
Northeast of Mexico City

Chichen Itza
Yucatan Peninsula

Uxmal
Yucatan Peninsula

MONACO

Monte Carlo Casino
Monte Carlo

MOROCCO

Fez medina
Fez

Hassan Tower
Rabat

Mohammed V Mausoleum
Rabat

MYANMAR

Mandalay
Central Myanmar

Pagan
Near Mandalay

Shwe Dagon Pagoda
Yangon (formerly Rangoon)

NEPAL

Bodnath Stupa
Kathmandu

Durbar Square
Kathmandu

Mount Everest
Northeast Nepal

NETHERLANDS

Anne Frank's House
Amsterdam

Rijksmuseum
Amsterdam

Keukenhof Gardens
Near Haarlem

Efteling
Southwest Netherlands

NEW ZEALAND

Bay of Islands
North Island

Lake Taupo
North Island

Rotorua
North Island

Waitomo Caves
North Island

Milford Sound
South Island

Mount Cook
South Island

Lake Tekapo
South Island

NORWAY

North Cape
Near Hammerfest, north Norway

Frogner Park
Oslo

Kon-Tiki Museum
Oslo

PAKISTAN

Shah Faisal Masjid
Islamabad

Quaid-i-Azam's Mazar
Karachi

Badshahi Mosque
Lahore

PERU

Macchu Picchu
Near Cuzco

Lake Titicaca
South-east Peru

PHILIPPINES

Banaue Rice Terraces
Luzon

Boracay Island
The Visayas

POLAND

Auschwitz
Near Krakow

Wadowice
Near Krakow

Zelazowa Wola
Near Warsaw

PORTUGAL

Alfama
Lisbon

Jeronimos Monastery
Lisbon

St George's Castle
Lisbon

RUSSIA

Bolshoi Theatre
Moscow

Kremlin
Moscow

Moscow State Circus
Moscow

Pushkin Museum of Fine Arts
Moscow

Red Square
Moscow

St Basil's Cathedral
Moscow

Hermitage
St Petersburg

St Isaac's Cathedral
St Petersburg

St Peter and Paul Fortress
St Petersburg

SAUDI ARABIA

Mecca
Mecca

Medina
Medina

SEYCHELLES

Vallée de Mai
Praslin

SINGAPORE

Sentosa Island
Singapore

Raffles Hotel
Singapore City

SOUTH AFRICA

Cape of Good Hope
Cape Province

Garden Route
Cape Province

Table Mountain
Cape Town

SPAIN

Ramblas
Barcelona

Sagrada Familia
Barcelona

Great Mosque
Cordoba

Port Aventura
Costa Dorada, Spain

Alhambra
Granada

Prado
Madrid

Caves of Drach
Majorca

Montserrat Monastery
Montserrat

Bellver Castle
Palma, Majorca

Cathedral
Palma, Majorca

Corrida
Pamplona

Alcazar
Seville

Cathedral
Seville

Giralda Tower
Seville

Teide National Park
Tenerife

SRI LANKA

Anuradhapura
Anuradhapura

Dambulla
Dambulla

Temple of the Tooth
Kandy

Polonnaruwa
Polonnaruwa

Sigiriya
Sigiriya

Adam's Peak
Southern Sri Lanka

SWEDEN

Drottningholm Castle
Near Stockholm

Skokloster
Northwest of Stockholm

Vasa Museum
Stockholm

Gripsholm Castle
West of Stockholm

SWITZERLAND

Kapellbrucke
Lucerne

Jungfrau
Near Interlaken

Matterhorn
Southwest Switzerland

St Gallen Cathedral
St Gallen

TANZANIA

Kilimanjaro
Northeast Tanzania

Ngorongoro Crater
Northern Tanzania

Serengeti Plain
Northern Tanzania

THAILAND

Floating Market, Bangkok
Bangkok

Grand Palace, Bangkok
Bangkok

Royal Barges, Bangkok
Bangkok

Bridge over the River Kwai
*Kanchanaburi, west of
Bangkok*

Phang Nga Bay
Near Phuket

TUNISIA

Carthage
Near Tunis

Matmata
South of Gabes

TURKEY

St Sophia, Istanbul
Istanbul

Suleimaniye Mosque
Istanbul

Topkapi Palace
Istanbul

Pamukkale
Near Denizli

Ephesus
South of Izmir

UNITED KINGDOM

Giant's Causeway
Antrim, Northern Ireland

Blackpool Pleasure Beach
Blackpool, England

Royal Pavilion
Brighton, England

Caernarfon Castle
Caernarfon, Wales

Cambridge
Cambridge, England

Canterbury Cathedral
Canterbury, England

Edinburgh Castle
Edinburgh, Scotland

Holyroodhouse
Edinburgh, Scotland

Royal Mile
Edinburgh, Scotland

Buckingham Palace
London, England

Houses of Parliament
London, England

Madame Tussaud's
London, England

St Paul's Cathedral
London, England

Tower Bridge
London, England

Tower of London
London, England

Trafalgar Square
London, England

Westminster Abbey
London, England

Ben Nevis
Near Fort William, Scotland

Stonehenge
North of Salisbury, England

Oxford
Oxford, England

Alton Towers
Staffordshire, England

Shakespeare's Birthplace
Stratford-upon-Avon, England

Windsor Castle
Windsor, west of London, England

York Minster
York, England

USA

Grand Canyon
Arizona

Death Valley
California

Everglades
Florida

Hollywood
Los Angeles, California

Graceland
Memphis, Tennessee

Niagara Falls
Near Buffalo, New York state

Disneyland, California
Near Los Angeles, California

Sea World, Florida
Near Orlando, Florida

Walt Disney World, Florida
Near Orlando, Florida

Las Vegas
Nevada

Broadway
New York

Empire State Building
New York

Statue of Liberty
New York

World Trade Center
New York

Independence Hall
Philadelphia, Pennsylvania

Alcatraz Island
San Francisco, California

Golden Gate Bridge
San Francisco, California

Mount Rushmore
South Dakota

Capitol, Washington DC
Washington DC

White House
Washington DC

VENEZUELA

Angel Falls
Canaima National Park, eastern Venezuela

ZIMBABWE

Great Zimbabwe
Near Masvingo, Zimbabwe

APPENDIX 7A
Travel Associations - UK

This section provides contact details for a selection of travel trade organisations in the UK. The brief descriptions have generally been provided by the organisations themselves.

AA
Automobile Association,
AA Travel,
Norfolk House,
Priestley Road,
Basingstoke RG24 9NY
Tel: 0990 448866
Provides an information, support and breakdown service for motorists.

AAC
Association of Airline Consolidators,
Beaumont House,
Lambton Road,
London SW20 0LW
Tel: 0181 288 1430
Keeps members abreast of current legislation as it affects their business, and provides a platform for members to voice their views to opinion formers.

ABPCO
Association of British Professional Conference Organisers,
PO Box 286,
Worcester WR2 6YA
Tel: 0704 405 5207

Fax: 0704 405 5207
A trade association offering advice and services to professional conference organisers.

ABTA
Association of British Travel Agents,
68-71 Newman Street,
London W1P 4AH
Tel: 0171 637 2444
Fax: 0171 637 0713
Promotes and regulates the activities of its members, and protects the interests of consumers.

ABTOF
Association of British Tour Operators to France,
PO Box 54,
Ross-on-Wye HR9 5YQ
Tel: 01989 769140
Fax: 01989 769066
E-mail: abtof@dial.pipex.com
Promotes travel to France and represents the interests of its member companies.

ABTOT
Association of Bonded Travel Organisers Trust Ltd,
86 Jermyn Street,
London SW1Y 6JD
Tel: 0171 930 2388
Fax: 0171 930 7718
A simple, economical and fully DTI-

approved bonding scheme, enabling travel organisers to provide financial protection for their non-licensable arrangements.

ACE
Association for Conferences and Events,
Riverside House,
High Street,
Huntingdon,
Camb PE18 6SG
Tel: 01480 457595
Fax: 01480 412863
E-mail: ace@martex.co.uk
Provides a service to, and forum for, its members who are involved in all aspects of the conference and meetings industry.

AEO
Association of Exhibition Organisers,
113 High Street,
Berkhamstead,
Herts HP4 2DJ
Tel: 01442 873331
Fax: 01442 875551
E-mail: info@aeo.org.uk
Works to increase the significance of exhibitions within the marketing mix, and to satisfy an increasing number of visitors.

AIRC
Association of International Rail Companies,
c/o John Edmonds,
Canadian National Railway Companies,
17 Cockspur Street,
London SW1Y 5BS
Tel: 0171 930 2150
Fax: 0171 839 6193
E-mail: edmonds@cn.ca
An umbrella organisation for its rail

company members to meet regularly to discuss matters of mutual interest and new developments in the industry.

AITO
Association of Independent Tour Operators,
133a St Margaret's Road,
Twickenham TW1 1RG
Tel: 0181 744 9280
Fax: 0181 744 3187
E-mail: aito@martex.co.uk
Represents the smaller tour operator to the trade and the public through joint marketing and promotional activities.

ANTOR
Association of National Tourist Office Representatives in the UK,
211 Picadilly,
London W1V 9LD
Tel: 0171 917 9536
Fax: 0171 917 9537
Promotes travel and tourism world-wide, to the trade and the public, and represents member tourist organisations.

AOA
Airport Operators Association,
3 Birdcage Walk,
London SW1H 9JJ
Tel: 0171 222 2249
Fax: 0171 976 7405
E-mail: keithjowett@the-aoa.demon.co.uk
Representative for all UK airports and regulatory body for airport standards.

APTG
Association of Professional Tourist Guides,
50 Southwark Street,
London SE1 1UN

Tel: 0171 717 4064
The professional body of London's 'Blue Badge' guides. It seeks to promote the highest possible standards in tourism in general and guiding in particular.

ARMTA
Association of Regional Multiple Travel Agents,
c/o Greg Mould,
Premier Travel,
Westbrook, Milton Road,
Cambridge CB4 1YG
Tel: 01223 500444
Fax: 01223 516240
A grouping of like-minded but non-competitive travel agents who discuss common issues.

ASVA
Association of Scottish Visitor Attractions,
County House,
20-22 Torphichen Street,
Edinburgh EH3 8JB
Tel: 0131 623 6630
Fax: 0131 623 6631
Improves the quality and viability of visitor attractions, and assists with tour development by identifying appropriate places to visit.

ATII
Association of Travel Insurance Intermediaries,
66-72 High Street,
Wealdstone HA3 7AF
Tel: 0181 424 9014
Fax: 0181 424 8069

ATOC
Association of Train Operating Companies,
40 Bernard Street,
London WC1N 1BY
Tel: 0171 904 3033

Represents the interests of the train operating companies to government and key opinion-formers, as well as managing a range of network services, products and responsibilities on their behalf.

ATTC
Association of Travel Trade Clubs,
22 Queens Road,
Southend SS1 1LX
Tel: 01702 351111
Fax: 01702 433563
An umbrella organisation for local travel trade clubs, each serving a social and educational purpose for their their members.

AUC
Air Transport Users Council,
CAA House T3,
45-59 Kingsway,
London WC2B 6TE
Tel: 0171 240 6061
Fax: 0171 240 7071
As the Civil Aviation Authority's official consumer watchdog, protects the interests of users of aviation services.

AWTE
Association of Women Travel Executives,
23 High Street,
Wealdstone HA3 5BY
Tel: 0181 427 5678
Fax: 0181 861 4459
Provides a social forum for female executives employed in the travel industry.

BAA
British Airports Authority,
130 Wilton Road,
London, SW1V 1LQ
Tel: 0171 834 9449
Fax: 0171 932 6699

Manages airport facilities at various airports in the UK and overseas.

BACD
British Association of Conference Destinations,
1st Floor Elizabeth House,
22 Suffolk Street,
Queensway,
Birmingham, B1 1LS
Tel: 0121 616 1400
Fax: 0121 616 1364
E-mail: info@bacd.org.uk
Represents and promotes all the major British conference destinations, providing information, venue finding and related services in respect of 3000 venues countrywide.

BAHA
British Activity Holiday Association Ltd,
22 Green Lane,
Hersham,
Walton-on-Thames KT12 5HD
Tel: 01932 252994
Works towards improving quality and safety in the activity holiday industry.

BAHREP
British Association of Hotel Representatives,
127 New House Park,
St Albans AL1 1UT
Tel: 01727 862327
Fax: 01727 862327
Promotes sales through marketing and representation companies for member hotels.

BALPA
British Airline Pilots Association,
81 New Road,
Harlington UB3 5BG
Tel: 0181 476 4000
Fax: 0181 476 4077

E-mail: balpa@balpa.org.uk
The professional union representing pilots and flight engineers in the UK

BAR UK Ltd
200 Buckingham Palace Road,
London SW1W 9TA
Tel: 0171 707 4147
Fax: 0171 707 4182
E-mail: peter.north@bar-uk.org
Encourages and promotes the interests of scheduled passenger and cargo airlines operating from and within the UK.

BATA
British Air Transport Association,
5-6 Pall Mall East,
London SW1Y 5BA
Tel: 0171 930 5746
Fax: 0171 321 0970
Encourages the safe, healthy and economic development of UK civil aviation.

BAWTA
British Association of Wholesale Tour Agents,
137 Station Road,
Impington,
Cambridge CB4 9NP
Tel: 01223 560513
Fax: 01223 566533
Promotes the quality, public image and growth of coach tourism, and represents and promotes the interests of British wholesale tour agents and operators.

BCH
Bonded Coach Holiday Group,
Imperial House,
15-19 Kingsway,
London WC2B 6UN
Tel: 0171 240 3131
Fax: 0171 240 6565
E-mail: bch@cpt-uk.org

Provides a government-approved bonding scheme for the operators of coach holidays.

BH&HPA
British Holiday & Home Parks Association Ltd,
6 Pullman Court,
Great Western Road,
Gloucester GL1 3ND
Tel: 01452 526911
Fax: 01452 307226
E-mail: jspencer@bhhpa.org.uk
Represents the parks industry including caravans, chalets, tents and self-catering accommodation.

BHA
British Hospitality Association,
Queens House,
55-56 Lincoln's Inn Fields,
London WC2A 3BH
Tel: 0171 404 7744
Fax: 0171 404 7799
E-mail: bha@bha.org.uk
Website: www.bha_online.org.uk
Protects and develops the interests of its members in the British hospitality industry.

BITOA
British Incoming Tour Operators Association,
Vigilant House,
120 Wilton Road,
London SW1V 1JZ
Tel: 0171 931 0601
Fax: 0171 828 0531
E-mail: info@bitoa.co.uk
Represents members of the inbound tourism industry and provides them with services such as research, lobbying and training.

BRA
British Resorts Association,
8 Post Office Avenue,
Southport,
Merseyside PR9 0US
Tel: 0151 934 2286
Fax: 0151 934 2287
A national organisation promoting the mutual interests of all member resorts (inland and coastal) and tourist regions.

BTA
British Tourist Authority,
Thames Tower,
Blacks Road,
London W6 9EL
Tel: 0181 846 9000
Fax: 0181 563 0307
E-mail: 101657.335@compuserve.com
Promotes tourism to Britain, and ensures that the national and regional Tourist Boards respond effectively to the needs of government, the industry and the public.

BVRLA
British Vehicle Rental & Leasing Association,
River Lodge,
Badminton Court,
Amersham HP7 0DD
Tel: 01494 434499
Fax: 01494 434747
E-mail: bvrlamail@bvrla.co.uk
Represents the short- and long-term vehicle rental and contract hire industry, and presents their views to government.

BW
British Waterways,
Willow Grange,
Church Road,
Watford, WD1 3QA
Tel: 01923 226422
Fax: 01923 201400

Cares for 2,000 miles of Britain's canals and rivers.

CAA
Civil Aviation Authority,
CAA House,
45-59 Kingsway,
London WC2B 6TE
Tel: 0171 379 7311
Fax: 0171 240 1153
Provides air navigation services, regulates the civil aviation industry including the licensing of air travel organisers, and advises government on civil aviation.

CIMTIG
Chartered Institute of Marketing Travel Industry Group,
Home Cottage,
Old Lane,
Tatsfield,
Westerham TN16 2LN
Tel: 01959 577469
Fax: 01959 577469
Improves the success and profitability of its members and their organisations by understanding and applying modern marketing techniques.

CITA
Confederation of Independent Travel Agents,
Central Chambers,
98 High Street,
Rayleigh SS6 7BY
Tel: 01268 777667
Fax: 01268 777687
Represents the commercial interests of its members, which are generally small travel agents. and secures tour operators' deals.

CPT
Confederation of Passenger Transport UK,
Imperial House,
15-19 Kingsway,
London WC2B 6UN
Tel: 0171 240 3131
Fax: 0171 240 6565
E-mail: admin@cpt-uk.org
Represents the views of bus, coach and light rail operators to government, the European Union and the media and protects the commercial environment of the industry.

CRAC
Continental Rail Agents Consortium,
c/o Gerry Harris,
Ultima Travel,
424 Chester Road,
Little Sutton,
South Wirral L66 3RB
Tel: 0151 339 6171
Fax: 0151 339 9199
Represents the interests of those selling European rail travel and provides a forum for discussion with European rail principals

CTC
Coach Tourism Council,
2 Sandown Road,
Toton,
Nottingham NG9 6GN
Tel: 0115 973 2260
Fax: 0115 973 2260
Promotes travel and tourism by coach.

CTO
Caribbean Tourism Organisation,
42 Westminster Palace Gardens,
Artillery Row,
London SW1P 1RR
Tel: 0171 222 4335
Fax: 0171 222 4325
E-mail: cto@carib-tourism.com
Represents its members from the

travel and tourism industry, and promotes travel to and within the Caribbean region.

CTT
Council for Travel & Tourism,
LGM House,
Mill Green Road,
Hayward's Heath,
W.Sussex RH16 1XQ
Tel: 01444 452277
Fax: 01444 452244
Provides a forum for member organisations to exchange information, news and views on current developments and lobbies government on issues of concern to the travel and tourism industries.

EATA
East Asia Travel Association,
c/o Romanski Ltd,
Barbican Business Centre,
132-140 Goswell Road,
London EC1V 7DP
Tel: 0171 490 4082
Fax: 0171 608 1851
E-mail: cecily@romanski.com
Promotes travel to and within the East Asia region.

ESITO
Events Sector Industry Training Organisation,
Riverside House,
High Street,
Huntingdon PE18 6SG
Tel: 01480 457595
Fax: 01480 412863
E-mail: ace@martex.co.uk
Acts as the forum for training and development in the events industry, and to pursue issues with government, education and other bodies.

ETB
English Tourist Board,
Thames Tower,
Blacks Road,
London W6 9EL
Tel: 0181 846 9000
Fax: 0181 563 0302
E-mail: 101657.325@
compuserve.com
Promotes tourism to and within England.

ETOA
European Tour Operators Association,
6 Weighhouse Street,
London W1Y 1YL
Tel: 0171 499 4412
Fax: 0171 499 4413
E-mail: tjenkins@etoa.org
A trade association to represent the interests of its members - mostly tour operators, but also including other sectors of the travel industry.

EVA
Exhibition Venues Association,
Mallards,
Five Ashes,
Mayfield TN20 6NN
Tel: 01435 872244
Fax: 01435 872696
E-mail: eva@martex.co.uk
Promotea quality and service in the exhibition industry, provides a one-stop shop for event organisers, and undertakes industry research.

FHA
Family Holiday Association,
16 Mortimer Street,
London W1N 7RD
Tel: 0171 436 3304
Fax: 0171 436 3302
E-mail: fha@ukonline.co.uk

A charity to provide holidays for families in need.

FTO
Federation of Tour Operators,
170 High Street,
Lewes BN7 1YE
Tel: 01273 477722
Fax: 01273 483746
Brings about change and improvement in all areas affecting customers' holidays on the journey and in resort.

GBCO
Guild of British Coach Operators,
Mill House,
Church Lane,
East Drayton,
Retford, DN22 0LP
Tel: 01777 248698
Fax: 01777 248549
A consortium of independently owned coach operators who are driven by quality.

GBTA
Guild of Business Travel Agents,
Artillery House,
Artillery Row,
London SW1P 1RT
Tel: 0171 222 2744
Fax: 0171 976 7094
E-mail: gbta@btinternet.com
Provides a forum for business and corporate travel agencies, and seeks the highest standards for its members and their clients.

GPCA
Guild of Professional Cruise Agents,
Quadrant House,
London W1R 6JB
Tel: 0171 734 4404
Fax: 0171 434 1410

Represents a group of over 60 travel agents who concentrate on the sale of cruises, each achieving cruise sales in excess of £250,000 per year.

GTOA
Group Travel Organisers Association,
c/o Jim Pickett,
4 Drake Road,
Eaton Socon,
St Neots PE19 3HS
Tel: 01480 406662
Fax: 01480 392306
E-mail: APIC413752@aol.com
Enhances the status and professionalism of group travel organisers and represents their interests in dealing with industry suppliers and official bodies.

GRTG
The Guild of Registered Tourist Guides,
Guild House,
52d Borough High Street,
London SE1 1XN
Tel: 0171 403 1115
Fax: 0171 357 7866
E-mail: guild@blue-badge.org.co
Acts as the national professional association of tourist board-registered guides in the UK.

GTT
The Guild of Travel and Tourism,
Suite 35,
Eldon Chambers,
30 Fleet Street,
London EC4Y 1AA
Tel: 0171 583 6333
Fax: 01895 834028
Acts as a forum for anyone in the travel, tourism or transport sectors, to provide benefits for its members,

*and to lobby for industry issues
of concern.*

HCA
Holiday Centres Association,
Ridge Lane,
Watford WD1 3SX
Tel: 01923 801121
*Represents all of the major holiday
centres providing an inclusive
entertainment, sporting and leisure
package in the UK.*

HMA
Hotel Marketing Association,
1 Glade House,
High Street,
Sunninghill SL5 9PU
Tel: 01344 876234
Fax: 01344 876187
*Promotea good marketing practice in
the hotel industry, through
educational events, industry-wide
research studies and recognition of
hotel marketing excellence.*

IBTA
**International Business Travel
Association,**
28 Church Street,
Rickmansworth WD3 1DD
Tel: 01923 711242
Fax: 01923 711522
E-mail: info@ibta.com
*A federation of business travel
organisations around the world,
providing a global forum for its
members to network with travel
managers and suppliers.*

IFTO
**International Federation of Tour
Operators,**
170 High Street,
Lewes BN7 1YE
Tel: 01273 477722

Fax: 01273 483746
*Enables tour operators throughout
Europe to cooperate in order to solve
the major problems which confront
package holiday makers.*

ILAM
**Institute of Leisure and Amenity
Management,**
ILAM House,
Lower Basildon,
Reading RG8 9NE
Tel: 01491 874800
Fax: 01491 874801
E-mail: info@ILAM.CO.UK
*The professional institute for the
leisure industry.*

ITM
Institute of Travel Management,
Easton House,
Easton on the Hill,
Stamford PE9 3NZ
Tel: 01780 482210
Fax: 01780 482310
E-mail: secretariat@itm.org.uk
*Provides networking opportunities for
its members, comprising Travel
Managers and suppliers.*

ITMA
**Incentive Travel & Meetings
Association Ltd,**
PO Box 195,
Twickenham TW1 2PE
Tel: 0181 892 0256
Fax: 0181 891 3855
E-mail: itma@martex.co.uk
*Represents the best in the motivation
and event management industry.*

ITT
Institute of Travel & Tourism,
113 Victoria Street,
St Albans AL1 3TJ
Tel: 01727 854395
Fax: 01727 847415

E-mail: ltt@dial.pipex.com
Develops the professionalism of its
members within the industry.

MTAA
Multiple Travel Agents' Association,
90 Church Street,
Sudbury CO10 9QT
Tel: 01787 248054
Fax: 01787 248080
E-mail: javatony@btinternet.com
A services -supply association which
currently comprises the five largest
UK travel agents.

NAITA
National Association of
Independent Travel Agents,
Kenilworth House,
79-80 Margaret Street,
London W1N 7HB
Tel: 0171 323 3408
Fax: 0171 323 5189
E-mail: 101703.3044@
compuserve.com
Enables independent agents to
compete with the 'multiples' without
losing their personal service and
independent management.

NT
National Trust,
36 Queen Anne's Gate,
London SW1H 9AS
Tel: 0171 222 9251
Fax: 0171 447 6701
E-mail: traveltrade@ntrust.org.uk
Promotea the permanent preservation,
for the benefit of the nation, of
lands and buildings of beauty or
historic interest.

NEA
National Exhibitors Association,
29a Market Square,
Biggleswade SG18 8AQ

Tel: 01767 316255
A national organisation of
exhibiting companies, offering
information and seminars on all
aspects of exhibiting.

NITB
Northern Ireland Tourist Board,
St Anne's Court,
59 North Street,
Belfast BT1 1NB
Tel: 01232 231221
Fax: 01232 240960
E-mail: general.enquiries.nitb@
nics.gov.uk
Promotes tourism to and within
Northern Ireland.

PSA
Passenger Shipping Association Ltd,
Walmar House,
288-292 Regent Street,
London W1R 5HE
Tel: 0171 436 2449
Fax: 0171 636 9206
E-mail: psarapsa@aol.com
Represents member organisations
from the cruising and ferry industry.

PSARA
Passenger Shipping Association
Retail Agents Scheme
Walmar House
288-292 Regent Street
London,W1R 5HE
Tel: 0171 436 2449
Fax: 0171 636 9206
E-mail: psarapsa@aol.com
The training arm of the PSA (see
above).

RAC
Royal Automobile Club,
Motoring Services,
PO Box 700,
Great Park Road,

Bradley Stoke.
Bristol BS32 4QN
Tel: 01454 208000
Fax: 01454 208277
*Provides and information, support
and breakdown service for motorists.*

SAGTA
School & Group Travel Association,
Katepwa House,
Ashfield Park Avenue,
Ross-on-Wye HR9 5AX
Tel: 01989 567690
Fax: 01989 567676
*Provides a forum for businesses within
the school travel industry, and a focus
for members to explore and act on
industry issues.*

SATH
**Society for the Advancement of
Travel for the Handicapped,**
Whiteridge,
Chalkpit Lane,
Marlow SL7 2JE
Tel: 01628 487494
Fax: 01628 487494
*Creates a forum for the exchange
and development of information
within the travel industry and to
promote barrier-free access to
travel for those with disabilities.*

SEO
Society of Event Organisers
29a Market Square
Biggleswade SG18 8AQ
Tel: 01767 316255
*A membership group of organisations
involved in organising events,
offering advice, publications and
seminars.*

SPAA
**Scottish Passenger Agents
Association**

135 Wellington Street
Glasgow G2 2XE
Tel: 0141 248 3904
Fax: 0141 226 5047
*A trade association to represent
the interests of retail travel agents
in Scotland.*

STB
Scottish Tourist Board,
23 Ravelston Terrace,
Edinburgh EH4 3EU
Tel: 0131 332 2433
Fax: 0131 313 2023
*Promotes tourism to and within
Scotland.*

TC
Timeshare Council,
23 Buckingham Gate
London SW1E 6LB
Tel: 0171 821 8845
Fax: 0171 828 0739
*Develops the professionalism of its
timeshare company members, and
provides advice to consumers.*

TS
The Tourism Society,
26 Chapter Street,
London SW1P 4ND
Tel: 0171 834 0461
Fax: 0171 932 0238
E-mail: tour.soc@btinternet.com
*Leading tourism network. A
membership body promoting
professionalism in travel &
tourism.*

TTA
Travel Trust Association Ltd,
Parkway House,
Sheen Lane
London SW14 8LS
Tel: 0181 876 4458
Fax: 0181 876 5756

Trade association to license travel agents and tour operators to trade within the industry, providing financial protection for their customers.

WTB
Wales Tourist Board,
Brunel House, 2 Fitzalan Road,
Cardiff CF2 1UY
Wales
Tel: 01222 499909
Fax: 01222 485031

E-mail: info@tourism.wales.gov.uk
Website: www.visitwales.com
Promotes tourism to and within Wales.

YHA
Youth Hostels Association,
St Albans AL1 2DY
Tel: 01727 855215
Fax: 01727 844126
E-mail: yhacustomerservices@
compuserve.com
Provides economical accommodation for the active holidaymaker.

APPENDIX 7B

Travel Associations - USA

This section provides details of a selection of travel trade associations in the USA.

AH&MA
American Hotel & Motel Association,
1201 New York Avenue N.W.,
Suite 600,
Washington, DC 20005,
USA
Tel: 202 289 3100
Web site: www.ahma.com
A federation of state lodging associations which provides operations, technical, educational, marketing and communications services plus governmental affairs representation to the lodging industry.

ARTA
Association of Retail Travel Agents,
501 Darby Creek Road, Suite 47,
Lexington, KY 40509-1604,
USA
Tel: 606 263 1194
Fax: 606 264 0368
E-mail: artalexhdq@aol.com
Web site: www.artaonline.com
The largest non-profit trade assocation in North America that represents travel agents exclusively.

ASIRT
The Association for Safe International Road Travel,
11769 Gainsborough Road,
Potomac, MD 20854,
USA
Tel: 301 983 5252
Fax: 301 983 3663
E-mail: asirt@erols.com
Web site: www.asirt.org
An international, non-profit organisation to promote road safety through education and advocay. Alerts individuals and corporations to road conditions in individual countries.

ASTA
American Society of Travel Agents,
1101 King Street,
Alexandria, VA 22314,
USA
Tel: 703 739 2782
Fax: 703 684 8319
E-mail: asta@astanet.com
Web site: www.astanet.com
Enhances the professionalism and profitability of members worldwide through effective representation in industry and government affairs, education and training, and by identifying and meeting the needs of the travelling public.

ATA
Air Transport Association,
1301 Pennsylvania Avenue,

Suite 1100,
Washington, DC 20004-1707,
USA
Tel: 202 626 4000
Fax: 202 626 4181
Web site: www.air-transport.org
*Advocates and supports measures to
enhance safety, ensures efficiency,
fosters growth and promote
economic health of the industry.*

CLIA
**Cruise Lines International
Association,**
500 5th Avenue,
Suite 1407,
New York, NY 10016,
USA
Tel: 212 921 0066
Fax: 212 921 0549
E-mail: CLIA@cruising.org
Web site: cruising.org
*Represents the North American cruise
line industry, and works to expand
and promote cruise vacations.*

HEDNA
**Hotel Electronic Distribution
Network Association,**
303 Freeport Road,
Pittsburgh, PA 15215-3131,
USA
Tel: 412 784 8433
Fax: 412 781 2871
Web site: www.HEDNA.org
*Promotes the use of electronic
distribution in the booking of
hotel rooms.*

IATAN
**International Airlines Travel
Agent Network,**
300 Garden City Plaza, Suite 342,
Garden City, NY 11530,
USA
Tel: 516 747 4716

Fax: 516 747 4462
Web site: www.iatan.org
*Promotes professionalism,
administers business standards, and
provides a vital link between the
supplier community and the U.S.
travel distribution network.*

IFTTA
**International Forum of Travel and
Tourism Advocates,**
693 Sutter Street, 6th Floor,
San Francisco, CA 94102,
USA
Tel: 415 673 3333
Fax: 415 673 3548
E-mail: ANOLIK@travellaw.com
Web site: www.tay.ac.uk/iftta or
www.travellaw.com
*Travel Law Attorneys, professors
and industry personnel dealing
with legal issues from 40 countries
worldwide.*

IFWTO
**International Federation of
Women's Travel Organisations,**
13901 N. 73rd Street,
Suite 2108,
Scottsdale, AZ 85260-3125,
USA
Tel: 602 596 6640
Fax: 602 596 6638
E-mail: ifwtohq@primenet.com
Web site: www.ifwto.trav.org
*International organisation that
addresses the concerns of women
in the sale or promotion of travel
and tourism.*

NACOA
**National Association of Cruise
Oriented Agencies,**
7600 Red Road, Suite 128,
Miami, FL 33143
Tel: 305 663 5626

Fax: 305 663 5625
E-mail: NACOAFL@aol.com
Web site: www.nacoa.com
*Non-profit trade assocation
dedicated to the cruise product and
the cruise professionals who sell it.*

NACTA
**National Association of
Commissioned Travel Agents,**
P.O. Box 2398,
Valley Center, CA 92082,
USA
Tel: 760 751 1197
Fax: 760 751 1309
E-mail: nacta@aol.com
Web site: www.nacta.com
*National association of travel agents
whose members include independent
contractors, outside sales agents,
cruise/tour oriented agents and their
host agency partners.*

SATH
**The Society for the Advancement
of Travel for the Handicapped,**
347 5th Avenue, Ste 610,
New York, NY 10016,
USA
Tel: 212 447 7284
Fax: 212 725 8253
E-mail: sathtravel@aol.com
Web site: www.sath.org
*A non-profit organisation which
assists and advises on travel
arrangements of all kinds for people
with disabilities.*

STAG
**Society of Travel Agents in
Government Inc,**
6935 Wisconsin Avenue,
Bethesda, MD 20815-6109,
USA
Tel: 301 654 8595
Fax: 301 654 6663

E-mail: govtvlmkt@aol.com
Web site: www.government-travel.org
*National association focusing on
research, education, buyer/seller
opportunities, networking,
mentoring and advocacy.*

TIAA
**Travel Industry Association of
America,**
1100 New York Avenue NW,
Suite 450 West,
Washington, DC 20005,
USA
Tel: 202 408 1832
Fax: 202 408 1255
Web site: www.tia.org
*The national, non-profit
organisation representing all
components of the $502 billion
US travel industry. Mission is to
represent the whole of the US
travel industry, to promote and
facilitate increased travel to and
within the US.*

USTI
United States Tourism Industries,
International Trade Association,
Department of Commerce,
Room 1860,
Herbert C Hoover Building,
14th and Constitution Ave NW,
Washington, DC 20230,
USA
Tel: 202 482 4028
Fax: 202 482 2887
Web site: www.tinet.ita.doc.gov

USTS
United States Travel Service
The forerunner of USTTA.

USTTA
**United States Travel and Tourism
Administration**
A body disbanded by the US

government in 1996. Its function now partly taken over in the UK by the Visit USA Association,

Visit USA Association
US Embassy,
24 Grosvenor Square,
London W1A 1AE,
UK
Tel: 0171 499 9000
A body of some 140 member organisations from the private sector whose aim is to promote tourism to and within the USA.

APPENDIX 7C

Travel Associations - Other

This section provides details of the travel agency associations in a selection of countries of major touristic importance. Details of associations in the UK and the USA may be found in the appropriate sections above.

Australia

AFTA
Australian Federation of Travel Agents,
309 Pitt Street,
Sydney, NSW 2000,
Tel: 00 61 2 92643299

Austria

ORV
Austrian Travel Agent Association (Osterreich Reiseburo Verband),
Hofburg 1010,
Vienna
Tel: 00 43 1 587 366623

Belgium

UPAV
Union Professionelle des Agences de Voyages,
Christian Vanderwinnen,
Rue de la Metrologie 6,
B-1130 Brussels
Tel 00 32 2 215 9823

Canada

ACTA
Association of Canadian Travel Agents,
Suite 201, 1729 Bank Street,
Ottawa,
Ontario, KIV 7Z5
Tel: 00 1 613 521 0474

CITC
Canadian Institute of Travel Counsellors,
41 Richwood Drive,
Markham,
Ontario, L3P 3Y7
Tel: 00 1 905 472 8533
Fax: 00 1 905 472 5691
E-mail: citcnat@sympatico.ca

China

CTA
China Tourism Association
9a Jianguomen Avenue,
Beijing
Tel: 00 86 10 6513 5383
Fax: 00 86 10 6513 5383

Czech Republic

ATA
Association of Travel Agencies,
Na Zderaze 6,
12000 Prague 2,
Tel: 00 42 02 291262

France

SNAV
Société Nationale des Agences de Voyage,
6 rue de Villaret de Joyeuse,
75015 Paris
Tel: 00 33 1 44 09 3699

Germany

DRV
Deutscher Reiseburo Verband,
Mannheimer Strasse 15,
60329 Frankfurt,
Tel: 00 49 69 273 90727

Greece

HATA
Hellenic Association of Travel & Tourism Agents,
15, Panetistimiou Avenue,
10564 Athens,
Tel: 00 30 1 9234 143

Hungary

AHTA
Association of Hungarian Travel Agents,
Petöfi Sándor u. No 2,
1053 Budapest
Tel: 00 36 1 318 4977
Fax: 00 36 1 318 4977
E-mail: muisz@mail.datanet.hu

Japan

JATA
Japan Association of Travel Agents,
Zen-Nittsu Kasumigaseki Bldg,
3-3 Kasumigaseki 3 Chome,
Chiyoda ku,
Tokyo
Tel: 00 81 3 3592 1271

Ireland

ITAA
Irish Travel Agents Association,
32 South William Street,
Dublin 2
Tel: 00 353 1 670 7679

Italy

FIAVET
Federazione Italiano Agenti di Viaggo e Turismo,
Via Ravina 8,
00161 Roma
Tel: 00 39 06 440 2552

Mexico

AMATUR
Mexican Association of Tour Operators,
Florencia Street. 57,
CP 06600,
Mexico City
Tel: 00 525 5208 9750

Netherlands

ANVR
Algemene Nederland Vereniging Reisburo
Gupiterstraat 234-236,
2132 HG Hoofddorp
Tel: 00 31 23 56 73 822
Fax: 00 31 23 56 22 080

New Zealand

TAANZ
Travel Agents Association of New Zealand,
Paxus House,
79 Boulcott Street,
Wellington,
PO Box 1888 Wellington
Tel: 00 64 4 499 0104
Fax: 00 64 4 499 0827

Poland

PIT
Polska Izba Turystyczna
ul. Hoza 42/8,
00–094 Warsaw
Tel: 00 48 22 827 0166
Fax: 00 48 22 827 0127

Portugal

APAVT
Association of Portugese Travel Agencies and Tourism,
Rua Dukue de Palmela 2 (first direito),
1050 Lisbon
Tel: 00351 1 355 3010

Russia

RATA
Russian Association of Travel Agents,
11 Stoleshnikov Per,
Moscow 103031
Tel: 0070 952922464

Spain

AEADVE
Asociación Empresarial Agencias de Viajes Españolas,
Plaza Castilla 3–18° E2,
28046 Madrid
Tel: 00 34 91 314 18 30
Fax: 00 34 91 482 71 31

AMAVE
Asociación Mayoristas Agencias de Viajes Españolas,
Leganitos, 35-2°,
28013 Madrid
Tel: 00 34 91 541 19 14
Fax: 00 34 91 559 78 42

South Africa

ASATA
Association of South African Travel Agents,
P.O.Box 6266,
Johannesburg 2000
Tel: 0027 118800562

Switzerland

SFTA
Swiss Federation of Travel Agents,
Etzel Strasse 42,
8038 Zurich
Tel: 00 41 14 87 30 50
Fax: 00 41 14 80 09 45

Turkey

TURSAB
Association of Turkish Travel Agencies,
Fulya Asikkerem Sokak 48-50,
Dikilitas,
Istanbul
Tel: 0090 212 259 8404

APPENDIX 7D

Travel Associations - Global

This section provides details of a selection of regional or international travel trade associations.

AEA
Association of European Airlines,
350 Avenue Louise,
Postfach 4,
B-1050 Brussels
Belgium
Tel: 00 32 2 6270600
Fax: 00 32 2 6484017

ECTAA
Group of National Travel Agents' and Tour Operators' Associations within the EU,
Rue Dautzenberg 36,
Box 6,
B-1050 Brussels
Belgium
Tel: 00 32 2 6443450
Fax: 00 32 2 6442421
E-mail: ectaa@skynet.be

ERA
European Regional Airlines Association,
The Baker Suite,
Fairoaks Airport,
Chobham,
Woking
Surrey GU24 8HX
UK
Tel: 00 44 1276 856495
Fax: 00 44 1276 857038

ETC
European Travel Commission,
61, rue du Marche aux Herbes,
B-1000 Brussels
Belgium
Tel: 00 32 2 5040303
Fax: 00 32 2 5040377

ICCA
International Congress and Conference Association,
Entrada 121,
1096 EB,
Amsterdam
The Netherlands
Tel: 00 31 20 398 1919
Fax: 00 31 20 699 0781
E-mail: icca@icca.nl

IATA
International Air Transport Association,
IATA-Genf,
Route de l`Aeroport 33,
Postfach 416,
CH-1215 Genf
Switzerland
Tel: 00 41 22 7992525
Fax: 00 41 22 7993553

PATA
Pacific and Asian Travel Agents Association,
1 Montgomery Street,
Telesis Tower,
Suite 1000,
San Francisco CA
USA
Tel 00 1 415 986 4646

WATA
World Association Of Travel Agents,
PO Box 2317,
CH-1211,
Geneva 1,
Switzerland
Tel 00 41 22 731 4760

WTO
World Tourism Organisation
Capitán Haya 42,
28020 Madrid,
Spain
Tel 00 34 91 567 8187

APPENDIX 8A

UK-USA English Differences

The English language as used in America (and other parts of the world) has evolved in different ways and there are significant variations in style, spelling, punctuation and pronunciation. While the changes do not generally cause problems, the interpretations that follow are a selection of those that are of particular relevance in the travel industry. The interpretations are shown both from UK to US English and vice versa although some terms will appear in only one interpretation.

There are certain common differences between UK and US English and not all examples of these are shown in the interpretative listing. These include the following constructions:

Words ending ...*ise* (such as enterprise) are not generally accepted by US speakers who prefer the ...*ize* construction. In UK English either ending is acceptable for most constructions. Although the ...*ize* termination is less common in the UK it is, in fact, the older of the two. The ...ise ending is a French influence that entered UK English after America was colonised. However, words ending ...*yse*, such as analyse and paralyse will be spelt analyze and paralyze in US English and this usage is not generally acceptable in UK English.

In UK English the ending ...*ise* usually denotes a verb (license) and the ending ...*ice* a noun (licence). This distinction does not usually apply in US English where the ...*ise* ending is commonly used for both. There are exceptions, most notably *practise* and *practice*, which in US English form exactly opposite parts of speech from their UK English equivalents.

Words ending ...*our* (e.g. colour) are generally spelt ...*or* (e.g. color) in US English.

The French-derived ending using a double consonant followed by "e" (cigarette, programme), common in UK English, is not normally used in US English. The usual US ending is a single consonant (cigaret, program). It should be noted, though, that the US spellings are now accepted in applications where the word is applied to a US-originating term. A particularly important example is the word program, spelled the US way when used to describe a computer program but spelled programme when used to describe a sequence of events.

In UK English the letter *l* in a word is usually doubled if it follows a single vowel, for example, labelled or travelled. In US English this does not occur and labeled or traveled would be used.

The UK English ending ...*re* is often replaced by ...*er* in US English. Thus, centre becomes center and theatre becomes theater.

Americans usually show dates in the form *month/day/year*, not *day/month/year* as is usual in the rest of the world. Thus

9/5/00 would be interpreted by an American as 05 September 2000 and not 09 May 2000. So ingrained is this habit that it is not unknown for air tickets issued in the USA to be written in the "month-first" format although this does, of course, contravene IATA ticketing rules.

Americans always express personal weights in pounds; the stone is not used. Thus a 14 stone man would be referred to as weighing 196 pounds.

UK (British) English → US (American) English

A

accommodation → accommodations
aerial → antenna
aeroplane, aircraft → airplane, or simply, plane
afters, sweet → dessert
air hostess → flight attendant (female)
aluminium → aluminum
annexe → annex
antenatal → prenatal
anticlockwise → counterclockwise
articulated lorry → tractor-trailer
aubergine → eggplant
autumn → fall
axe → ax

B

baby's dummy → pacifier
baggage reclaim → baggage claim
Bank holiday → public holiday
banknote → bill, (e.g. $10 bill)
bap → hamburger bun
barrister → trial lawyer, attorney
bath → bathtub, tub
beetroot → beet
bill (in restaurant) → check
billion → a million million
bin liner → trash bag
biscuit (savoury) → cracker
biscuit, sweet → cookie
Black Maria → paddy wagon

blancmange → vanilla pudding
bloke → guy
boiler suit → overalls, coveralls
bonnet (car) → hood
booking → reservation
booking office → reservation office
boot (car) → trunk
braces → suspenders
bubble and squeak → cabbage and potato
bumbag → fanny pack
bumper, wing → fender (car)
busker → street performer
bypass → detour

C

cake shop → bakery, pastry shop
candy floss → cotton candy
car park → parking lot
car silencer → muffler
caravan → motorhome, trailer, campervan, RV
carriageway → highway
carry on → continue, drive on
cash dispenser, cashpoint → ATM (Automated Teller Machine)
casualty unit → hospital emergency room
cat's eyes (on road) → reflectors
central reservation (of a highway) → median strip
centre, centred → center, centered

charity → non-profit organisation
cheap → inexpensive
chemist's shop → pharmacy, drugstore
cheque → check
chilli → chili
chips (potato) → French fries
cinema → the movies
cinema (building) → cinema, moviehouse
coach → bus
coach (railway) → car (railroad)
collection (car rental) → pickup
colour → color
condom → rubber
confectionery → candy
conserves, jams → preserves
constable → police officer
cooker → oven
corn → grain
corn on the cob → corn
cosy → cozy
cot → crib
couchette → sleeper car, sleeping compartment
courgette → zucchini
crib → crèche, manger
crisps → chips
crossroads → intersection
crumpet (attractive women) → unknown in the USA
crumpet (toasted foodstuff) → unknown in the USA
cul-de-sac → dead end
current account → checking account
cuttings (newspaper) → clippings

D

dear → expensive
defence → defense
demister → defroster
deposit account → savings account
dialling → dialing

dialling code → area code
dialling tone → dial tone
diarrhoea → diarrhea
diary → appointment book
dinner jacket → tuxedo
dipped headlights → low beam
dirt road → unpaved road
discount store → outlet, factory outlet
diversion → detour
double glazing → storm windows
draught → draft
drawing pin → thumb tack
driving licence → driver's license
dual carriageway → divided highway, two-lane highway
dummy (for crying child) → pacifier
dustbin → trashcan, garbage
duvet → comforter
dyke → dike

E

elastic band → rubber band
Elastoplast (brand name) → Band aid (brand name)
electric fire → electric heater
electrical socket → outlet
encircle → circle
engaged → busy, occupied
enquire, enquiry → inquire, inquiry
ensuite (bathroom) → private (bathroom)
ensure → make sure, insure
enthusiasts → fans, buffs
entitle → title
entrecôte steak → rib steak, prime rib
estate agent → realtor

F

favour → favor
filling station → gas station
film (noun) → movie
fire brigade → fire department
fire station → fire house

first floor → second floor
fishmonger → fishstore, fishmarket
fizzy → carbonated
flat → apartment
flavour → flavor
flyover → overpass
football → soccer
fortnight → two weeks
foyer → lobby
front stalls → orchestra seats
fulfil → fulfill
full headlights → high beams, brights
funfair → amusement park

G

gammon → ham, hamsteak
gaol → jail
garden → yard
gas fire → gas heater
gear lever → gearshift
gearbox → transmission
gents → men's room
good value → bargain
greaseproof paper → wax paper
grey → gray
grilled (meat) → broiled
ground floor → first floor
guard (on a vehicle) → conductor
guard's van → caboose
gully → gutter

H

hand luggage → carry-on bags, carry-on
handbag → purse
harbour → harbor, port
headmaster, head teacher → principal
high season → tourist season, peak
    season
high street → main street
hire → rent
hoarding (advertising) → billboard
hockey → field hockey

hold up (noun) → traffic jam, backup
holiday → vacation (but holiday for
    public or religious holidays)
holidaymaker → vacationer
honour → honor
hood (of a convertible car) → top
horse riding → horseback riding
housing estate → tenement

I

ice lolly → popsicle
ill → sick
in hospital → in the hospital
indicator (vehicle) → turn signal

J

jam → jelly
jelly → jello
jewellery, jeweller → jewelry, jeweler
join (a highway) → enter
jumper → light pullover or sweater

K

kerb → curb
kilometre → kilometer
knickers (lady's) → panties

L

ladies' → women's restroom
land for development → real estate
laundrette → laundromat
lavatory → bathroom
lay on → provide, arrange for
lay-by → rest stop
left-luggage office → baggage room,
    storage
lemonade, squash → pop or soda
letterbox → mailbox
level crossing → train crossing
licence → license
lift → elevator

liqueur → after-dinner drink
liquid baby food → formula
litre → liter
lobster tail and steak → surf-and-turf
loo → bathroom, rest room
lorry → truck
luggage → baggage
luggage trolley → baggage cart

M

mackintosh → raincoat
main course → entrée
maize → corn
mange-tout → snow pea
marrow → squash
mend → fix, repair
metalled (road) → paved
metre → meter
metro → subway
mileometer → odometer
mince → ground beef, ground meat
mincemeat → unknown in the USA
motoring → driving
motorway → highway, expressway,
    freeway, interstate, turnpike
muesli → granola
muffin → a circular cake made from
    yeast dough. Unknown in the USA
    and not the same as the cake known
    there as an English Muffin

N

nappy → diaper
nature reserve → nature preserve,
    wildlife refuge
newsagent → news stand
nil → nothing, zero
no admittance, no entry → no entrance
note (banknote) → bill
number plate → license plate

O

off-licence → liquor store
on offer → for sale, offered
on show → on display, displayed
on stream → on line
one-off → one-of-a-kind
open day → open house
orbital road → beltway
orientated → oriented
out-of-hours → off-hours
overtaking → passing

P

pack of cards → deck of cards
paddle steamer → side wheeler
paddle-steamer with rear propulsion →
    sternwheeler
page (in a hotel) → bell-hop, bell boy
pants → underpants
paracetamol → acetaminophen
paraffin, aviation fuel → kerosene
parasol → umbrella
parcel → package
pardon? → excuse me?
pavement → sidewalk
pelican crossing → pedestrian crossing
penknife → pocket knife
petrol → gasoline, gas
petrol station → gas station
phone box → pay-phone
pickle → relish
pillar box → mailbox
plimsolls → gymshoes, tennis shoes,
    sneakers
plough → plow
porridge → oatmeal
post → mail
post box → mailbox
postcode → zip code
postman → mailman
practice (noun) → practise

practise (verb) → practice

pram → baby carriage

prawn → shrimp

programme → program

prom → a walkway or kind of musical concert

proper → standard

pub → bar

public school → private school

pudding → dessert

pull down (building etc) → tear down

pulses → legumes

puncture → blowout

purpose built → built to order, specially designed

put paid to → finish, put an end to

pyjamas → pajamas

Q

quay → dock

queue → line

queue (verb) → stand in line

R

railway → railroad

railway goods wagon → boxcar

railway station → train station

rates (domestic) → local property taxes

read (for a degree) → study

rear lights → tail lights

recovery vehicle → tow truck

redundant → laid off

return (ticket) → round trip (ticket)

reverse-charge telephone call → collect call

ring (to telephone) → call

ring road → beltway

rise (in salary) → raise

roadside embankment → berm

roadworks → construction

roast beef, entrecôte steak → prime rib

roundabout → traffic circle, rotary (New England)

rowing boat → rowboat

rubber (pencil) → eraser

rubbish (bin) → garbage (can)

rucksack → backpack

S

sack (verb) → fire

sailing boat → sailboat

saloon car → sedan

savoury → savory

scheme → project, plan

seafront → waterfront

self-catering → efficiency apartment, efficiency

Sellotape (brand name) → Scotch tape (brand name)

serviette → napkin

shop → store

sidewalk → pavement

sign-posted → marked, well-marked

silencer (car) → muffler

single (ticket) → one-way ticket

situated, situation → located, location

skilful → skillful

sledge → sled

sleeper (railway) → railroad tie

sleeping policeman → speed bump

smoked salmon → lox

snowplough → snowplow

socket (electrical) → outlet

soft drink → soda

solicitor → lawyer, attorney

spanner → wrench

speciality → specialty

spirits → liquor

spring onion → scallion

squash (drink) → juice concentrate

stalls (theatre) → orchestra seats

starter → appetizer

steam train driver → engineer

steward (aircraft) → flight attendant
stewardess → flight attendant
sticking plaster → bandage, band-aid
stone (weight) → 14 pounds
stop lights → traffic lights
stopover → layover
storey → floor, story
straight on → straight ahead
subway (pedestrian) → underground (pedestrian) passage
surname, family name → last name
suspenders → garter belt
swathe → swath
sweet (confectionery) → candy
sweet (dessert) → dessert

T

take-away (meal) → carryout
tannoy → public address system
tap (noun) → faucet
tariff → rate-sheet
taxi rank → taxi stand
tea towel → dish towel
telephone box → telephone booth, pay-phone
tender (noun and verb) → bid
terminus → terminal
theatre → theater
tights → panty-hose
till → cash register
tinned → canned
toilet → restroom
toll road → turnpike
torch → flashlight
tower block → high rise
train driver → engineer
trainers (footwear) → sneakers
tram → trolley, streetcar
transmission → power train
transport → transportation
travel sickness → motion sickness
traveller, travelled → traveler, traveled
treacle → molasses

trolley → baggage cart
trousers → pants
tsar → czar
tyre → tire

U

underground → subway
unsurfaced road → dirt road, unpaved road
upmarket → upscale

V

value for money → affordable
van → minibus
venue → place, spot, arena
vest → undershirt
vet → veterinary surgeon, animal doctor

W

waistcoat → vest
washing → laundry
way in → entrance
WC → toilet, restroom
wellies, wellington boots → gumboots
whisky → whiskey
Whit Monday → Whitmonday
Whit Sunday → Pentecost
white coffee → coffee with milk or cream
wholemeal → whole wheat
windscreen → windshield
wing, bumper (car) → fender
woman's handbag → purse
worshipped → worshiped

Y

Y-fronts → men's underpants

Z

Z (zed) → Z (zee)
zebra crossing → pedestrian crossing
zip fastener → zipper

APPENDIX 8B

USA-UK English Differences

US (American) English → UK (British) English

A

accommodations → accommodation

acetaminophen → paracetamol

affordable → value for money

after-dinner drink → liqueur

airplane → aeroplane, aircraft

aluminum → aluminium

amusement park → funfair

animal doctor → vet

annex → annexe

antenna → aerial

apartment → flat

appetizer → starter

appointment book → diary

area code → dialling code

ATM (Automated Teller Machine) → cash dispenser

attorney → solicitor, lawyer

ax → axe

B

baby carriage → pram

backpack → rucksack

baggage → luggage

baggage cart → luggage trolley

baggage cart → trolley

baggage claim → baggage reclaim

baggage room, storage → left-luggage office

bakery, pastry shop → cake shop

Band-aid (brand name) → Elastoplast (brand name), sticking plaster

bar → pub

bargain → good value

bathroom → lavatory, toilet, WC

bathtub, tub → bath

beet → beetroot

bell-boy, bell hop → page (in hotel)

bell-captain → head porter

beltway → ring road, orbital road

berm → roadside embankment

bid (for a contract) → tender

bill, (e.g. $10 bill) → banknote

billboard (advertising) → hoarding

billion → a thousand million (archaic, a milliard)

block (city block) → area bounded by streets on four sides, distance between two streets

blowout → puncture

boondocks, boonies → remote location, backwoods

boxcar → railway goods wagon

broiled (meat) → grilled

brownie → small rich chocolate biscuit

buff → enthusiast

buns (slang) → part of body you sit on, posterior

bus → coach

busy (phone) → engaged

C

cabbage and potato → bubble and squeak

caboose → last wagon on goods train, guard's van

call (on the phone) → ring

call collect → reverse the charges

candy → confectionery

candy → sweet (confectionery)

canned → tinned

car (railroad) → coach (railway)

carbonated → fizzy

carry-on bags → hand luggage

carryout (meal) → take-away

center, centered → centre, centred

check (banking) → cheque

check (in restaurant) → bill

checking account → current account

chili → chilli

circle → encircle

clippings (newspaper) → cuttings

coffee with milk, or cream → white coffee

collect call → reverse charge telephone call

color → colour

Columbus Day → second Monday in October

comforter → duvet

conductor (on a vehicle) → guard

continue, drive on → carry on

cookie → biscuit (sweet)

corn → corn on the cob, maize

cotton candy → candy floss

counter clockwise → anticlockwise

cozy → cosy

cracker → biscuit (savoury)

crib → cot, crèche

curb → kerb

czar → tsar

D

dead end → cul-de-sac

deck of cards → pack of cards

defense → defence

defroster → demister

dessert → afters, sweet, pudding

detour → diversion, bypass

dial tone → dialling tone

dialing → dialling

diaper → nappy

diarrhea → diarrhoea

dike → dyke

dirt road → unmade, unsurfaced road

dishtowel → tea towel

divided highway → dual carriageway

draft → draught

driver's license → driving licence

driving → motoring

drugstore → chemist's shop, pharmacy

E

efficiency → self-catering apartment, room with kitchenette

eggplant → aubergine

electric heater → electric fire

elevator → lift

emergency room → casualty unit

engineer → train driver

English muffin → a small spongy cake made with eggs and baking powder (unknown in England)

enter → join (a highway)

entrance → way in

entrée → main course

eraser → rubber (pencil)

excuse me? → pardon?

expensive → dear

expressway → motorway

F

fall → autumn

fanny pack → bumbag

faucet → tap

favor → favour
fender → wing, bumper (car)
fender (car) → bumper, wing
field hockey → hockey
fire (remove from job) → sack
fire department → fire brigade
firehouse → fire station
first floor → ground floor
fishstore → fishmonger
fix → mend, repair
flashlight → torch
flavor → flavour
flight attendant (female → stewardess, air hostess
flight attendant (male) → steward
floor, story → storey
for sale → on offer
formula → liquid baby-food
four lane road → dual carriageway
fourteen pounds (weight) → one stone
freeway → motorway
french fries → chips
fulfill → fulfil

G

garbage (can) → rubbish (bin)
garters → suspenders
gas heater → gas fire
gas station → filling station, petrol station
gas, gasoline → petrol
gearshift → gear stick, gear lever
granola → muesli
gray → grey
ground meat, ground beef → mince
gumboots → wellingtons
gutter → gully
guy → bloke

H

half and half → half cream/half milk

mixture for coffee
ham, hamsteak → gammon
hamburger bun → bap
harbor → harbour
high beams, brights → full headlights
high rise → tower block
highway → road, carriageway
highway construction → roadworks
hockey → ice hockey
honor → honour
hood (car) → bonnet
horseback riding → horse riding
huddle → planning or tactics meeting or conference

I

in the hospital → in hospital
Independence Day → July 4th
inexpensive → cheap
inquire, inquiry → enquire, enquiry
insure → ensure
intersection → crossroads
interstate highway → motorway

J

jail → gaol
jello → jelly
jelly → jam
jewelry, jeweler → jewellery, jeweller
john (the john) → toilet, lavatory
juice concentrate → squash

K

kerosene → paraffin, aviation fuel
kilometer → kilometre

L

Labor Day → first Monday in September
laundromat → laundrette
laundry → washing

layover → stopover
legumes → pulses
license → licence
license plate → number plate
line (of people) → queue
liquor → alcoholic spirits
liquor store → off-licence
liter → litre
lobby → foyer
located → situated
longshoreman → dock worker
low beams → dipped headlights
lox → smoked salmon

M

mail → post
mailbox → letterbox, pillar box, post box
mailman → postman
main street → high street
Martin Luther King Jr. Day → third Monday in January
mean (adjective) → nasty
median strip → central reservation (of a highway)
Memorial Day → last Monday in May
men's room → gents, gent's toilet
meter → metre
minibus → van
mobile home → motorhome, trailer, caravan
motion sickness → travel sickness
motorhome, trailer → caravan
movie → film
movie theater → cinema
muffler (car) → silencer

N

napkin → serviette
nature preserve → nature reserve
news stand → newsagent
night crawler → worm used by fishermen

no entrance → no admittance

O

oatmeal → porridge
odometer → milometer
off-hours → out-of-hours
on display → on show
one-of-a-kind → one-off
one-way ticket → single
online → on stream
open house → open day
orchestra seats → front stalls
oriented → orientated
out to lunch → empty-headed, stupid, drugged
outlet → electrical socket
outlet (electrical) → socket
outlet (factory) → discount store
oven → cooker
overalls, coveralls → boiler suit
overpass → flyover

P

pacifier → baby's dummy
package → parcel
paddy wagon → Black Maria
pajamas → pyjamas
pants → trousers
panty-hose → tights
parking lot → car park
passing → overtaking
paved (road) → metalled
pavement → sidewalk
pay-phone → phone box
Ped Xing → pedestrian crossing, zebra crossing
Pentecost → Whit Sunday
pharmacy → chemist's shop
pickup (car rental) → collection
plow → plough
police officer → constable
pop → soft drink (such as lemonade)

popsicle → ice lolly

potato chips → crisps

potlatch → celebration among native Americans of Northwest region with the exchange of gifts

power train → transmission

practice (verb) → practise

practise (noun) → practice

prenatal → antenatal

preserves → conserves, jams

President's Day → third Monday in February

prime rib → roast beef, entrecôte steak

principal (school) → head teacher

private (bathroom) → en suite

private school → public school

program → programme

prom → a school or university formal ball or dance

provide, arrange → lay on

public address system → Tannoy (brand name)

public holiday → Bank holiday

purse → lady's handbag

purse → woman's handbag

quay → dock

R

railroad → railway

railroad tie → sleeper

raise (in salary) → rise

rate-sheet → tariff

real estate → land, developed or to be developed

realtor → estate agent

reflectors (embedded in road) → cat's eyes

relish → pickle

rent → hire

reservation → booking

reservation office → booking office

rest stop → lay-by

restrooms → toilets

rotary (New England) → traffic roundabout

roundtrip (ticket) → return (ticket)

rubber → condom

rubber band → elastic band

RV (recreational vehicle) → motor home, caravan

S

savings account → deposit account

savory → savoury

scallion → spring onion

Scotchtape (brand name) → Sellotape (brand name)

second floor → first floor

sedan → saloon car

shellac → high-gloss varnish

shrimp → prawn

sick → ill

side wheeler → paddle-steamer

sidewalk → pavement

skillful → skilful

sled → sledge

sleepercar, compartment → couchette

sneakers → plimsolls, trainers

sneakers → trainers

snow pea → mange-tout

snow plow → snowplough

soccer → football

soda → soft drink (such as lemonade)

specialty → speciality

speed bump → sleeping policeman

squash (vegetable) → sort of marrow

stand in line → queue

standard → proper

sternwheeler → paddle-steamer with rear propulsion

stick shift (car) → manual transmission

stoplights → traffic lights

store → shop

storm windows → double glazing
street musician → busker
subway (train) → underground railway, tube
surf-and-turf → lobster tail and steak
suspenders → braces
swath → swathe

T

tail lights → rear lights
taxi stand → taxi rank
tear down (building etc) → pull down, demolish
tenement → housing estate
Thanksgiving Day → fourth Thursday in November
the movies → cinema, film
theater → theatre
thumbtack → drawing pin
tire → tyre
title → entitle
top → hood (of a convertible car)
tourist season → high season
tow truck → recovery vehicle
tractor-trailer → articulated lorry
traffic circle → roundabout
traffic jam, backup → hold up
train crossing → level crossing
train station → railway station
transmission → gearbox
transportation → transport
trash bag → bin liner
trashcan → dustbin
traveler, traveled → traveller, travelled
trial lawyer, attorney → barrister
truck → lorry
trunk → boot (car)
turn signals → indicators
turnpike → motorway with tolls, toll road
tuxedo → dinner jacket

U

umbrella (for use in the sun) → parasol
underpants (men's) → Y Fronts
underpants (women's) → knickers, panties
underpass → subway
undershirt → vest
unpaved road → dirt road

V

vacation → holiday
vacationer → holidaymaker
vanilla pudding → blancmange
vest → waistcoat
vet → ex-serviceman, veteran
Veterans Day → November 11

W

waterfront → seafront, dock
wax paper → greaseproof paper˙
whiskey → whisky
whole wheat → wholemeal
wild life refuge → nature reserve
windshield → windscreen
worshiped → worshipped
wrench → spanner

Y

yard → garden (around a house)
you're welcome → don't mention it, no problem

Z

Z (zee) → Z (zed)
zero → nothing, nil
zip code → postcode
zipper → zip fastener, zip
zucchini → courgette

Appendix 9

The Greek Alphabet

Capital	Lower-case	Nearest equivalent English letter or sound
Α	α	a
Β	β	b
Γ	γ	g
Δ	δ	d
Ε	ε	e
Ζ	ζ	z
Η	η	ē
Θ	θ	th
Ι	ι	i
Κ	κ	k
Λ	λ	l
Μ	μ	m
Ν	ν	n
Ξ	ξ	x
Ο	ο	o
Π	π	p
Ρ	ρ	r
Σ	σ	s
	(at the end of a word ς)	
Τ	τ	t
Υ	υ	u
Φ	φ	ph
Χ	χ	kh
Ψ	ψ	ps
Ω	ω	ō

Appendix 10

The Russian Alphabet

Capital	Lower-case	Nearest equivalent English letter or sound
А	а	a
Б	б	b
В	в	v
Г	г	g
Д	д	d
Е	е	e
Ё	ё	ë
Ж	ж	zh
З	з	z
И	и	i
Й	й	ĭ
К	к	k
Л	л	l
М	м	m
Н	н	n
О	о	o
П	п	p
Р	р	r
С	с	s
Т	т	t
У	у	u
Ф	ф	f
Х	х	kh
Ц	ц	ts
Ч	ч	ch
Ш	ш	sh
Щ	щ	shch
Ъ	ъ	˝ ('hard sign')
Ы	ы	y
Ь	ь	´ ('soft sign')
Э	э	é
Ю	ю	yu
Я	я	ya